AF413647

ADVANCE PRAISE FOR *RE-CULTURE*

"A concise and practical guide for creating healthy, high-performing cultures."

—Brian Deveaux, CEO Hussey Seating

"Adam has captured the essence of successfully leading through the transformation of today's workforce. He has blended action, humility, and inspiration into a road-map for leaders who care about supporting their teams."

—Rob Gelb, CEO Valenz Health

"I started reading it last night and couldn't stop until halfway through. I just finished reading it. Great job in making *Re-Culture* an actionable guide. While most organizations know what the right thing to do is, the issue is always of execution. Urgent becomes the enemy of important. I plan to use the book's suggestions in 2026 and will share any success stories with you."

—Sandeep Mor, Senior Strategy Officer, Sempra

"Adam delivers an insightful and operationally grounded guide to culture—one that helps leaders build trust, resilience, and long-term strength."

—Mike Lepper, CEO, Impact Networking

"In a time when many are focused on AI and technology, Adam reminds us of the importance of our people and building resilient, people-centered cultures. This book provides us with a clear map to that goal."

—Chris King, Director, Corporate Services, INPO

"When the AI bubble finally bursts, Markel reminds us that the most powerful algorithm will remain: human connection. *Re-Culture* shows you how to unlock the exponential power of teams to create amazing results."

—Dr. Nick Morgan

"Adam cuts through the noise and delivers a simple, actionable manual for building culture that actually works in the real world. And I should know, since we hired his firm and saw great results across our organization."

—Ken Tripp, CSCO ZB

"Adam writes like he talks: thoughtful and fun, with punchy, useful wisdom and humanity. You'll learn a lot and enjoy what he has to offer."

—Brian Lott, CCO, Mubadala

"Having worked directly with Adam's team, I've seen first-hand how effectively *Re-Culture* principles translate into real results. It gives leaders a clear, practical path to building cultures that protect people, reduce burnout, and elevate performance. It's timely, deeply relevant, and exactly what organizations need right now."

—Kara Wilson, VP HR Flex

"*Re-Culture* hits right at the heart of what real leadership is about. Culture isn't a poster or a program; it's the everyday behaviors that show people they're safe, valued, and part of something bigger than themselves. This book gets that right.

"It reminds us that belonging is built through dignity, accountability, and genuine care. It champions resilience, shared responsibility, and the simple truth that culture is a 'we' thing, not a memo from HR. That's the work that creates teams who grow, contribute, and go home happy.

"If you're ready to stop inheriting culture and start intentionally shaping it, *Re-Culture* is your roadmap. And the good news? Any dumb ass can do it if they choose to lead with love and purpose."

—Garry Ridge, Former CEO and
Chairman Emeritus, WD-40 Company

"Entrepreneurs and fast-growing companies will find Adam's work invaluable. He shows exactly how to build a culture that supports growth without burnout."

—R. Read Davis, Vice Chairman,
Marsh & McClennan Agency

"Adam and his team do extraordinary work to advance and transform corporate culture with a focus on leadership capabilities and development."

—Lori Winkler, SVP and CHRO, Zimmer Biomet

"In an era obsessed with technology, Adam Markel delivers what leaders need most—a clear, actionable framework for building strong, people-centered cultures. *Re-Culture* is a must-read for anyone serious about sustainable success."

—Joel G. Carson, Executive Director,
Geoprofessional Business Association

"Adam delivers an insightful and operationally grounded guide to culture—one that helps leaders build trust, resilience, and long-term strength."

—James Healy, CEO of Reece

"I've had the privilege of learning from Adam for years, *Pivot*, *Change Proof*, and now this, and what I appreciate most is that he never sugarcoats the truth. He tells leaders what we *need* to hear: Culture isn't built on charisma, memos, or mission statements. It's built when people bring their full selves and take full ownership. As a CEO, I value Adam's perspective because he equips teams to stop waiting, stop assuming, and start leading from where they stand. When everyone steps up, we become not just a stronger organization, but a grounded one."

—Suzanne Ogle, President and CEO
SGA Natural Gas Association

"Stop what you're doing and read this book now! In the 47 years since receiving my MBA, I have worked for several global automakers in leadership positions, nearly 30 years at Honda and most recently as the COO of Kia America. This journey provided me with exposure to many corporate cultures composed of a wonderfully diverse collection of people, personalities and nationalities, each molded from their own life experiences.

I wish I would have read then what Adam has to say here about the need to Re-Culture and how to go about it. Adam has really nailed it.

Culture is not an asset in the same sense that a patent or proprietary technology is. Culture is really the connective tissue. Culture must be cared for, nurtured, just as a farmer would maintain his (or her) acreage.

In the same sense that "your body is your temple" so is your culture and Adam's book is THE guide for its care… to paraphrase a famous political retort: 'it's the people, stupid!'"

—Steve Center, Former COO of
Honda and Kia, North America

RE-CULTURE

RE-CULTURE

*A Leadership Guide to
Restore Connection, Collaboration,
and Trust in Today's
Disconnected Workplace*

ADAM MARKEL

A POST HILL PRESS BOOK
ISBN: 979-8-89565-634-1
ISBN (eBook): 979-8-89565-635-8

Re-Culture:
A Leadership Guide to Restore Connection, Collaboration, and Trust in Today's
Disconnected Workplace
© 2026 by Adam Markel
All Rights Reserved

Cover design by Conroy Accord

Post Hill Press
New York • Nashville
posthillpress.com

Published in the United States of America
1 2 3 4 5 6 7 8 9 10

"Good and evil both increase at compound interest.
That is why the little decisions you and I make every
day are of such infinite importance. The smallest good
act today is the capture of a strategic point from which,
a few months later, you may be able to go on to victories
you never dreamed of."

—C. S. Lewis

"Me, We."

—A Poem by Muhammad Ali

Table of Contents

HOW TO WORK

HOW WE GET FROM WORK TO WORK WELL

HOW TO WORK WELL

HOW WE GET FROM WORK WELL TO WORK WELL TOGETHER: THE CODE OF CULTURE

HOW TO WORK WELL TOGETHER

Foreword

I know from experience that when my friend Adam Markel asks you a question, it's rarely the simple kind. He goes straight to the core with the kind of inquiry that makes you pause, breathe, and rethink the assumptions you may have been carrying around for years. He has a rare ability to challenge you without scolding you, to stretch your thinking without overwhelming you, and to bring you into a bigger, more honest conversation about leadership, culture, and the human experience at work.

I've built my professional career around helping leaders understand that love is just damn good business. Not the soft, sentimental kind of love. The operational, disciplined kind—the kind that chooses belief over cynicism, contribution over self-protection, and collaboration over fear. Adam and I share that worldview. We both believe that organizations rise or fall on their willingness to honor the humanity of the people who make them run. And we both know how rarely that actually happens in practice.

That's where *Re-Culture* comes in.

This book is a wake-up call wrapped in a set of practical, accessible tools. Adam is inviting us to stop admiring the idea of a better culture and start building one—or re-building one—intentionally, persistently, and together. He's not offering shortcuts, and he isn't pretending this work is easy. Culture isn't a poster on a breakroom wall. It's the sum of a thousand daily choices—how we communicate, how we recover from setbacks, how we hold one another accountable, and how willing we are to reexamine the habits we keep insisting are "normal."

Adam has always had a natural gift for storytelling, and in this book, he takes us inside organizations we recognize from our own experience—even if we've never worked there—places where people are burnt out, leadership is reactive, and everything feels like a crisis. Then he shows us what's possible when we ask the right questions and choose a different path: a culture built on shared responsibility, psychological safety, and the courage to speak the truth, even when—or especially when—it shakes things up.

Adam's advocating for shared care and commitment is deeply aligned with my Radical LEAP framework, in which I challenge business leaders to cultivate love, generate energy, inspire audacity, and provide proof. We've both seen that culture isn't created by an internal PR campaign; it's created by people. It's created in the spaces between us—how we show up for one another, how we collaborate, how we navigate challenges, and whether we choose fear or accountability in moments of pressure.

Adam understands that better than almost anyone I know. He reminds us that culture doesn't shift because the CEO says so. It shifts when everyone, at every level, participates in its creation. Because they want to, not because they've been ordered to. And because they have each other's backs.

And he has a clear and compelling point of view on why so many organizations struggle: they're running at full capacity with no margin, no pause, no time to reflect or refine. They tell themselves they're too busy to deal with culture… until the culture becomes the problem they can't ignore. Adam doesn't just diagnose that problem—he offers a roadmap out of it by giving us practical questions, rituals, and frameworks that help leaders at every level build resilience—not the individual, "grit-your-teeth-and-push" kind, but the collective kind that makes team members stronger together than they are alone.

You're about to feel the benefit of Adam's decades of experience, his joy in human potential, and his refusal to accept the false divide between performance and well-being. He knows—because he's lived it—that organizations succeed when people succeed, and people succeed when they feel connected, trusted, valued, and seen. He's been in the rooms where things fall apart, and he's helped build the rooms where they come back together. That's why his guidance lands the way it does: it comes from experience, reflection, and a genuine desire to help people thrive.

So, here's my suggestion to you: read this book not as a prescription, but as a partnership. Let Adam challenge you, provoke you, support you, and occasionally nudge you out of your comfort zone. Let him walk beside you as you consider what you want your organization—and your own leadership—to become.

Culture is not a storm to survive. It's a craft to be mastered. A promise to be kept. A shared creation you constantly renew, even if the winds are high… and especially when they are.

Herein is your invitation to build something better. It starts with yourself, extends to your team, and ripples outward in ways you can't predict but will absolutely feel.

So, turn the page. Your Re-Culture journey starts here.

—Steve Farber; Author, *The Radical Leap, Greater Than Yourself* and *Love is Just Damn Good Business*; Founder and CEO, The Extreme Leadership Institute

The Storm

Imagine...

You are on a ship, a thousand tons of steel, being tested to its absolute limit by a raging sea about to capsize your vessel. You're about to learn about the strength of your hull, the skill of your crew, and the true meaning of your ship's culture.

In the midst of the storm, the deck is a wild, unpredictable surface, but your feet know how to find purchase. Your body has learned to move with the lurch and heave, not against it. The wind screams, but you hear it as a warning of the next great wave, a call to tighten your grip and brace yourself for the inevitable.

Salt spray stings your face. You taste it. It is the taste of the work, and, like it or not, you have no choice but to be in it.

The storm is here, and for some reason, the ship's captain has been absent for hours. The helm was unattended, so you took your place even though you don't feel ready to lead. The old charts, which promised a safe and predictable passage, are now irrelevant because the wind is howling and the rain is sideways, and you're the one in charge.

And yet, the ship continues to run. The engines are still turning. The lights are still on.

Why?

Because the crew is still here, and you're terrified they're looking to the Executive Officer (you!) for answers, because you're the one leading them. You expect chaos and panic.

But you find the opposite.

Through the wind and the rain and your terror, you take a breath and look around.

You don't see a collection of terrified individuals. You see a single, breathing organism. You see the first mate, not waiting for an order, but already directing a team to reinforce the starboard rail with cargo nets and spare line. You see the navigator, her face lit by the radar screen, calling out a new heading (not a perfect one, but the best possible one) to the first mate. You see the youngest deckhand, blood drying on his temple from a falling crate, helping a fellow crewmate to their feet and checking their harness.

No one gave them a memo. No one held a meeting. Their response is instinctual, cultural. It is the product of a thousand small rehearsal interactions, a shared sense of responsibility, and an unspoken agreement that they all have each other's backs. This is not a hierarchy responding to commands. This is a network responding to a threat.

This is collective resilience. And it is the only thing standing between your ship and the abyss.

You feel a pull to join them, not because you are in charge, but because you are one of them. You move to help secure the rail, your hands working in rhythm with the others. A voice calls out a warning about the next wave, and the message ripples through the crew not as panic, but as preparation. Everyone shifts, braces, and becomes part of the ship's structure itself.

Later, when the storm has passed, the sun is out, and the sea is calm, you give a tentative knock on the captain's door. He invites you in.

He shows no signs of a night spent in the storm. In fact, he looks as though he had a full night of sleep. Stunned, you ask him, "Why did you not come to the deck during the storm?"

With a slight smile, he says, "Because I believed in you. I believed in our crew. I believed in what you could do together. And I slept like a baby."

In this moment, the central truth becomes stunningly clear:

The strength of your ship is not found in its captain's cabin. It's forged in the spaces between her crew members. It is the trust in a knot tied by human hands. It is the confidence in a heading called out by a voice you recognize. It is the shared breath before a wave hits, and the collective exhale when it passes. It's a crew working well together.

The locked door of the captain's berth is no longer a symbol of leadership failure. It has become the catalyst for your greatest discovery. You were waiting for a leader to emerge, only to realize that leadership had already emerged: It was all of you.

The storm did not break the crew. It revealed it.

When I'm asked to speak to organizations about resilience and culture, I like to do an experiment from the stage. It's the same call-and-response we learned from high school cheerleaders. Holding my arms out wide, I call to the assembled workforce, "I say, 'MARGIN,' you say…"

Invariably, the response comes back in one voice, "PROFIT!"

Then I pull up a quote from John Mark Comer's *The Ruthless Elimination of Hurry* and I say "Today, we're gonna think about margin a little differently.

I want you to catch this one. We're gonna talk about margin as the space between your load and your limits. That's a different margin. Most people have no personal or professional margin. They're at 100% capacity most of the time. There is no margin between their load and their limits. This is a problem. Now and in the future."

While the room sits in a sort of bewildered silence, I continue, "Our relentless push to be everywhere, do everything, all of the time, has all of us at the absolute margin of both our load and our limits. There's nowhere to go; and we all know that a business that has no margin will be out of business before very long."

Dawn rises in their eyes as they realize that most people are all operating in the dangerous, burnout area of the red.

This book is about that realization. We're all operating without margins. The world is a storm of constant change, of economic shifts, technological disruptions, and global challenges. The dollar is down, and prices are up. Organizations that wait for a single captain at the top to navigate it all will be swallowed by the waves.

The organizations that will navigate the coming storms are those that understand the fundamental truth of this book:

Re-Culture is collective resilience.

I can't make it any simpler than that. It's the capacity of a group of people to work well together through uncertainty and change. Culture, resilient culture, is the ability to turn and face the storm, not as a leaderless crowd, but as a crew that leads itself.

It is not about getting the captain to come and set things right. It is about realizing that the captain is already here. It is in all of us.

This is not a book just for leaders, but also for those who want desperately to be lead.

Let's begin the work of building a new culture that works for you, for your business, and for the people that make it work.

Your Re-Culture ship is waiting.

Introduction

A WORD ABOUT THE TITLE

I'll be the first to admit that *Re-Culture* might be a strange title. You might be thinking, "What does that mean? Is it a noun or a verb?" Actually, it's both. The title boils down to this: Most people think "culture" is something you have. It's the ping-pong table in the breakroom and the holiday party. It's static. But that's a myth. Culture isn't just a noun; it's also a verb. It's not what you have, it's what you do. And if what you're doing is creating burnout machines instead of resilient innovators, then you don't need a fifteen-minute culture hack; you need a fundamental reset.

If you'll excuse the tautology: To get Re-Culture (noun), you need to re-culture (verb).

Re-Culture is about renewal, not just repair. You don't just patch a hole in a boat that's taking on water; you dry-dock it, sand it down, and reseal the entire hull. Re-Culture means a proactive renewal of your company's core values and how those values are practiced through your actions. It's not a one-time fix for a toxic manager or a bad policy. It's the conscious, every day, in-the-trenches practice of rebuilding your organization so it generates resilience day after day.

Like penicillin, most great cultures are accidents. They just seem to happen, like they've always been there, because they're built from leftover habits, past leaders' egos, and "the way we've always done it." That's not building a culture; that's inheriting one.

Re-Culture means stopping the autopilot and grabbing the tiller. It's about driving your culture with intention, a clear heading, and with everyone on board pulling in the same direction. You have to repeat habits to build culture.

That's why it will REWIRE your team's collective brain. A Re-Cultured environment actively rewires your team from a reactive, threat-based mindset to a challenge-seeking, resilient mindset. It's not about eliminating stress; it's about changing your relationship with it so that pressure creates diamonds instead of dirt.

Okay, this one is a stretch, but, like the poets, I'm going for the rhyme. Re-Culture is a collective "WE" journey, not a solo "ME" fix. It's "We-Culture." You can't outsource culture to an HR memo. The "Re-" is a collective call to action. It's about we, not me. It means every single person, from the C-suite to the front desk, owns a piece of the culture. It's about rebuilding together, creating a shared responsibility for the organization you work in every day.

It's about getting real, measurable results. This isn't touchy-feely stuff. This is about the bottom line. A Re-Cultured organization sees results you can take to the bank: higher retention, sharper innovation, and a team that adapts to market shifts instead of crumbling under them.

Re-Culture is a return to what's real and measurable, the blue-ribbon competitive advantage of a truly resilient culture that wants to be both profitable and a place in which people are excited to meet new challenges together.

WHO THIS BOOK IS FOR

The Parable of The Storm was inspired by a true moment from my life. There I was, out on *"Moondust"* near a lovely spot we call Our Haven. That's my twenty-one-foot bow rider we keep in a little harbor in Martha's Vineyard, outside Oak Bluffs (where I'm routinely surrounded by Boston Red Sox Fans). Her name comes from a song that appears in the cinema classic *Meatballs*, which is one of our favorite movies. It's also the song my wife Randi and I danced to when we tied the knot. Our Harbor is a quaint, sweet spot where you can't have a big boat, so the water traffic is mostly fishing boats. For me, that boat is peace. It's where I go to get out of my own head, away from the anxieties and fears. The colors out there are a painter's paradise with every shade of green you can imagine, and those Cape Cod blues. For me and Randi, it's a restorative place. A perfect resilience spot.

This particular afternoon, it was gorgeous. We were over near Chappaquiddick. My wife, Randi, looks at the sky and says, "Adam, we should probably head back. Looks like rough weather's coming."

I glanced up. It was still beautiful. The sun was on the water. It was warm. I said, "Ah, we're good. We'll head in about twenty20 minutes." I wanted just a little more of that peace before heading back to our phones and the world.

Well, in nineteen minutes, I kid you not, the fog rolled in. And I'm not talking about a little mist. This was the proverbial pea soup. We couldn't see five feet in front of the boat. One minute, it's all blues and greens, the next, it's just this thick, gray wall from stern to bow. In a moment, the wind shifted, the temperature dropped, and just like that, we went from a peaceful cruise to a potentially dangerous situation.

I had my instruments to guide me. I knew my heading. I knew where I was supposed to go. But knowing your destination and getting there safely are two completely different things when you're blind. My family's on board—Randi and, the kids—and the tension spikes. Everyone's got an opinion, a fear, they're speaking their minds, and as the captain, you feel that weight. You're trying to project ease and calm, but inside, you're hyper-vigilant, your knuckles are white on the wheel, listening for any-thing, anything in that fog. And then, out of nowhere, a massive sailboat just materializes, a ghost through the mist, maybe fifty yards away, which seems like a lot but for boats is like inches. It passed us by safely, but the anxiety remained.

That moment on the water is exactly why I wrote *Re-Culture*.

You see, that sailboat was always there. It was on the same water, heading somewhere. The danger wasn't that it suddenly appeared; the danger was that my visibility suddenly disappeared. I was caught off guard. I was complacent in the sunshine. And in that fog, with my family counting on me, I had to rely on more than just a heading. I had to rely on my instruments, my gut, and a calm focus that I had to really dig deep for. Let's also not forget that I didn't listen to my XO–my wife, Randi–whose instincts are eerily accurate, almost always.

So, who is this book for? I'll tell you exactly who it's for. It's for you, the guy or the gal at the helm of a business, a team, a department. You're the captain. You've been sailing in decent weather for a while. Maybe the sun's been out, the profits are okay, and people aren't quitting in droves–even if they don't seem to be OK. It's not perfect, but it's fine. You're telling yourself, "We'll head in and deal with that…whatever it is…in twenty minutes."

Culture is like that.

You know the "fog" is coming. You can feel it. It's in the quiet discontent of your best people. It's in the email that says, "We've always done it this way." It's in the Monday morning dread that you feel walking in, and you know your team feels it ten times worse. It's the innovation that never happens, the meeting that solves nothing, the constant, low-grade anxiety that your engine, your core business, might just blow its engine and leave you floating, not too far from shore, but far enough to be in real trouble.

You're not stupid. You're not a bad leader. Maybe you're just a little complacent. Maybe you stopped listening to your people or you listened to the devil, and you think you've got more time than you do. But buddy, on the ocean and in the boardroom, the weather changes faster than you think.

This book is for the leader who knows their culture is the boat they're all sailing in, and they can hear the creaking of the boards. They see the rust on the rail. They know they need to renew it, to refit it, to Re-Culture it, but they don't have the first clue how to do it without sinking the whole damn ship.

You think, "If I start poking around, if I start asking hard questions about accountability and purpose and psychological safety, I might open a Pandora's box. I might make it worse. I may lose everything." So, you stay quiet. You keep heading in the general direction you think is right, hoping the fog doesn't roll in before you make it to port.

Let me talk straight with you: That's a losing strategy.

Re-Culture is your navigation system for when the fog is so thick you can't see your own hand in front of your face. It's the step-by-step process for moving from being reactive, constantly swerving to avoid sailboats you never saw coming, to being proactive, trusting your headings, and believing in your crew.

It's for the leader who is tired of:

The meetings where no one says what they really think, and then the real meeting happens in the hallway afterward, leading to everyone pulling in different directions.

Watching your talented people slowly disengage, their passion fading, until they're just collecting a paycheck. Or collecting themselves for the walk to HR.

Knowing you need to change, needing to pivot, but feeling like you're trying to turn a cruise ship with a canoe paddle.

Feeling the weight of being the "captain," where every problem, every drama, every failure ultimately lands on your desk. It's lonely at the helm when the storm hits.

This book isn't theoretical, academic fluff. It's a practical playbook. It's how you build a culture that is your competitive advantage. A culture that doesn't just survive the fog, but can navigate through it with confidence. A culture where your team isn't adding to the panic in the pea-soup moment, but is instead checking the instruments, spotting for obstacles, and trusting you to get them home safely.

Because the truth is, the fog is inevitable. Market disruptions, key people leaving, a global pandemic, a shift in technology, at the end of the day, it's all just weather. You can't control it. But you can control your boat by strengthening your hull, training your crew, and then trusting your compass.

Re-Culture is how you stop being a victim of the weather and start being the master of your vessel. It's how you turn your workplace from a source of distress into a haven where people do the best work of their lives, and where you, as the leader, can finally take a deep breath and enjoy the ride, even when the blue skies turn to black.

So, if you're the one holding the wheel, feeling that first chill of the wind change, let's stop waiting for the fog to hit. Let's get your ship in shape.

CULTURE MYTHS

A culture built on resilience thrives on change, but a culture that lurches from crisis to crisis with no learning is holding on to myths from the past.

In my work with organizations and teams, I've collected the Six Myths of Culture that are keeping them from renewing, reimagining, and rebuilding their culture from the ground up.

Myth 1: Culture Will Take Too Long

We live in a world where if something doesn't happen right away, the feeling is that it might as well never happen, because we don't have time to institute real, lasting change.

That's nonsense.

I've been lucky to travel to Europe quite a few times in my life, and I'm always struck by the cathedrals and churches that are the centerpiece of nearly every city, town, and village across the continent. When I stand outside these architectural marvels, I think about the fact that the people who laid the first stone were rarely alive to see the last stone laid in its place. The people who built those structures had to imagine a world blessed by a monument to faith, beauty, and wonder, but with the knowledge that they wouldn't be able to partake in that delight. They were like Moses, taken up to the Promised Land, and, in a cruel twist of fate, not allowed to enter and enjoy.

Re-Culture is not a cathedral. It's not going to take decades to turn things around.

Strangely, though, that's not how our brains work, is it? We can only fixate on the road in front of us, without thinking about where we're headed. We want an organizational culture that we can be proud of, but we think it'll take more time than we have.

Then the limited beliefs crowd in with thoughts like, "I just have to get through the next quarterly report with our heads above water." All the while, the culture fix we desperately need waits patiently in its place on the back burner. Then the next quarter comes, with its challenges and its obstacles, and we're in the same predicament, playing the corporate version of musical chairs on the deck of the Titanic. We think we're busy, but we're failing to see the real problems.

But though we're aiming to be around for the long term, resilience culture, if done correctly and in good faith, will bear fruit almost immediately.

Myth 2: Culture Is One Size Fits All

Culture is deeply tied to our organization's unique values and context. The very spark that lit the flame of your organization is loaded with this stuff. It's hard to look back to go forward, but sometimes that's the only way. We have to return to why we got into this in the first place. Because that's what sets us apart from the rest of the pack.

If we're honest, we're all looking for the formula, the quick fix, or the easy solution to the problems that ail our culture. But Re-Culture is about seeing our organizations with their specific problems. The challenges of a health-care provider aren't the same as those of an energy management corporation. Sometimes the problem is us. We just have to admit it.

When we go to therapy, we bring with us our entire history, from our childhood to the present moment. In some cases, we bring the history that existed before we were born. Then, with help from an objective person, we explore the patterns that have shaped who we are.

Imagine if a therapist said, "Tom was just in here. He has a similar problem. You should do what Tom did." Our backs might bristle at this. But sometimes, looking at how someone else addressed their cultural challenges helps us look at ours with fresh eyes.

There will be examples in this book about other companies and other leaders, but it's not a prescriptive ask. It's more about finding a culture that works within our organizations and our teams. To know our culture is to love it, and to love it means we can change our culture into something better.

Re-Culture isn't a formula; it's a choice.

Myth 3: Culture Is a Solo Job

Nobody knows your culture better than you do. For real resilience culture, we've got to own up to what we've created. Maybe the culture of the organization we're in predates our arrival, and we want to fix it. Either way, admitting that yes, there is a problem, is the first step.

But most of the time, we know what we're good at, and we're not aware of what we're bad at, and we don't want to know the difference. That's why we've got to reach out for help. Sometimes, that means finding money in our budgets to address our cultural issues. Maybe we've got to bring someone in from the outside who can see our structures through fresh, compassionate eyes.

The attributes of ambition, drive, and focus define most entrepreneurs. If we've built a business from nothing, then we've got to have a single-minded ego capable of distorting the energy fields that stand in our way. Like Steve Jobs.

But those days are over. Culture is, by its very nature, collective. We're all in this together. If I want to change my organization, then I can't go in, guns blazing, hoping that my will is enough to create a new culture. I've got to get buy-in from all my stakeholders. Toxic leadership says, "It's my way or the highway." Collective leadership says, "We're all going to have to drive to get where we want to go."

Life is a highway, but we can't drive it alone. Re-Culture drives in the HOV lane.

Myth 4: Culture Can't Be Measured

We think of culture as ephemeral, light as air, and impossible to quantify. Well, I'm here to say that it can.

My organization runs thousands of surveys and assessments on the companies we work with. And we can drill down into the benchmarks and trends that provide the data that back up the feelings that something just doesn't feel right.

But if we want something more direct and immediate, we can take a walk through our organization (if we're in the office) or observe virtual meetings (if we're remote) to actually hear and see how our people interact with one another. We can tell immediately if the culture is healthy or if it's in need of intervention.

In this case, when it comes to culture, intervention is innovation. The "just leave it alone and hope things change" strategy is gone. We've got to get active.

Myth 5: Re-Culture = Happiness

One of the more interesting cultural developments of the last decade is the notion of "toxic positivity" and its quest to eliminate difficulty from our daily lives. In her book on the subject, Whitney Goodman writes, "Positive thinking is often a Band-Aid on a bullet wound. Instead of helping, it leads to emotional suppression, which is destructive to our bodies, minds, relationships, and society."

There's a moment from C. S. Lewis's *The Chronicles of Narnia* where a previously arrogant and terrible boy is turned into a dragon. He's huge, ungainly, but still dangerous. It's a sad, pathetic spectacle as he's mocked and chased and feared even though he's trying to communicate the depth of his pain. At one point, he cries huge tears that drop, steaming onto the dirt. But eventually, he begins to turn his new nature to the advantage of the group: He's moving huge logs and trees to help repair a ship and giving flying rides around the island. Not despite, but because of his nature, he finally becomes part of the group.

Then, Aslan, the Lion, meets the dragon, recognizes the pain he's in, and volunteers to turn him back into a real boy. But Aslan doesn't wink or wiggle his nose or say a spell to do it. He takes his sharp lion's claws and digs into the dragon's hide to dig for the scared boy inside. The process is painful for the boy, but it also feels kind of good, like pulling off a scab.

That's what Re-Culture is. We're going to dig into the discomfort of our culture with friction, discomfort, and hard truths, and we're going to look at our failures with fresh eyes.

If we're truly called to Work Well Together, we have to adapt to the type of adversity that breeds resilience, not happiness.

We have to have a pain tolerance greater than our potential to get to Re-Culture.

Myth 6: Re-Culture Is a Sunk-Cost

Many of us resist cultural change because we believe the time, resources, and effort already poured into existing structures would be wasted. This mindset traps organizations in the "sunk-cost fallacy" that afflicts all risk-averse leaders. There's a line from Shakespeare's *Macbeth* that encapsulates this perfectly:

> "I am in blood/Stepp'd in so far that, should I wade no
> more, Returning were as tedious as go o'er."

Which is a fancy way of saying, "We've come too far to turn back now."

Whether it's retaining outdated processes, clinging to legacy systems, or preserving toxic traditions that came with past successes, the fear of "wasting" what's already been spent paralyzes progress. Deep inside our hearts, a voice whispers, "But we've always done it this way. What about the years and capital we invested?"

Sunk costs are irrecoverable, but they should never dictate future decisions. Imagine refusing to replace a broken-down delivery truck because "we've already spent so much repairing it." Every extra dollar thrown at the truck is money not spent on faster, more efficient vehicles that could transform a business. Similarly, clinging to a harmful culture because of past effort ignores the compounding cost of not changing: lost talent, stifled innovation, and eroded trust.

Re-Culture isn't about discarding your history; it's about composting it. Those years in a cutthroat sales culture were about the value of collaboration with those who disagree with us. I spent years as a Manhattan lawyer swimming with sharks, and I don't regret a single moment. It taught me how to survive in deep water filled with predators. And it's shown me a different way to achieve success: Love. Even toxic patterns serve as a map of where not to tread. As with a forest after a wildfire, the richest, most resilient growth often emerges from what's been burned away.

Like a chef who stops adding salt to a ruined dish, courage lies in saying, "This no longer serves us," not in stubbornly eating the meal. Your past built resilience. Don't let it become an anchor. Re-Culture thrives when we trade "We've come too far to quit" for "We've learned too much to stay."

Then, once we start seeing results and experiencing what that tastes like, we'll get hungry for more ways to get better and deeper with our intentions. Then, the rewards will snowball, and the next thing we know, we'll have a renewed, resilient culture that we can not only be proud of but one we can enjoy for as long as we choose.

That's no myth. It's real.

THE RE-CULTURE CURIOSITY QUESTIONS

1. How can you rebuild culture without tearing everything down?
2. Do leaders make culture, or does culture make leaders? Give three examples of each.
3. Where will your workplace culture be in ten years?
4. Why does a healthy culture lead to better results?
5. When should leaders intervene to address the culture of their business?
6. What's the one action every organization can do to change its culture?
7. Does this cultural practice still coordinate with who we're becoming?
8. What lessons from our "investment" can we carry forward?
9. What's the cost of staying silent versus the cost of changing?

STEERING INTO THE STORM

"Culture is the widening of the mind and of the spirit."

—Jawaharlal Nehru

Since the global pivot of 2020, everything has changed. The pause of that strangest of springs asked us to choose resilience—and choose it we did.

Sort of.

One thing that hasn't changed since those days of masks, elbow bumps, and disinfecting groceries is that change is here to stay.

In fact, time is moving faster than ever—for the young and the old. Most days, there seems to be too much change in the air. It's swirling around us. We feel like the velocity of change is picking up speed so that we're on a bullet train to somewhere. And that unknown destination terrifies us, because, in the age of chaos and disinformation, it's nearly impossible to know what's real.

Not only has the spending power of a dollar decreased to almost nothing, but so too has an hour of our day. We've got disruptions in our business that are happening constantly, everything from supply chains to AI to the shrinking workforce to trade wars. There's not a single business out there that has its wing tips perfectly oriented to the winds of change. It's coming for everyone. Uncertainty is no longer a rip current that pops up randomly, sucking us out to sea, but a constant, pounding, daily churn of change. At every moment, we have to adjust everything, from our strategies to our expectations. In the current climate, whether we like it or not, change is our business.

How we navigate that change together is culture.

THE 20 PERCENT NAIL

Many of us have heard (and used) the phrase, "To a hammer, everything looks like a nail." It's an old axiom that goes back to Victorian England, but it was Abraham Maslow who brought it into popular consciousness. Mr. Maslow was speaking about confirmation bias and something called the law of the instrument, which posits that overreliance on the same tool, no matter the problem, masks the deeper, more insidious problems.

In the world of Re-Culture, the hammer is a CEO, and the nail is 20 percent workforce cuts. We've seen this hundreds of times in the business pages of our newspaper: Facing tough economic headwinds, a CEO will slash the workforce by up to 20 percent, signalling a willingness to get tough and cut costs, and, as a result, the stock price will jump. It's a story, repeated over and over, and it usually results in a depleted and over-stretched workforce while the CEO is pushed out of the airplane with a golden parachute.

Forget the long-term, foundational challenges the business is facing; institute sweeping layoffs and live off the sugar rush of boosted investor value.

Rinse, repeat.

Now, we're all facing major headwinds if we want to reimagine and renew our culture, but the windiest of all is how to build culture while still maintaining profitability. A recent interview with Chevron's CEO, the aptly named Mike Wirth, gives us a powerful, real-world case study of this central tension in modern business: the struggle between building a human-centric culture that ensures long-term resilience and balancing that with the relentless pressure for short-term shareholder value.

When asked about the difference between his company and his main competitor, Exxon, this is what Mr. Wirth said: "The difference is in the culture of the companies. We put a real premium on partnership. We put a premium on diversity and inclusion. We put a premium on getting the best out of our work force and using that to deliver solutions for communities, governments and customers."

So far, so good, right? This is exactly what we're building when we're talking about resilience culture. But, for our purposes, it gets even better when he goes on to say, "In our industry, strategies are easy to copy. Assets you can buy, technologies you can license. Cultures are harder to build, and they are a differentiator." When I read this, I wanted to put down my paper and throw a parade in the street! Each and every one of us knows that culture is the true measure of an organization's ability to not only survive but thrive in the storms that used to come once a generation and now seem to come every quarter.

Now for some straight talk: Let's be real about what's happening at Chevron. The company is in the process of cutting 15 percent to 20 percent of its global workforce (up to nine thousand employees) by the end of 2026. This includes over 200 jobs in Midland, Texas, and another 575 in Houston.

In the same interview, here's what Mr. Wirth has to say about that: "In a commodity business, costs always matter. We have to stay competitive, and the most difficult thing we do is downsize our work force. The way we protect the most jobs for the most people is by remaining competitive. Companies that don't remain competitive at some point either don't exist anymore, or they get acquired by somebody else, or an activist investor comes in and changes things. We have to take control of our own future."

Now, the easy thing for us to do is sit up on the highest road in the county on the highest horse and judge Mr. Wirth and his gimlet-eyed appraisal of their value. It's easy to say, "Well, Mr. Wirth, you can't claim culture is your differentiator while simultaneously dismantling it person by person."

The real question isn't whether he's right or wrong. The question is: Is this a strategic pivot or a strategic failure?

To see this as a simple choice between "people" and "profits" is a false binary. The same principle applies at an organizational level. The goal isn't perfect balance, but a dynamic harmony where valuing people is how you create enduring value.

But we all know that's not how business works. To build resilient cultures, we have to be honest about the pressures that we face. Like Odysseus, we have to steer our ship between the twin rocks of sustainable culture and shareholder value. If we don't, at best, we're out of a job. At worst, the company turns to Chapter 11.

The truth is, this isn't just a business problem; it's a human dilemma, and it's at the very heart of what we teach about resilient leadership.

Mr. Wirth laid out the two competing interests with stunning clarity and honesty.

So, what is the solution? How do we bridge the gap between these competing interests? We have to consciously pivot from a reactive stance to a proactive, resilient culture.

ExxonMobil, according to reports, has taken a different path, avoiding sweeping layoffs and instead focusing on performance-based adjustments and leveraging innovative technologies to streamline operations. I'm not here to say which is better, but it's *wirth* (couldn't help myself) noting that there is more than one way to stay competitive and agile.

Chevron has chosen a path of large-scale layoffs while Exxon has, so far, chosen a different method of reshaping its business.

But again, this isn't about which approach is the correct one, because the correct approach is rarely obvious. Leaders usually have to choose between the lesser of two evils.

In my previous book, I took aim at the binaries inherent in work-life balance. We're not aiming for one-to-one perfect balance. Our goal is harmony between the two states. As we move from individual resilience to organizational resilience, we have to recognize that it's not just about bouncing back from layoffs or cuts. It's about the dynamic process of how we adapt to a world that's changing every moment of every day. It's about building a system where our people are the resilient markers that allow the entire organization to thrive amid adversity.

That's why we, as leaders, must do the inner work to build our own resilience first. We cannot foster a resilient culture if we are operating from a place of fear and scarcity. We have to leverage uncertainty to build long-term resilience.

A resilient culture is built on daily organizational rituals and habits that spark innovation and growth. Re-Culture is about providing teams with tangible, daily actions to center themselves, access creativity, and maintain momentum in the face of the kind of uncertainty that forces us to choose between people and the bottom line.

Here's something simple that you can practice with your teams: Replace a few of those predictable, mind-numbing status updates with forward-looking responses from team members who, rapid-fire, answer three questions:

- "What did I learn yesterday that changes my approach today?"
- "What one deliverable will I commit to completing today?"
- "What specific roadblock could sink my week, and who here has an idea to overcome it?"

The idea is not to overthink. The goal is that the team will learn and work together, rather than zoning out in their Zoom windows. Bad ideas become good ideas. Perfect ideas stay in the brain. The latter is the enemy of the former.

That's why, in our work, resilient cultures utilize two principles: articulation and reflection. If you can articulate the problem, then you can reflect on how best to solve it, and if you do both, there's a non-zero chance the problem can be solved by the close of business. Individual learning is a collective advantage. That's why, with all due respect to Mr. Wirth, the ultimate differentiator isn't a few head-fakes toward culture in pull-quotes from an interview. It's the one we demonstrate with our hardest decisions. Protecting the most jobs isn't about being the last company standing after cuts; it's about innovating and pivoting our business model before the cuts become necessary.

And then, when cuts come, we have to manage them so that they don't poison our organizational culture.

If we know where the storms are, we can sail away from them, or around them, or, if those aren't options, then we have to build resilient teams for when the unavoidable storm drops upon us.

Mike Wirth has presented us with the defining business challenge of our time. The old paradigm of "cut costs to please shareholders" isn't going away any time soon. This is the world in which we live. When I go swimming in the Pacific Ocean early in the morning, I don't complain that the water's cold. It's supposed to be cold. That's the point.

The other paradigm that will never go away is the fact that organizational cultures so resilient and invested in people are the ultimate, undeniable value driver for shareholders, customers, and the below-the-line workers who bring it to life every day.

Let's go back to the parable of the storm. Put yourself back in the position of having to lead your crew through the storm. Imagine, if you will, that in response to the squall and the panic spreading through the entire system, you push two crewmembers overboard to lighten the ship. Maybe you make it through the storm. Then what? The rest of the surviving crew will never trust you again. And what happens when you sail into the next storm and you need a line rigged or a joist tightened? Well, that was Rodney and Kathleen's job, and you pushed them into the murky depths.

The jig is up. It's time for new tools.

SOMEBODY UP THERE NEEDS CULTURE

How does this happen? How did we get here? And what does it look like when the stock price is the only god we serve?

A couple of years back, I was invited to meet with an organization that had brought me in to work with them on their resilience culture. We were gathered together at a resort they'd booked for their core management team and the entire workforce. The night before I was due to speak to all of them, we were about to go to a cocktail party when someone grabbed me by the elbow and said, "I want to show you something."

This Somebody with something to show me was high up in the Somebody Suite. He pulled me into a small room with a laptop and hooked it up to the television. Like a proud father, he took me through a PowerPoint presentation of the strategic vision for his organization for the next five years. It was amazingly detailed and lovingly laid out. I would have felt like he was showing me an investor pitch deck if it weren't a publicly traded Fortune 500 company.

The heart of the presentation was what they'd identified as the top five risks to their strategy—risks like market volatility and economic shifts, technological disruption, regulatory compliance, and operational efficiency.

I listened politely, and then I said, "I don't see culture anywhere in your whole deck. I don't see any risks associated with your workforce."

Mr. Somebody looked at me like I'd just struck him in the face with a rhubarb pie. He sat in silence for at least a minute, staring at the final slide.

Then he said, "That's…really interesting."

And then he left the room.

This organization had thought about their strategy and worked it with the finest of the fine-toothed combs, and in all of that thinking, they'd never once thought about their company culture being a risk to their workforce. This is a good organization, full of tremendously smart people, and with good intentions for the world and their teams.

But it didn't even occur to them that the biggest risk to their organizational strategy was their people.

In my last book, *Change Proof,* I wrote about the Dust Bowl and how it was a historical warning or metaphor for how we were treating our bodies, minds, hearts, and spirits, driving them hard, without understanding their nature, and burning them out, unable to work, let alone grow. The Dust Bowl was caused by East Coast speculators, who rushed into the Plains, drawn by cheap government land (stolen from the Native American nations). But without the intrinsic understanding or appreciation of the soil and earth that they were going to farm, they grew too much, too fast. Consequently, within a generation, the top layer of soil was gone with the wind, and famine, disease, and poverty nearly wiped out the central farms of the United States. The fast money was in and out, and landowners, the actual people who lived there, saw their livelihood disappear. It was a land bubble, and when that bubble burst, it was full of dust.

Since then, the problem has only gotten worse. Instead of farmers burning through layers of soil, we have organizations burning through layers of their workforce. That's how we get toxic cultures where fear trumps trust, power silences voices, and the bottom-line silos teams from each other and their well-being.

Our corporate culture is an ecosystem, rotting slowly from the inside, where burnout is normalized, and psychological safety is a mythical island in a book somewhere.

The rot festers under unprepared leaders who mistake control for strength, where employees navigate minefields of micromanagement, gaslighting, and sixteen-hour grinds.

Toxic cultures thrive on widening inequity. From the top, favoritism and exclusion wear the costume of tradition. Dissent is seen as disloyalty.

The result? A workforce paralyzed by chronic stress, creativity stifled by conformity, and talent turnover. We've lost sight of the basic truth that thriving people drive thriving organizations. Until accountability replaces apathy, these cultures will keep trading human potential for KPIs, leaving scars far deeper than the bottom line.

THE GREAT RESIGNATION

"Work takes on new meaning when you feel you're pointed in the right direction. Otherwise, it's just a job, and life is too short for that."

—Tim Cook

Make no mistake, the global virus that kept us in our homes for the better part of two years changed culture irrevocably, because when offices opened again, an unprecedented number of us changed jobs or dropped out of the workforce entirely.

It was called "The Great Resignation" by economist Anthony Klotz in response to the almost one hundred million people who quit their jobs in 2020–21. As the virus spread, so did the quiet quitting in sectors like health care, hospitality, and tech.

For the first time, organizations were forced to confront a workforce that demanded hybrid office options and rejected rigid office hierarchies. The organizations that failed to adapt witnessed a mass exodus of talent. The world was pivoting away from the guardrails that had sustained it for so long.

During the lockdowns, we all rethought our relationship to a work-life harmony that was woefully out of tune. Being out of the office helped many of us realize that we were in situations that were stagnant at best and toxic at worst.

Russ Hill wrote, "To some, the pandemic exposed how much work had become like adult daycare. Everyone is expected to be in at a certain time. They're expected to stay till a certain time. And it's best to look busy in between."

The people who didn't exit the workforce took advantage of the shortage and negotiated for higher-paying jobs. They pivoted to entrepreneurial organizations in new industries that eschewed traditional offices.

Organizations scrambled to improve retention rates with well-meaning but mostly cosmetic fixes like raises, flexibility, mental health support, and diversity initiatives.

The Great Resignation reshaped workplace culture, and it remains to be seen whether it will survive, but one thing's for certain: We can't be resigned to our fate.

Let's see what the data has to say.

CULTURE NUMBERS

Corporate culture is being scrutinized in a way it's never been before. It's conventional wisdom that people in the workforce, of all ages, are looking for culture over money. But let's dig into the numbers to see what things look like at a granular level.

A comprehensive workplace study by the Arbinger Institute has some staggering numbers that should be bright warning lights for you and your organization.

They found that 86 percent of job seekers avoid companies with bad reputations, and it's easier than ever for them to find out who the bad apples are on sites like Glassdoor.

On the other hand, strong cultures had retention rates above 40 percent and four times the revenue growth. They can also boast higher engagement from their teams (72 percent), while their disengaged counterparts cost $450–$550 billion every year.

Poor culture is driving people away at a 33 percent clip, while toxic workplaces are ten times more likely to cause attrition. Team members say that leadership defines an organization's culture. When those leaders communicate transparently with their teams, motivation goes above 85 percent.

Fifty percent of the workforce is quiet quitting (clocking in and clocking out and just doing the bare minimum). The fact that we call doing the job we were hired to do and for which we collect a paycheck, as laid out in our contract, "quiet quitting" suggests that our workplace culture has historically been "overworking audibly" for far too long. If we want our people to take initiative and go the extra mile for our organizations, we have to give them meaning, purpose, and, inevitably, more resources.

Simply put, healthy workplace cultures consistently outperform the S&P by 20 percent. Team satisfaction and retention lead to long-term success.

Leaders can shape it all by creating a positive environment that rewards all the actions that create a healthy culture.

To sum up the numbers:

- Workplace culture is a critical driver of satisfaction, retention, and business success.
- Poor culture leads to high turnover, disengagement, and financial losses.
- Leadership plays a pivotal role in shaping and maintaining a positive culture.
- Remote and hybrid work models require intentional efforts to sustain cultural connection.

HOW TO USE THIS BOOK

"Many of life's failures are people who did not realize
how close they were to success when they gave up."

—Thomas A. Edison

In my book *Pivot*, I laid out a challenge to my readers: Read through fifty pages before giving up on the book. Fifty pages. That was it. If you can get through fifty pages, you'll build up the mental discipline and adaptability to not only finish the book, but you'll have the energy to pivot when the need arises.

Then, in my follow-up, *Change Proof*, I went further and set down a one-hundred-page marker. Make it to one hundred pages before deciding to give up. If you want resilience, you have to be a resilient and voracious reader.

But the time for such challenges is over. If you want to renew, regenerate, and remake your organization's culture, you've got to use every part of this book.

Consume it from beginning to end. Re-Culture means no shortcuts. There's no "fifteen-minute hack" for culture. It's time to do the work.

It's designed in such a way that you can read it from cover to cover the first time, but what I want for you is to be able to check in when you find yourself and your organization not living up to the values that birthed it. You might say, "We're getting too serious. We need to vibe. We need to open up new possibilities." Then you can thumb back to the appropriate chapter to remind yourself of the lessons and questions.

WHAT TO EXPECT IN RE-CULTURE

This book is a guide to transforming your workplace culture from the inside out with clarity and purpose. In these pages, there's something for everyone who wants to renew their organization's culture.

Think of *Re-Culture* as a recipe book, like Julia Child's *Mastering the Art of French Cooking* or Samin Nosrat's *Salt, Fat, Acid, Heat*, where you might find fine restaurant-level recipes to make in your humble home kitchen. A great cookbook promises that, with patience and diligence, you, too, can create the kinds of dishes the great chefs make every day for high-paying customers. A recipe is a kind of algorithm: A set of instructions to make, say, beef bourguignon.

That's what this book is: A recipe for culture. As you make your way through these pages, you'll see what I mean.

To renew your culture, you don't have to be great at it. You really don't. You just have to ignore Yoda (*do or do not*) and try. You'll find that just by the very fact that you're trying to create culture around you, you'll start to notice culture where you didn't before. Culture is vital to your organization, but it isn't an impossible dream you'll have to dream. It's something we can all do. Provided we do it together.

So, how exactly will *Re-Culture* equip you to lead meaningful and lasting change in any organization?

A Navigational Blueprint

Throughout this book, I've created a navigational blueprint to guide teams and organizations stuck in a fractured, anxious past into a reimagined future rooted in trust and shared values. Businesses don't start with a storefront. They need people. People are culture. We need to plan. Anyone who's built something knows you can't just stick a shovel in the ground and build a house, write a book without an outline, and you can't just pack a bag and hop in the car, hoping to get somewhere amazing. Culture can be created by accident, but that's not why you're here. It's not something you can manufacture out of nothing. In Re-Culture, the shifts we make have to be intentional. We can't luck our way into change. Hope is not a strategy, nor is it culture. I can't cross my fingers, click my heels, and expect my business to run itself. This book is the roadmap for how you get to a culture that works for you.

Stories of Cultural Evolution

The key to Re-Culture is that it's not just about how organizations can work well together; it's about how people can work better with themselves. Evolution travels upward from the foundation, and the foundation is you.

On an airplane, what do the flight attendants say to you in the event of a loss of cabin pressure? Put your oxygen mask on first and then take care of your family. It's the same in Re-Culture: Go through the book once for yourself. Get real with where you are right now. It's not enough just to say, "Something is wrong, but I don't know what it is."

Inside to outside. That's how we moved in *Pivot, Change Proof,* and now, with *Re-Culture.* We move from inside to outside.

Re-Culture is an inner process first. It starts with individuals trying to make the world a better, more productive place and then letting that change their world.

In this book, you'll learn from organizations, leaders, and teams who've successfully redefined their cultures. Just like we have at WORKWELL Labs, where we've collected blueprints from across the corporate spectrum—from big businesses to fledgling start-ups, from the boardroom to the locker room, from Wall Street to Main Street, and found that, in business and life, the two buildings of success and failure often look the same on the outside.

You'll read about breakthroughs, setbacks, and the hard-won wisdom won through resolve and actionable insights. Maybe you'll recognize yourself and your organization. Or maybe you'll see that, in many ways, you're already on the right path to renewed culture.

Grounding in Reality

Every golfer would like to play Augusta on Sunday at The Masters. The fairways, the greens, the trees, even the rough, there's not a blade of grass or pine straw out of place. Sadly, most of us won't be lucky enough to play golf's cathedral before we die. My "Amen Corner" is wherever my grandkids are playing. The vast unwashed among us have to make do with a public course full of divots, stones, and imperfections. Re-Culture is the same. You want to create a perfect organization from a perfect set of circumstances. I get it. But in Re-Culture, the perfect is the true enemy of the good. It's imperfect. It doesn't happen in the correct order at the right moment. Real cultural change isn't about utopian ideals or reckless overhauls. It's about getting real with yourself and your organization.

In the pages that follow, you'll find strategies that honor your organization's history, resources, and day-to-day realities while creating space for bold, sustainable evolution.

Practical Tools for Collective Impact

Now that we've gotten real, let's get practical and collaborative. If there's a secret to working well together, it's that. We can't learn to swim by reading a book. We've got to dive into the deep end. This book will move you beyond theory with exercises, frameworks, and rituals designed to embed cultural shifts into daily instructions and questions. There's a reason I practice the Code of Conduct (we'll speak more of this in a few pages) every morning: I can't set it and forget it. Like you, I need constant reminders of who I am and what I'm trying to achieve. And I need the Code of Conduct at night so I can check in with myself. In this book, you'll learn why.

Like the case of Steve Kerr, the NBA coach and player who's been a part of some of the greatest teams of all time, has a very simple approach to culture. He has four values that he adheres to in any situation: joy, mindfulness, compassion, and competition. If he finds himself or his team in a difficult situation, he can lean on the daily practice of those values to lead the Golden State Warriors to seasonal success.

From communication practices to decision-making protocols, Re-Culture will help you build systems that turn values into action.

Faith without works is dead. Tactics without values are desiccated.

That's why we need practical tools that are built on shared values to help our teams build their own culture. The future will be made by those who realize that they can't do it alone.

"Me, We"

One of the epigraphs for this book comes from the shortest poem ever written, credited to the great boxer and human rights hero, Muhammad Ali. Though he was accused of being the most egotistical, arrogant sportsman of his day, he understood that the value of collective action was nonnegotiable. It took an army of people to get him into the ring in Kinshasa, Zaire, against the heaviest punching heavyweight of all time, George Foreman. He knew that, even though it was only a "me" in the ring against Big George, he needed a "we" to rally the crowd to his aid.

That's why you'll notice throughout that I'm going to be using the words "we" and "us" and "ours" more than I'm using "me" and "I" and "you." There's a very simple reason for this: If we want to Work Well Together, it's going to take all of us. We are the program, our team is the algorithm, and our business is the "if/then" instructions that create culture. It's not a lonely path. We're collectively building something together.

That's why this isn't a manifesto. It's an invitation. From "me" to "you" to "we." That's how I help my grandchildren learn math <u>and</u> pronouns.

ME + YOU = WE

Whether we're reshaping our teams, our department, or our entire enterprise, Re-Culture will meet you where you are and help you lead change that lasts beyond your organization and into the wider world where the rest of us are waiting for you.

Ready to rewrite the rules and become Re-Cultured?

Note:

At the end of each section, you'll find a space called "The Re-Culture Curiosity Questions." These are meant to be reflective prompts designed to spark critical inquiry, challenge assumptions, and deepen engagement with the book's principles.

For me, they're rooted in the idea that cultural transformation begins with curiosity; these questions are meant to encourage you to interrogate your organizational dynamics, personal biases, and systemic habits.

There's no right answer. There won't be a test. That's because they're not meant to be answered quickly or definitively. They're there to trigger ongoing dialogue, experimentation, and self-awareness as you apply Re-Culture to your life and your organization.

You can use them during individual reflection, team workshops, or strategy sessions to bridge the gap between theory and practice.

I like to think of the Re-Culture Curiosity Questions as speed bumps, meant to keep you in an analytic headspace. Some readers among you might be speed readers, binging and gorging on a text, but when you get to the end, you may have forgotten what you've read.

And that's fine. Scrolling on our devices has made reading harder than it used to be. That's why you can use the Re-Culture Curiosity Questions to ground yourself after each chapter so you can process what you've read and keep that information as you move forward.

That's why you'll want to write in this book. Make notes in the margins. Use Post-it notes. Stain it with coffee mugs water marks from reading in the hot tub or sauna. The goal is to embrace imperfections and failures. Nothing is final.

My wish for you is to turn passive reading into the kind of active, adaptive problem-solving that will make you a living, breathing, walking Re-Culture machine.

Now, let's move from the water into the sky…

THE RE-CULTURE CURIOSITY QUESTIONS

1. How might prioritizing your "inner work" disrupt your traditional leadership models and unlock deeper, more sustainable cultural transformation across your teams?
2. If culture is a "recipe" rather than a rigid blueprint, what risks and rewards emerge when you honor your organization's unique history, values, and imperfections?
3. How could embracing setbacks as inherent to the Re-Culture process, rather than evidence of failure, reshape how your organization measures progress and cultivate resilience in uncertain times?

Work Well Together

WORK WELL LABS, OR HOW ROBERT DENIRO
GAVE ME THE IDEA FOR THIS BOOK

Maybe you have seen a movie called *The Intern*, starring Robert DeNiro and Anne Hathaway. It's about a late-in-life widower named Ben, once an executive, now retired and empty of the purpose and meaning that used to define him. He gets wind of a "senior intern" program at a fast-rising e-commerce startup run by Jules, the type-A CEO who's trying to raise a company and a daughter. The two generations and styles clash, but they grow to appreciate one another's differences. They both realize that in business, and in life, things are pretty much the same: It's not about what we make, it's how we make it and who we make it with.

> "You are going to participate in the ovarian lottery. And that is going to be the most important thing in your life, because that is going to control whether you are born here or in Afghanistan or whether you are born with an IQ of 130 or an IQ of 70.
>
> What type of world are you going to design?"
>
> —Warren Buffett

My own experience with the Oracle of Omaha's "Ovarian Lottery" dropped me into one of New York's finer boroughs a long time ago, when

I was a budding entrepreneur, buying baseball cards and then reselling them to my friends and kids in the neighborhood at a healthy markup.

On the mean streets of Queens, I learned more about supply and demand, market efficiency, opportunity cost, and incentives than any freshman-level class in microeconomics could ever teach me.

- Business requires commitment, bravery, and a healthy dose of delusion.

For as long as I can remember, business was in my blood.

Let me be clear, I don't just love business merely as an idea. I love businesspeople. I love everything about them (well, almost everything, but we'll get to that later).

I love the power of people in teams to work together to achieve something none of them could do on their own. As Phil Jackson says, "The strength of the team is every member. The strength of the members is the team."

I love that I'm blessed to live in a country where smart, dedicated people use their talent, capital, and ingenuity to start from nothing, just an idea, the ghost of a chance, and then they build that idea into a real, living, breathing business that stands the test of time.

Like the founder of FedEx, Fred Smith, who was denied a loan that would keep the company afloat, and chose to pivot his approach. He took the last $5,000 in the company's account, hopped on a plane to Vegas, and turned that $5,000 into $27,000 on blackjack in a single night. And the company was able to make payroll and stay open for one more week. It's crazy. But it's true.

- How far would you go to keep your business afloat?

The fact of the matter is that almost a third of all new businesses fail within the first two years. And when you get to the five-year mark, that number goes above fifty percent. As founders, the numbers are staggeringly stacked against us. If we were gamblers, we wouldn't do it. Like marriages: Fifty percent fail. And yet, we do it anyway.

The simple fact is that organizations are made to produce profit for stakeholders. The conventional wisdom is that high performance is at odds with longevity. Teams are only loyal to their paycheck plus benefits. The well-being of individuals is subservient to the stock price.

But around eight years ago, when I was extolling the virtues of the pivot, I started to become obsessed with what made a company last beyond the two-to-five-year window of death. It seemed to me that the reasons for failure were obvious: lack of a market need, ineffective leadership, and poor financial management. But the markers for success are often murkier and more unrepeatable. After all, if there were a formula, not a single person would lose money. We know that isn't true.

What specific ingredient allows a company to last for at least ten years? Or even twenty? What helps the captains of industry weather the slings and arrows of an ever-changing world to make an outrageous fortune?

If having a great product that a lot of consumers want, combined with effective and knowledgeable leadership with a dash of financial literacy, was all it took to make a successful business, there wouldn't be a need for this book. Every company would be a roaring success, and the streets would be paved with gold.

- The odds are stacked against you. So what?

The more research I did, the more data I collected, the more businesses that I worked with, I came to see one salient principle: Every business is measured not by the stock price or awards or the plaudits of journalists, but by the people who work there. Our most precious resource is human: the people, the flesh-and-blood beings, that make up the fabric of each and every organization. They show up every day, punch their time card, and give their best for more than just a paycheck plus benefits and vacation days.

Walt Disney said, "It is the little things that give you a great lift." Those little things are actual flesh-and-blood humans who are more than just spreadsheet numbers.

When I'm called in to work with a company, these are the folks, the daily employees, the day-time players, that get my focus. Because I want to make sure that they're healthy—their minds, their bodies, and their hearts. The spirit of an organization is the work they do together.

If these folks are healthy, happy, and fired up to be better, then the company will be healthy and strong for the long term. But if they're bummed out and miserable and just showing up to pay their bills? Then that company is on life support and fading fast.

But, strangely, that's not the conventional wisdom in organizations. Oh, they might have some pretty words on their website about diversity, inclusion, mental health, and collaborative solidarity. But when these words are sent into the arena against the twin gladiatorial demons known as "efficiency" and the "bottom line," they get cut to ribbons while Wall Street cheers its lungs out.

I hear it from leaders all the time: "Why? Can't we just get new employees? Isn't great leadership pushing your people to places they didn't even know they could go? We've got a stock price to meet, and if our people can't help us meet it, then shouldn't we find newer, better people?"

For most of human civilization, the answer was Yes. Then, in March 2020, a different answer stepped to the front of the line.

A global pandemic paused everything about the way we live and work. For the first time, we really began to question the relationship between our lives and our work.

For me, in those strange months that followed, I began to see the connection between an organization's long-term success and the health of the humans that are its most precious resource.

I began to see that resilience was the true coin of the realm. The companies that were resilient were the ones that not only survived but also returned value in the marketplace.

But even as I went from company to company, business to business, evangelizing the gospel of resilience, I kept seeing a depleted workforce, anxious managers, generational conflicts, stress levels dangerously in the red, topped off with a pervasive sense of mistrust between leadership and employees.

Organizations were falling out of the sky because they weren't resilient.

I wrote in *Change Proof* that it's not enough to talk about resilience. You have to live it. Every day. You have to practice resilience before you need it, so when the change and uncertainty come to tear down what you've built, your foundation holds firm and fast.

Resilience, I discovered, is built through culture. It's got to be in everything you do. It's not enough that YOU are resilient; every aspect of your organization must be.

That's why, in early 2024, we created Work Well Labs with one mission in mind: to foster innovative, inclusive, and people-centered solutions that empower individuals and teams to work well together—creating thriving workplaces where collaboration, well-being, and purpose drive collective success.

It begs the question: Is it possible to create a healthier and more productive ecology of work by developing greater individual and team resilience?

We brought together some of the most fascinating business thinkers and keynote speakers about workplace culture, organizational resilience, and employee well-being. We've got founders, re-founders, former and current CEOs, lawyers, psychological counselors, mentors, coaches, teachers, physicians, and metaphysicians. Of course, there's my brilliant wife, Randi, and me too.

We refer to these special people as "WORKWELLians."

All apologies to the Justice League's Hall of Justice, I like to think of Work Well Labs as the Hall of Resilience. Or maybe it's The Resilience Avengers. I don't know, my kids will have to tell me. It's been a "minute" since my comic book days.

Most of the team had previously successful lives in business, and now, rather than retiring to a beach somewhere with little drinks with umbrellas, we still feel like our work isn't done. They're like Robert DeNiro in *The Intern*. They've come to the place in their professional careers where they want to give back, create growth, and continue their own research and development process.

One such WORKWELLian team member is Greg, an impressive individual with over thirty-five years of experience in sales.

Do you know how resilient you have to be to last for three and a half decades in sales?

Greg's one of my favorite people, and one day, out of the blue, he and I happened to find ourselves in a conversation about turnover and attrition, the workforce bleed that every organization faces every single year.

Attrition is when a team member leaves, and the job isn't filled by someone new, whereas turnover is when we replace the ones our organizations lose.

Greg laid it out for me, saying that both categories can both be broken down into two sub-categories: "regrettable" and "non-regrettable." Regrettable is when a team member leaves of their own choice:

- Recruitment by another organization
- Seeking growth opportunities
- Embarking on a new career path
- Retirement
- Relocation

Non-regrettable is that they were fired, let go, or a part of structured layoffs. That's pretty clear. Even though there's a lot of regret when it comes to layoffs. Nobody enjoys it.

All of that is to say: there's a certain amount of an organization's workforce that is going out the door every single year.

Healthy organizations have 10 percent or less. Anything more than that, and the cost to replace or retrain or combine roles is now greater than what we would have spent on that team member if they'd stayed.

Every organization is trying to cut down or eliminate regrettable losses, Greg told me.

While we were talking, Greg told me that in the world of Work Well Labs, he wanted to own the area of talent bleed because at companies he'd worked for, they not only accepted an unacceptable amount of attrition, but they also didn't do exit interviews with talent on their way out the door.

It blew my mind.

Organizations were losing people at a rate that was unsustainable, and they weren't gathering data as to why.

Eyes wide, Greg said, "There's all this information that organizations are just leaving on the table."

Like St. Paul on the road to Damascus, this was when the scales fell from my eyes.

In a certain way, it's like the dumpsters and garbage cans behind our restaurants and grocery stores: There's all this wasted food. We have hungry people on our streets and in our neighborhoods, and yet there's more than enough food to feed everyone.

It's the same way with the data about our organizations.

There's all this data just whooshing out the door.

Greg says, "This is because of shareholder supremacy." By this, he means we care more about looking up and forward to raising the stock price in the future, but we're not paying attention to the hole in our boat that's leaking water.

It's, well…regrettable!

What we're seeking is healthier workplaces. It's about building resilience—not just for individuals, but for entire organizations. Resilience, in this context, isn't just about bouncing back from challenges; it's about thriving in the face of change, uncertainty, and stress.

And that's where the heart of the work lies: helping leadership operationalize resilience in a way that's practical, sustainable, and impactful.

We've spent years gathering research and data—working with more than eight thousand business leaders globally—to understand what truly drives well-being in the workplace and to help organizations foster mental, emotional, physical, and even spiritual well-being. And when I say "spiritual," I'm talking about helping people connect with a sense of purpose and meaning in their work.

That's why this book is the story of what we know so far, and yet, how far we have yet to go.

Our abiding belief is that our work can be better; our work should be better. It begins with leaders, bringing their resources to bear on making their organization work with and for its people. Not the other way around.

• In every success story, the unsung hero is resilience.

WORK WELL TOGETHER

"A major reason capable people fail to advance is that they don't work well with their colleagues."

—Lee Iacocca

In *Change Proof,* I developed a three-step tool that I first learned as a lifeguard on Jones Beach, which I called:

Pause, Ask, Choose

These three words may seem deceptively simple, but they represent a structured framework for resilience and decision-making. The essence of this process is expressed as we move from mindfulness to self-awareness and then acting with intentionality. It's about breaking the automatic, reactive patterns our minds have learned and instead cultivating a proactive approach to how we move through our work and our lives.

In many ways, Pause, Ask, Choose is less a process and more a tool to use when the rip current of life's changes and uncertainties pulls us away from the relative safety of consistency and routine. When changes come, as they always do, and we feel ourselves rocketing out to deep water, we have to do the hardest, most counterintuitive action possible. We pause and lift our feet and go with the current so we can conserve our energy. In that space, we're able to ask ourselves, "What do I gain from struggling against the ocean? What if the thing I'm asked to do is *not* do?" Then, when the rip current eventually spits us out, we choose to swim home.

So, for those of you who are new to class, let's do a quick Pause, Ask, Choose refresher course.

The Pause Is a Reset.

Pausing allows us to interrupt the momentum of stress or emotion before it careens us into reactions that are unproductive at best and harmful at worst. It's a conscious act of stopping to breathe, reflect, and recalibrate. It's the STOP soldiers are taught to do when they're lost on a mission.

- **S**top
- **T**hink
- **O**bserve
- **P**lan

Rather than stumbling blindly through the trees, we have to gather our wits about us and wait. That may seem impossible, but solutions come to calm minds, while panicked minds eventually become bleached skulls discovered by hunters. That's why pausing is about regaining control and creating the mental and emotional bandwidth to bounce forward with clarity.

Asking Isn't About Answers.

Okay, now you've paused. The next step is to ask a series of meaningful questions. That's all. In individual resilience training, asking questions allows us to probe the situation, our emotions, our assumptions, and what options might be available to us.

Here are some examples:

- What am I feeling right now?
- What is really happening here?
- What outcome do I want?
- What's within my control?
- Am I reacting, or am I responding thoughtfully?

These questions are meant to disrupt knee-jerk reactions and surface deeper insights. They encourage us to confront not just the external situation but also our internal state—the biases, fears, and motivations we've learned through a lifetime of survival. But we're not here to just survive; we're called to thrive.

Sometimes, the answers that bubble up for us are immaterial. Just through the exercise of asking questions, we unclench our thoughts to allow for new possibilities for action.

Asking questions creates in ourselves a culture of curiosity.

Curiosity opens the door to creativity and flexibility, qualities that are essential for resilience. When we approach challenges with curiosity, we're more likely to see them as opportunities rather than threats.

Which leads us to—

Choosing Is Not a Choice.

Having paused and asked, we're now ready to make a decision and take intentional action. We decide on a path forward that meets our values, goals, and the insights gained from the first two steps.

Without action, reflection becomes stagnant. Choosing is the moment when clarity transforms into commitment. When we exercise agency and take ownership of our response, even in the face of uncertainty, the universe begins to conspire with us.

It's important to remember that choosing doesn't guarantee the perfect outcome. When we choose, we make the best decision we can with the information available, and then we must be willing to adapt as new information arises.

Something that we all have to face—the hardest part of making a choice, any choice at all—is the fear of making the wrong choice. Resilience isn't about avoiding mistakes. It's about learning and adapting from them. The more mistakes we make, the more resilient we'll be. Our research and anecdotal experience confirm that less resilient individuals and teams don't make enough mistakes along the way. Fear, thanks to Frank Herbert, truly is the mind killer. And the one thing we have to fear isn't actually fear itself, but the status quo.

Lastly, we need to remember the obvious: Choosing isn't the end of the process. It's part of an ongoing cycle. After we choose, we observe the results, reflect on what we've learned, and repeat the process. In this way, Pause, Ask, Choose becomes a continuous practice rather than a special response.

> "Life doesn't get easier or more forgiving, we get stronger and more resilient."
>
> —Steve Marabol

But, as we now know, a lot has happened in the world since I conceived this simple three-step tool for resilience. The world has gotten stranger, and the changes seem to come faster than our ability to process them. More and more, organizations are dying from the attrition and churn cycling through the workforce. Force is a word that means strong, but our work is making them weak.

Since 2020, I have learned a very important lesson:

We can't practice resilience alone.

What I began to realize was that the Pause, Ask, Choose process, useful though it certainly is, is limited. It can only describe our relationship to individual resilience. If we want true cultural transformation that meets the moment and all the moments to come, then we need to go deeper. We need to travel further.

We need culture.

We're all searching for a way to regenerate our culture, to transform it into something lasting and real that will stand the test of time. Cultural transformation can only occur in groups, teams, and organizations. It's like Napoleon Hill said, "…two or more minds coming together in harmony…create a third mind known as the mastermind." Collaboration is a group endeavor that builds culture, brick by brick.

For our organizations to thrive into the unknown future, we need a new tool, a new process that builds upon our internal resilience work. We need a cultural tool.

That's how I came to the three words that build upon our previous tool and turn them into something that can recreate culture. And the name we've given to that is "Re-Culture."

Maybe you can imagine these words dissolving into something new.

WORK, WELL, TOGETHER

The whole reason why you picked up this book in the first place is that you want to work well together with the people around you.

At first glance, these three words may seem straightforward, but they hint at a profound philosophy for navigating work and life with a group of people. This new framework is about fostering our values, our skills, and our creative collaboration, whether with ourselves or others.

In organizations, how we inspire disparate individuals to work together is the conundrum of leadership. Somehow, we have to protect both the organization and that part of each team member that wants to be a part of something greater than themselves. That's where Work Well Together lives: It's where singular effort meets organizational communication and becomes a collective culture that both celebrates and protects resilience.

I'll say it again: If culture is collective resilience, then you get it through the Work Well Together formula. And what do you achieve? Resilience culture.

That's Re-Culture.

You can use the Work Well Together tool to make your organization better, and rather than it being an interesting story to tell at parties about this book you heard about but mostly forgot, it'll be the moment that your organization went from just working together to working well together.

WORK

There's no way of getting around the fact that work is why we're all here. We're here to make something new. That requires effort, discipline, and sweat equity. Work is where we separate the wheat from the chaff. If we want our organizations to succeed, we've got to be prepared to work long, hard hours that will take us to our breaking point. Or so the theory goes.

As leaders, when we work, we model action, effort, and progress. Work is where we engage in the process, where we get our hands dirty, where we roll up our sleeves and commit to purposeful effort, whether that's solving a problem, pursuing a goal, or supporting a team. However, not all work is equal. In a resilience culture, our work must be tied to clear intentions. Otherwise, we're just working for the sake of work.

Work Comes First

If we want to grow and harness that growth for maximum impact, there's no escaping the fact that it's, well, work. It's hard. That's the system we have. We wake up every morning, five days a week, for fifty weeks of the year, for our entire adult lives. It's a habit.

Work is where everything begins. We're building something out of nothing. That takes time, effort, and people. It's through our effort that we learn, adapt, and contribute to the greater good of our organizations. But the "Work" in this framework is not just about doing for the sake of doing.

It's about why we choose to do it, what we choose to do, and how we do it.

Blindly running through walls without meaning will burn us out.

That's why the work has to have meaning.

Meaningful work starts with getting clear about our purpose. We take our values and our priorities, and we marry them to the needs of the moment.

Re-Culture is about our individual effort, say solving a specific challenge and finding out where it meets collective collaboration, where different people have sometimes competing responsibilities, and pointing them toward a common goal. Re-Culture is about breaking down barriers and fragmentation, creating an intentional movement away from silos and separation and toward coherence and unity. Such a workplace ecology solves for work-life balance because it makes it obsolete and irrelevant. What we seek in our bones is harmony, not competition for our attention and emotional loyalty.

Yin and Yang is more a symbol of interconnectedness than a scale of opposing forces to be balanced. In the work context, harmony is the interplay of what's most important to us—both work and not-work. The effective alternation of our endeavors is the ultimate goal. Like seasoning your food to your liking or blending the hot and cold water, the goal is a good experience in whatever you are doing.

We cannot trust in work alone. It will not set us free. Work must be met head-on with self-awareness. As leaders, if we do that, we can keep our teams from the hollowing out that comes from frustration and apathy.

"All happiness depends on courage and work."

—Honoré de Balzac

WELL

We cannot work without seeking to work well. That means two things:

- Working well is practicing impeccability, not perfectionism. It's doing the best job we can on any given day by being fully committed to what we're doing in the moment.
- Working well is protecting the well-being of ourselves and our people.

"Work" without "Well" is the first problem we need to solve. In our formulation, "Well" represents care, coherence, and habits that help us perform resilience.

To work effectively, we need to prioritize our well-being, physically, mentally, emotionally, and spiritually. This is about regenerating ourselves, creating space for rest and renewal, and ensuring our work is sustainable over the long term.

We've got to do the same for our organizations. That's the beautiful thing about resilience: The more we practice in ourselves, the more it spreads to the people around us. It's contagious!

It's the same with innovation and growth. The more we seek opportunities to learn, the more we create those opportunities for our teams. When we play and believe in one another, we're collaborating and trusting in each other's best abilities and not just the bare minimum.

Well-Being Is Essential

Without well-being, even the most purposeful work becomes unsustainable. Stress, fatigue, and disconnection can erode our ability to think clearly, collaborate effectively, and stay motivated. By prioritizing wellness, we cultivate resilience and energy, enabling us to engage fully with our efforts and relationships.

Practice Work Well

The iconic film director, David Fincher, is notorious for putting his actors through many takes of a scene. Some actors hate his process, and some love it. Fincher's basic point is: We've spent a lot of money and effort to bring everyone to this spot in the world where we're going to get one crack at this scene, so we don't want to regret not putting forth the effort to get the scene right.

> Part of the promise when I work with actors is that we may be on take 11 and I'll say, "We certainly have a version that we can put in the movie that will make us all happy. But I want to do seven more and continue to push this idea. Let's see where it goes." Now, I may go back to them after those seven takes and say, "It was a complete fucking waste of effort, but I had to try because I feel there's something to be mined from this." That's a lot of extra work for an actor, and sometimes it pushes them out of their comfort zone. In some cases they're not getting paid as much as they would on another movie. I go out on a limb, and people work harder for me than they do for other people. But I want them to be happy with the fact that we were able to do something singular, something unlike anything else in their or my filmography.

We're not all going to be geniuses like David Fincher, so it's not about burning our people out. But it is about giving them a North Star to head towards, so that they can feel like they're engaged in something that rhymes with their inner values.

Self-Awareness

Leading people who want to work well starts with our awareness of ourselves—not being "self-unaware"—and understanding when we need to pause, recharge, or adjust our approach to challenges. This requires tuning into our physical, emotional, and mental states. We want to know that we're getting the juice and the squeeze. If it's all squeeze, the juice runs out pretty quickly.

It's easy to prioritize work over well-being, especially in cultures that reward the hustle and the grind. But this disharmony leads to diminishing returns. When we're out of step with our bodies, we make poor decisions, strain our relationships, and eventually burn out. Harmonizing our effort with our deepest care is essential. We need more redefined "margin," that is, more space between our load and our limits.

> "We make a living by what we get, but we make a life by what we give."
>
> —Winston Churchill

TOGETHER

Now we come to the end of the magic trick. It's all well and good to make a rabbit disappear, but we've got to bring it back.

We can Work Well but if we're not doing it together, we're not creating resilience culture.

The idea of "Together" is about connection, collaboration, and shared success. No meaningful work happens in isolation. Whether we're collaborating with colleagues, seeking feedback, or drawing on the wisdom of others, togetherness reminds us of the power of working well with others.

Human beings are inherently social. Even in individual pursuits, we rely on others (mentors, colleagues, communities) for insight, support, and encouragement. Togetherness fosters innovation, resilience, and a sense of purpose. It also helps distribute effort, making challenges more manageable for everyone. If we do our jobs well, everyone's job should be easier.

In our work, togetherness starts with empathy and communication. It's about understanding others' perspectives, sharing goals, and working toward solutions collaboratively. It also involves creating spaces where people feel valued and included. For example:

- Are we listening to others' ideas?
- Are we fostering trust within our teams?
- Are we celebrating shared successes?

Harmonizing Independence and Collaboration

While togetherness is essential, it's important to harmonize it with personal autonomy. Not every decision requires consensus, and not every task needs collaboration. The key is knowing when to work together and when to take independent action.

As leaders, that's where our money is made.

It's our job as leaders to recognize the difference and which of our people need to run and which need the support of the group. The beauty of this work is that when our teams see in us this recognition, trust washes over the group, and then people feel safe to give their absolute best. Not because they're ordered to, but because they want to. Teresa Amabile writes, "Most people aren't anywhere near to realizing their creative potential, in part because they're laboring in environments that impede intrinsic motivation."

Intrinsic motivation is next to impossible individually, but collaborative groups ignite the flames within.

Being Together Is Hard

Collaboration isn't always easy. Miscommunication, conflicting priorities, and power dynamics can create friction. Our Work, Well, Together framework emphasizes creative communication, mutual respect, and resilience to deal with these complications as they arise.

The beauty of this framework lies in its interconnectedness.

- Work provides purpose and progress.
- Well ensures sustainability and growth.
- Together creates connection and shared success.

None of these elements can sing alone. They have to harmonize.

> "Members of a cohesive group feel warmth and comfort in the group and a sense of belongingness; they value the group and feel in turn that they are valued, accepted, and supported by other members."
>
> —Irvin D. Yalom

By practicing "Work, Well, Together," we can create a life that is not only productive but also meaningful, sustainable, and deeply connected. Remember: It's not about perfection. Working well together is about progress, balance, and shared purpose. Ultimately, this elegant framework invites us to engage fully with ourselves, our work, and the people around us, creating a foundation for lasting growth and resilience.

An organization that works well together—balancing effort, care, and connection—can reach unimaginable heights. An organization that prioritizes the well-being of its people without sacrificing productivity can foster creativity and long-term success.

When that happens, we've achieved Resilience Culture.

We've Re-Cultured.

THE RE-CULTURE CURIOSITY QUESTIONS

1. When do we work with greater clarity and purpose?
2. When do we prioritize well-being so that we bring our best selves to the work?
3. When we work together, how do we draw on the strength of collaboration, making our efforts more effective and meaningful?

Can Culture Crash a Plane?

On the morning of March 10, 2019, in Addis Ababa, a young, impeccably trained captain, the embodiment of Ethiopian pride and modern aviation, boarded Boeing's new 737 Max 8 for a routine flight carrying 157 people. Just six minutes after takeoff, the plane crashed into a field, a tragedy that would later be wrongly blamed on the pilot but was, in reality, the preventable result of corporate arrogance, a nation's pride in its airline, and a fatal denial of a known, flawed system.

Culture is serious business. Nowhere is this clearer than in the case of Boeing, the world's largest manufacturer of airplanes. If you're reading this book on an airplane, then you're probably on a Boeing plane. For generations, Boeing was the gold standard in safety and security for both passengers and investors.

Unfortunately, the once-unassailable reputation of Boeing was fundamentally shattered in the late 2010s by two catastrophic crashes that claimed 346 lives: the Lion Air Flight 610 crash in October 2018 and the Ethiopian Airlines Flight 302 crash.

I travel all the time to work with organizations all over the world. I feel safer in the friendly skies than I do on the highways of Southern California. That's the correct way to think—statistically, at least.

So, on the surface, the Boeing plane disasters could easily be dismissed as a lethal combination of pilot error and just plain bad luck. An aberration, nothing more. The reality of human flight is that sometimes mighty, heavy planes are brought down by the smallest factors, like something as light as a bird sucked into an engine at exactly the wrong moment.

But this wasn't one of those times.

The Ethiopian Airlines disaster, while tragic, was the result of corporate decisions made years earlier, decisions that prized results over safety, that relied on black box decision-making, and that were dependent on an insidious relationship between the company and the regulatory agency charged with keeping it in check.

This was a failure of culture.

***

Culture failures are like avalanches; things fail slowly, imperceptibly over time, and then, all at once, the slide buries all it touches.

It's a common story of corporate downfall, where a thriving culture undergoes a shift from resilient values to one that prizes profits and endless growth at the expense of its mission statement and, inevitably, crashes.

That's why Boeing's downfall began in 1997, when it acquired another aircraft manufacturer, McDonnell Douglas, a move that was akin to taking on a toxic mold that would eat away at the company from within. A company devoted to engineering excellence and safety became a business that worshipped stock prices and the S&P index.

Cut to the mid-2010s when Boeing faced intense pressure to develop the planes too quickly to compete with their main European rival, Airbus. The stiffness of the competition made them lose sight of the value system that had made them one of the most trusted companies in the world. They compromised through cost-cutting and a development process that stifled feedback and burned out its employees.

To save time and reduce costs, Boeing introduced an automated piloting system to rush their planes to market. Did they tell their pilots and put them through the rigorous testing process that would guarantee redundancy and safety?

No, they did not.

Every decision they made was driven by cost considerations and profit margins, because they didn't want to retrain pilots and anyone who spoke up was muffled by the invisible hand of self-interest.

Boeing's culture fostered a belief that automation could prevent human error and that any human who reported it was in error.

Later, internal communications revealed that some employees felt pressured to overlook safety issues to meet deadlines. On background, one such whistleblower said, "Boeing quit listening to their employees. Every time I'd raise my hand and say, 'Hey, we got a problem here,' they would attack the messenger and ignore the message."

Furthermore, Boeing's management ignored safety concerns and rushed through the certification process, relying heavily on delegated authority to internal engineers who would tow the company line rather than a thorough independent review by the proper authorities.

In business, this has become an all-too-familiar story.

After the Ethiopian Airlines disaster, the plane that they cut costs and corners to rush to market was grounded for over twenty months, causing financial losses that reverberated through the entire airline industry. The money they saved betraying their culture was a drop in the bucket compared to the consequences that followed.

The company faced a significant loss of trust from customers and the public.

Trust is the basis of safety. Even my grandkids know this. But Boeing's management team somehow forgot or didn't care. Later, internal memos revealed Boeing employees mocking management decisions and criticizing safety compromises, indicating a severe lack of trust in leadership.

Boeing shifted its focus from engineering excellence to profit-centered values and, in the bargain, distorted who they said they were. This resulted in a culture of cynicism where even its loyal employees doubted the organization's commitment to its values, like safety and innovation. Now, they were in service of the stock price and overly aggressive financial targets, leading to insane decisions like bypassing rigorous safety checks and pressuring engineers to meet impossible production schedules with no extra investment.

Instead of fostering a culture of collaboration, Boeing's culture became rife with animosity between executives and frontline engineers. To journalists, employees reported being ignored or overruled on critical safety concerns.

Lack of coherence within the company culture created impenetrable silos, where vital information was either withheld or disregarded, leading to systemic rot within the ranks. Employees told stories of intense pressure to meet deadlines, unrealistic demands, and a real fear of losing their jobs. This, of course, led to pervasive burnout and stress.

Boeing found itself with a demoralized workforce with low engagement and high turnover rates, which created massive inefficiencies and huge risks as the FAA publicly revealed the awful truth that on-the-line Boeing employees were aware of safety risks but failed to act decisively because they knew there was no institutional support for whistleblowers.

A once-proud engineering firm that was a model for American manufacturing was now cranking out subpar manufacturing processes so bad that a variety of safety lapses led to catastrophic failures, including two crashes in a single year. After which, blame was deflected onto individual employees rather than addressing systemic flaws that flowed from the very top.

To make matters worse, not only did employees feel disempowered, but the public perceived Boeing as evasive and irresponsible. Not a good place for any corporation.

Over a twenty-year period, Boeing's culture became excessively rigid and devoid of creativity by stifling innovation and morale, leading to unaddressed critical issues and an employee base brow-beaten to the point of disengagement.

That's the story about how Boeing's culture failed, and people died.

Now let's turn to a story that tries to show how culture may be able to land a plane.

BUILDING A REHEARSAL CULTURE

This year, Randi and I discovered a television show called *The Rehearsal*, created by the infamous awkward comic Nathan Fielder. Not only was it gripping and appointment television for us, but it also opened a completely new conversation about aviation, communication, and what it has to tell us about resilience culture.

What if you could rehearse life's most difficult conversations until you perfected them? What if you could simulate challenging scenarios to eliminate uncertainty? This is the provocative premise of Nathan Fielder's groundbreaking HBO series *The Rehearsal*, a show that, on one level, operates as cringe comedy but, for Re-Culture, functions as a laboratory that challenges everything that we know about how we work together.

For me, the really important lessons come in the show's second season when the show turns its uncanny lens toward airlines and aviation safety. Like Malcolm Gladwell in *Outliers*, Fielder is asking a simple question: Why do highly trained pilots sometimes fail to communicate critical information during emergencies?

A series of absurd experiments (building replica airports, creating fictional singing competitions, and even earning his pilot's license) illustrates for us the invisible (and flawed) architecture of culture that governs every organization.

When we examine the tragic story of Boeing's 737 MAX crashes through Fielder's unique framework, we discover an unsettling answer to this central question: Yes, culture can crash a plane. More specifically, a toxic organizational culture that stifles open communication, prioritizes results over safety, and discourages speaking up can indeed become a contributing factor in catastrophic failure.

The connection between Fielder's social experiments and Boeing's institutional breakdown reveals that the distance between comedy and tragedy, between safety and disaster, is often measured in the health of an organization's culture.

Throughout the masterful season two, Nathan Fielder pivots from helping individuals rehearse personal challenges to tackling the core systemic issue facing airline pilots: communication breakdowns in the cockpit. The season begins with Fielder researching black box transcripts from fatal plane crashes, where he identifies a disturbing pattern: First, officers often feel too intimidated to challenge captains, even when they see danger on the horizon. This power dynamic, reinforced by cockpit culture, creates something called "authority gradients," which, experts say, are the invisible barriers that prevent subordinates from speaking up, even when lives are at stake.

For our purposes, Fielder has given us fun, valuable, and actionable tools when he has pilots giving critiques to singing contestants to practice being direct and honest. From there, he builds realistic sets and environments so that pilots (not the most emotionally expressive people on their best day) can build the communication muscle memory needed to overcome authority gradients during genuine emergencies. As Steven Lantier notes in the *Toronto Guardian*, "The solution, Fielder posits, is to run pilots through various rehearsal scenarios and play-acting exercises, giving them the tools they need to communicate clearly and confidently, so that the wrong choice isn't made at thirty thousand feet in the air." In the world of organizational culture, Fielder's madness has the kind of method that creates real change.

Fielder's experiments demonstrate that psychological safety, the belief that one can speak up without fear of punishment or humiliation, isn't an abstract concept. It's a tangible cultural element that can be deliberately cultivated. We just need to practice and reinforce them. In one episode, Fielder deliberately makes his co-pilot uncomfortable, then works with him to "unpack that discomfort and strengthen the relationship," recognizing that this process ultimately benefits "the hundreds of passengers relying upon them."

If *The Rehearsal* diagnoses cultural communication breakdowns, it also proposes a radical solution: what if we deliberately designed our organizations to actually set aside time to practice difficult conversations and challenge scenarios before they become matters of life and death?

Fielder's approach, while exaggerated for television, contains powerful principles that any organization can apply:

1. **Normalize practice:** Create regular, low-stakes opportunities for team members to practice delivering difficult feedback or raising concerns.
2. **Flatten authority gradients:** Develop rituals and processes that make it safe for junior team members to speak up to senior ones. Again, you can "rehearse" them to create a zone of safety.
3. **Embrace simulation:** Use realistic scenarios rather than abstract discussions to build communication skills under pressure.
4. **Value psychological safety:** Recognize that comfort with discomfort is a cultural asset that requires deliberate cultivation.

Mr. Lantier went further on Nathan Fielder's exercise and gave us the means to repeat his mad method: "The point...is to make his copilot uncomfortable, then work with him to unpack that discomfort and strengthen the relationship, to the benefit of the hundreds of passengers relying upon them." This same principle applies to our organizations, where our safety, innovation, and performance depend on uncomfortable conversations

To get there, though, we have to Work. Let's find out how.

How to Work

"Without ambition one starts nothing. Without work one finishes nothing. The prize will not be sent to you. You have to win it."

—Ralph Waldo Emerson

WORK CULTURE GROWS FROM CULTURE

"One sometimes finds what one is not looking for."

—Alexander Fleming

The year is 1929, and a Scottish microbiologist returns from a holiday at the beach to the London lab where he had been studying a specific strain of staph bacteria. Accounts vary as to how one sample became contaminated (the story we were taught in school was that a half-eaten sandwich was close to hand), but a single petri dish was infected with a peculiar culture that would change the world. This new culture, Fleming observed, wiped out the infectious toxins in a way no one had ever seen before.

The microbiologist was Alexander Fleming, and the extraordinary culture was penicillin. And if it hadn't been discovered or perfected before World War II, millions around the globe would have died.

First, a language lesson:

The word "culture" comes from the Latin "cultura," which means "to tend, cultivate, or nurture" and derives from "colere," or "to till, inhabit, worship, or care for." Originally, culture was about farming and our relationship to the land. Culture was, quite literally, a garden that needed tending.

Then later, Cicero referred to something he called "cultura animi" or the "cultivation of the soul." For the first time, a garden could be outside in the fields and inside human beings. Philosophers like Cicero intuited that within the human mind, heart, and spirit were vast, seemingly infinite fields to cultivate.

As we advanced, explored, and spread throughout the world, culture began to refer to the local laws, customs, and modes of being in far-flung geographical areas, each with a complex network of values, symbols, and signifiers that are resilient from one generation to the next.

Later on, in Europe, the word came to refer to a kind of refinement or sophistication that indicated a higher level of class. It was the original "Finer Things Club" for you fans of the workplace comedy, *The Office*.

The word would develop a culture of its own, referring to everything from identity, ethics, patterns, and ideas.

In the 1960s, UNESCO defined culture as "a whole complex of distinctive, spiritual, material, intellectual and emotional features that characterize a society or social group. It includes not only the arts and letters, but also modes of life, the fundamental rights of the human being, value systems, traditions and beliefs."

I love their definition because it corresponds to the four building blocks of our humanity: the body, the mind, the heart, and the spirit. Our hardware and our software work together in harmony to create culture.

Like our bodies, an organization is not a bunch of isolated silos, but a living ecosystem. Another way of saying this is: An organization is an ecology of resilient systems. The intern who answers phones holds the client's trust, the foundation no AI can replace. The quiet analyst spotting risks is the immune system we can't afford to lose. When we divide and fragment ourselves into roles, we amputate our own potential.

We're not all the same. We don't have the same talents, gifts, and abilities. We don't have the same temperament. We're not all resilient in the same ways. And yet, we can come together to do things with one another. It's a beautiful process when it works. When it doesn't, it depletes our health.

Toxic work environments betray a fundamental idea of what makes us human. If we can no longer work together, then cultures start to erode much faster than they evolved. The social isolation that has come from technology and airborne viruses is attacking the soul of our society so that the bonds that once kept us united are frayed to their breaking point.

We hear the term "culture war" more than ever these days, especially in election years. And every year now seems to be an election year.

We hear about two opposing sides locked in a siege for the soul of a society struggling to stay sane and solvent.

Is that true?

Well, the different octopus arms of the information economy would like us to believe that it is. The media generates metric tons of engagement by pitting us against one another. They tell us we've got checklists of beliefs and values, and if someone doesn't check every single box, they're the enemy. On social media, "enragement" is the coin of the realm. Whatever is the most extreme, the most controversial, the hottest take, no matter how absurd, is what gets the most attention. We're told, as we scroll down endlessly, that the doom has no bottom.

Kanye West is pretty good evidence for this decline. He came up from nothing with nothing but his genius. He exploded into the culture with the fierce urgency of a prophet backed by beats that weren't like anything we'd ever heard before. He soared to the heights with money, power, and influence. He wasn't just a part of the culture: He was shaping it, molding it, and turning it to focus on the things he cared about. And then he became a sort of sad spectacle, engagement farming with more and more outrageous behavior. To break through in our cultural moment, you have to say and do the most bizarre thing of the day. Then you have to do it tomorrow. And the next and the next. The power structure that built and sustained Kanye the artist has consumed Kanye the man. He's richer than almost everyone, yet everyone mostly pities him.

So, we look at these power structures with a jaundiced eye. Yet we're trying to climb them. That's where the money is. We hate it, and we need it. So, we lose our belief in anything that's real or sustainable or resilient. Kanye West is a funhouse mirror that shows us exactly who we are.

Look around: We see it everywhere, this loss of faith in the cultural institutions that used to sustain us through hard times.

We don't trust our governments.

We don't break bread together.

We don't believe in science.

We don't listen to the media.

George Orwell nailed this when he wrote, "It is a mysterious thing, the loss of faith-as mysterious as faith itself. Like faith, it is ultimately not rooted in logic; it is a change in the climate of the mind." The change in the climate of the mind means the soil we've been cultivating together is in desperate need of regeneration, and the only way we'll do that is together.

How we work together can save our cultural ecosystem.

They say that you can't really know a person until you do a day's work with them. But how often do our beliefs come into the equation? Most of us work with people in situations where we don't talk about politics, religion, or the topic du jour. Instead, we share banal moments from our days and our weekends, things like movies, sports, errands, or small wins. As human beings, this is how we work together. It's how our species evolved from survival to revival.

We're built to work together. I guess you could say, we're built to build.

But what we've built is crumbling. We live in a culture of blame and shame, even though, underneath it all, we're pretty much the same. We're cut off from each other and our communities.

Let me give you an example: private planes. It used to be that we all traveled on the same planes. They were divided into classes, sure, but we were all in the same tube together. Rich, middle-class, and poor, we traveled as one. But with the rise of private air travel. Now, the rich and the super-rich can travel in a style that was once reserved for queens and sultans. It's not an accident, then, that air travel for the rest of us has gotten worse. Prices have gone up, but we're overstuffed on overfilled planes that sometimes sit on runways that never seem to end. We're less united than we've ever been—on air, land, and sea.

But there is something that unites us: work. In many ways, the workplace has become our new place of worship. The movement of capital has replaced the movement of the spirit. Just a cursory glance at LinkedIn will tell you that our relationship to work and working together fascinates, excites, and confounds us. Everywhere we look, someone has the answer, the ten-point plan for success that will turn my business from middling to profitable.

To realize how it's changed and evolved in just a handful of years, let's examine what culture can be for us.

CULTURE IS RENEWAL

Max McKeown nailed organizational culture when he wrote, "Ideas need constant renewal. A great idea will never be perfect and will never work perfectly in all markets and all seasons."

It's about shedding stagnation to reclaim our vitality. Renewal fuels growth in nature, individuals, and organizations. Think of it as the forest fire that clears the underbrush for new seedlings. Renewal springs from resilience because it confronts decay. We're not talking about recovery, a reactive process. In cultures, renewal is constantly embracing fresh possibilities. In a world of change and uncertainty, renewal isn't optional: It's oxygen. In creating sustainable strategies for ourselves and our people, we renew our relationship to how we do business.

CULTURE IS LEARNING

Ben Franklin gave me my kind of cultural definition of learning when he wrote, "Tell me and I forget, teach me and I may remember, involve me and I learn." In our work together, learning is the product of curiosity and experience. Learning takes our entire lives and spurs us to growth. When we actively pursue learning, we rewire the neural pathways of "This is how we've always done it" that wear old grooves into our new strategies. Cultural learning is active and humble and demands that we confront ourselves and our assumptions. Learning and leaning into the discomfort it brings builds resilience. It's the leap between what we know and what we need to know. Every question we answer creates an army of new questions, and every failure takes us deeper into our understanding of the world.

CULTURE IS COLLABORATION

"Coming together is a beginning. Keeping together is progress. Working together is success," says Henry Ford. Collaboration is the intentional act of uniting diverse skills, perspectives, and expertise toward a shared goal, creating outcomes greater than what we could have achieved on our own. We're going to talk about it a lot in the pages to come. In the main, it thrives on trust, open communication, and mutual respect, where we actively listen, challenge assumptions, and build on ideas together. A "Got Your Back" culture is based on creative collaboration between two or more people pulling in the same direction who all want the best for and from each other.

In an era of relentless change, where we're siloed off from one another, where trust in institutions erodes, and workplaces have become our modern tribes, culture is the antidote to the poison we've been drinking. But culture isn't easy. It demands we shed the "old ways" to embrace resilience through the renewal of our habits, assumptions, and strategies. It thrives on learning, rewiring rigid mindsets. It unites diverse voices into collective success. Culture is not passive; it's the soil we till daily. It requires of us deliberate acts of collective awareness in a world hurtling toward uncertainty. When we choose growth over decay, unity over isolation, and shared purpose over chaos, we heal, adapt, and thrive.

Together.

JOSH VS. EMMA VERSION 2

To introduce us to the concept of Work let me reintroduce you to two people you met in *Change Proof.*

These are two people you definitely have on your team: Josh and Emma. From the outside, they look the same. They've got the career, the family, the mortgage, the whole package. They both face massive pressure and uncertainty every single day.

But here's where it splits. Josh is drowning. He's stretched so thin that he's about to snap. His heart's racing, he's not sleeping, and he's one bad day away from curling up in a ball and letting go of the rope of reality. His brain is treating every email like a saber-tooth tiger. His status updates are anxiety-monsters let loose upon the rest of the team.

But what about Emma? She's got the same chaos, but she's thriving. She's energized, focused, and sleeping like a baby. She sees the same challenges Josh sees, but she sees them as a puzzle to solve, not a threat to survive. She's solving problems before they become problems that land on your desk.

- The difference in Change Proof (my manual of individual resilience) between the two was that it's not what's on their to-do list or in their inbox. Josh is stuck in a constant state of fight-or-flight. Emma has what I call resilient clarity of purpose. Their individual wiring is completely different. One seeks resilience while the other flees.
- Now, here's the tricky part: our organizational culture is directly responsible for which one of these people shows up to work. A toxic, fear-based culture amplifies the "Josh" in everyone. It burns out our best people and kills our ability to adapt.
- So, let's revisit our two protagonists and see where they've come in the last five years.

Emma is in her late forties, still with her partner, and her twins are now in private school, about to start looking at colleges. After the election of 2024, her government consulting firm was absorbed by a large tech company (funded by private equity) to leverage artificial intelligence to alter the bidding process for government contracts.

Oh, she made a whole lot of money in the deal, but she's proud of her business baby and wants to make sure that it's taken care of by its new parents. And she's not ready to start a new business, nor is she ready to throw in the towel.

In a blink, Emma's gone from the very top to the middle. For the first time in years, Emma's got a manager. You've met him before too. His name is Josh.

He's now in his mid-forties, and during the pandemic, he lost both his job and his marriage. He has a small condo and sees his daughter on the weekends. Because of his software experience, Josh was well-poised to take advantage of the push to AI, as his old firm had dozens of prototypes of AI bidding contracts. At heart, Josh is a coder, but he's now a manager across ten different teams. He's making more money than he ever has, but he's working twice as hard.

Emma, once autonomous, feels infantilized. Her confidence wanes as Josh second-guesses her expertise. Josh, anxious about his own job security, micromanages Emma's every move. He demands she CC him on every client email and submit hourly progress reports. "I need to stay in the loop," he insists, though Emma built her consulting firm from scratch.

Exhausted and resentful, Emma starts dreading Mondays. When Emma requests time off to attend her twins' school play, Josh scoffs, "If you can't handle deadlines, maybe this role isn't for you." He praises "hustle culture," urging her to work weekends to meet AI-driven targets.

Paranoia replaces teamwork. Emma isolates herself, fearing betrayal. Josh fuels division. He warns Emma, "Watch out for the AI team! They're gunning for your projects." He pits departments against each other, framing collaboration as a weakness.

Emma feels scapegoated, questioning her value. When a client rejects a bid, Josh blames Emma publicly: "This failure is on YOU." He takes credit for her past wins but distances himself from setbacks.

Emma's integrity clashes with Josh's profit-at-all-costs mindset. Josh pressures Emma to cut corners on ethics: "Enough with the compliance checks. We need this contract NOW." When she refuses, he implies she's "not a team player."

Creativity dies. The office becomes a joyless grind. Emma suggests a brainstorming session to reenergize the team. Josh shuts her down: "We don't have time for games. Stay on point!"

Stagnation sets in. Emma's skills atrophy as AI renders her expertise "obsolete." Emma asks about mentorship opportunities. Josh dismisses her: "You're here to execute, not be coddled." He cancels her training budget to cut costs.

Fear of mistakes paralyzes her. She stops taking risks. When Emma miscalculates a bid, Josh berates her: "This proves you can't handle the new system." He files a write-up instead of discussing lessons learned.

Feeling invisible, Emma's motivation plummets. Emma works nights to salvage a project. Josh says nothing. When she asks for feedback, he snaps, "Why should I thank you? You're paid to deliver."

Disillusioned, Emma scrolls through job listings during lunch breaks. Josh dismisses Emma's questions about the company's mission: "Just do what I say. It doesn't matter why." Work feels transactional, stripped of purpose.

One Friday, Emma resigns. "I used to love this work," she tells HR. "Now I'm just a cog in Josh's fear machine." Her exit interview cites every single one of Josh's cultural sins.

Across all of Josh's teams, morale collapses. Three more employees quit. Projects stall without Emma's institutional knowledge. HR investigates Josh's leadership, citing the Dust Bowl metaphor: "You've eroded our culture's 'soil,' and all our trust, joy, and purpose are gone."

Every company needs an Emma. And even though he was probably put into a position for which he wasn't suited, they need a Josh too.

A company with a healthy culture would have been able to keep both. If they'd swapped positions straight up, the organization would have been able to flourish and thrive.

> "Research indicates that employees have three prime needs: Interesting work, recognition for doing a good job, and being let in on things that are going on in the company."
>
> —Zig Ziglar

LEADERSHIP BLIND SPOTS

We've all got blind spots, and, though we don't want to admit it, they're hindering our ability to grow as individuals and as an organization.

Do you remember learning how to drive? I do. Especially now that I've survived teaching all my kids to drive as well.

When I'm driving, I've to keep an eye on my blind spots. Even though the technology of cars has advanced to the point that it does everything for me, I still check my mirrors, and when I'm changing lanes, I check my blind spots. When accidents happen, they're usually because someone didn't check their car's blind spot, the place that the mirrors can't show.

When we work with our teams, we have the same blind spots. They're those areas that we know we need to work on, but for a million reasons, we don't.

As we've said, Re-Culture isn't a top-down process, but culture regeneration begins at the top. Re-Culture is about checking our blind spots for the moments, the interactions, and the weak points in our culture so we can work well together. When we address our blind spots, we create a permission structure for others to do the same.

I learned this with the help of Antonio Garrido, the founder of My Daily Leadership and an expert in leadership transformation. Let's hop in the car with Antonio while he takes us on a tour through some of the three main leadership blind spots and how to fix them to create a lasting resilience culture in our organizations.

BLIND SPOT #1—OVERCONFIDENCE IN STRATEGIC ASSUMPTIONS

"Overconfidence in strategic assumptions" is the business way of saying "confirmation bias," the tendency of people to favor information or data that confirms prior beliefs or biases. Confirmation bias was first studied in the 1960s when we were finally confronting the racial biases of our country. But confirmation bias is about more than just race. It affects every aspect of how we perceive the world. It's something we are all subject to, and it's especially insidious to people in positions of authority.

If a cop pulls you over believing you're intoxicated at the wheel, then everything you do on that traffic stop is going to be seen through that lens. If you're black and the cop is white, then biases compound like interest.

We see what we want to see.

Another way of looking at strategic assumptions is the coach's maxim, "We do what we do no matter what they do, and we win." That's an example of playing to your strengths. A fine strategy based on maximizing your talents. But it will only take you so far.

Since we often operate on our strategies without questioning them deeply, this can lead to misguided strategies because our intuition is not synchronized with the market, no matter how much we'd like it to be.

Strategies get you in the game, and they may help you win a few, but eventually, other teams will figure you out.

The Re-Culture Fix: Disconfirm Your Bias

- Be clear about your expectations

Good leaders know that they have to guard against their teams' desire to please them. We all do it. Hierarchies exist for a reason. But that's not what makes our culture resilient. Our teams want clear expectations and autonomy to achieve them. At the end of that process, it's time for feedback. It's a simple system that's wickedly difficult to achieve.

- Seek out difficult conversations

In my own conversation with Antonio, he spoke passionately about speaking hard truths to the members of the C-suite. He told me, "It's about intelligent questioning of the senior people who recognize that if you always do what you've always done, you'll always get what you've always got. Therefore, if we want something different, then either the inputs have to be of a higher quality, or the process has to be of a higher quality."

You get better inputs and better processes with better questions. You have to be the one who asks them.

- Stay vigilant

A resilient culture where everyone has each other's backs means that we take nothing for granted. Assume nothing, question everything. That's what leaders do. Play devil's advocate, ask neutral questions, and regularly test the assumptions and roles of your company. In the military, they've got plans for every eventuality, because you just never know.

BLIND SPOT #2—RESISTANCE TO FEEDBACK

According to Antonio, this is one of the most common cultural problems that he sees when he works with organizations and teams. And it starts with the CEOs. They will not seek nor tolerate feedback from their employees. Oh, they may say that they want a constant, free flow of feedback that ebbs and flows between management and employees. But so few practice it. They view constructive feedback as threatening dissent rather than an opportunity for growth. C-suite leaders routinely ignore valid critiques and fail to create a Re-Culture environment where employees feel safe to voice concerns.

When I pressed Antonio on why, he said, "You don't want your feedback to be reflected in your next salary review, do you? You don't want that to reflect where you can park your car in the car park. Nobody tells a leader that they're doing a terrible job. Self-awareness is a key principle of leadership. If self-awareness is in short supply and nobody is going to tell you the truth, then how do you develop self-awareness?" In short, it has to start with us.

We can't assume people are with us. We have to ask. And when we ask, we have to be prepared for what our people are going to say to us, says Antonio. "Until you get to that point of self-awareness and until you admit to yourself you have a problem, then no one else can help you. We have to get over that hurdle as early as we can, as quickly as we can, and as painlessly as we can, because there are a lot of bruised egos associated with it. Once we get over them, then people's resilience starts to grow, and they can more easily accept critique."

Imagine a culture where everyone feels free to give one another feedback, with the knowledge and trust that they have each other's backs.

The Re-Culture Fix

- Trust and Verify

Creating a psychologically safe workplace is built on mutual trust and respect, but it's not a one-time project. It's an ongoing journey, requiring persistent effort to continually listen, refine, and adapt to change.

Leaders can install evolving feedback systems and actively support the culture of openness and vulnerability. We need to understand that things might not work right away. There will be pushback or discomfort with new feedback tools. These are part of a growth process, and we must persist until we're a confident, healthy, and open culture.

BLIND SPOT #3—FAILING THE EQ TEST

It used to be that leadership was about having a strong vision and then driving your team like horses toward a horizon that only you can see. Think of Steve Jobs and his "reality distortion field," and you'll be in the right place. For most of human civilization, that type of leadership was the norm. The bigger the company, the worse it got. Antonio told me, "The worst leaders we know have very low impulse control. They blow hot and cold and scream and shout and throw things." We've all had a boss like that. Maybe we've been that boss.

The truth is: The megalomaniacal way of management persists, but it's dying faster than the dodo.

As millennials age into management and Gen Z proliferates into the workforce, emotional intelligence is no longer the exception; it's the expectation. EQ has been bandied about in management consulting for three decades. But what exactly is emotional intelligence? Daniel Goleman, the trailblazer of the term, wrote, "If your emotional abilities aren't in hand, if you don't have self-awareness, if you are not able to manage your distressing emotions, if you can't have empathy and have effective relationships, then no matter how smart you are, you are not going to get very far."

These are the four markers for Emotional Intelligence:

> *Empathy*
> *Emotional Regulation*
> *Self-awareness*
> *Strong Interpersonal Relationships*

For leaders, these four markers are vital to increase our emotional intelligence—and not just because it's the right thing to do, but because it's more productive. That's the thing about resilient cultures: They don't just survive; they thrive. How? By helping mitigate conflict, identifying talent, creating change, and, our old friend, offering constructive feedback.

The bridge between leaders and their teams is emotional intelligence. And that bridge goes both ways. That's why team members need to possess emotional intelligence too.

Why?

A study done by the Niagara Institute in 2023 found that emotional intelligence was the highest predictor of workplace performance; that emotionally intelligent employees made, on average, $29,000 more; and that 75 percent of managers used emotional intelligence as the basis for promotion.

The Re-Culture Fix

- Journal your way to freedom

The simplest, the easiest, and the cheapest way to develop emotional intelligence isn't therapy, it isn't classes, and it isn't plant medicine in Costa Rica. It's keeping a daily journal—at least according to Antonio Garrido, who says that his coach (who coaches some of the most powerful people in the world) will not work with someone if they can't or won't journal. Antonio recommends that at the close of each day, you track your performance and give it a letter grade. It won't take years for the process to begin to work inside you. You'll notice a difference in just a few weeks. And then, Antonio told me, something interesting will begin to happen: "You'll find that situationally, instead of responding one way, you think, 'How would future Adam or what would future Adam be grateful for if I did or said or didn't do right now?' You'll find yourself situationally changing your behavior because you want to give yourself an A. You start to look ahead instead of looking backward."

It's like the line from *Almost Famous*: Be honest and unmerciful with yourself. And great things will begin to happen almost overnight. What could be better than that?

In a world of life hacks and easy fixes, this may be one of the easiest to do, but so few have the self-awareness to even attempt it. That'll tell you where your self-awareness level is.

I'll let Antonio sum things up for you: "Self-awareness is a keystone of emotional intelligence. We all know that emotional intelligence trumps IQ and technical skill by about 400 percent. People who come to me and tell me that they've got an MBA from Harvard don't impress me much. I am much more impressed by somebody who hasn't got a degree but is working on their EQ: empathy, self-awareness, social skills, and impulse control."

If we want to know why our organizations have high incidents of turnover, infighting, isolationism, and burnout, then we need to start with the person in the mirror.

THE RE-CULTURE CURIOSITY QUESTIONS

1. How might you systematically dismantle your strategic overconfidence by seeking disconfirming data? Are you strong enough to open yourself up to criticism from your team?
2. How could you weaponize vulnerability to crush feedback resistance? How can you foster psychological safety by showing your team that their voices reshape culture?
3. What daily EQ practice could bridge the gap between your self-awareness and your organizational reality?

BILL BELICHICK'S NO BULLSHIT CULTURE CAN WORK FOR YOU

"I am who I am. In the end, I feel that what I'm account-able for is doing a good job as a football coach."

—Bill Belichick

I'm a New Yorker. My record's pretty clear on that. I love the Knicks and the Yankees more than I love my life. And I love my life a whole lot. The New York football teams also have had my heart since the Jets' Joe Namath was guaranteeing Super Bowl wins and one of football's true Giants, Lawrence Taylor, was striking fear in the hearts of the entire NFL. For years, my New York football teams were pretty well useless until the New York Giants drafted Eli Manning, the unruffled little brother and giant-killer.

What giant did he kill? Oh, only the greatest coach-quarterback combo in the history of the NFL, Bill Belichick and Tom Brady. Twice. If I had a Hall of Fame vote, Eli would already be in just on the strength of those two Super Bowl wins over the New England Patriots, whom nobody seemed to be able to beat on the biggest stage. Except Eli, of course. Did I mention he beat them twice?

Even now, it seems even more improbable than David beating Goliath. It's more like some guy named Dave beating eleven Goliaths.

That's because Bill Belichick created a culture in New England that was nearly unbeatable. How? Through rigorous and ruthless accountability.

Together, Bill Belichick and Tom Brady forged the New England Patriots' culture of accountability through relentless, no-excuses leadership where everyone was responsible for the team's success.

The standard for everyone, from the backup long snapper to Tom Brady, was Belichick's mantra "Do Your Job," which demanded excellence as a habit. For almost twenty-five years. It's an understatement to call them dominant. It's not an understatement to say that it was dominance through culture. No matter how many players they lost or cut (some of whom still had good years left), they always found new players to integrate into their system.

Belichick and Brady were obsessive preparers, famously arriving first and leaving last, dissecting film, and publicly taking blame for losses even when others faltered. This dual standard of "extreme ownership" (no one above criticism) and "egalitarian expectations" (no one beneath responsibility) dissolved the egos that could wreck another, weaker team, creating a meritocracy where players trusted that accountability wasn't punitive but the shared currency of trust. When stars like Julian Edelman or undrafted contributors like Malcolm Butler bought in, they knew their effort would be matched by everyone. That was the test of trust in the system's fairness. They could buy in because winning, not individual glory, was the only bottom line that mattered.

I spoke to the Bill Belichick of leadership performance experts, Martin Moore, author and host of the podcast called *No Bullshit Leadership*. The few words he uses, he doesn't mince. One of the first things he told me was that he was a college dropout who tended bar for two years instead of finishing his schooling. Martin was adamant that bartending prepared him for the world of business and leadership performance: "To be able to read that in people by the way they walk, body language, and the expression on their face was important to me developing my emotional intelligence, my ability to see people for how they were feeling as opposed to looking at them and look through them. That was an incredibly important part of my growth for both human relationships and my leadership career."

But Martin's journey to accountable leadership wasn't exactly a straight growth line that went up forever. Like me, he pivoted out of a successful career working in a lot of different cultural environments and into an environment where he was helping others revitalize their culture. He's typically direct about how he works with leaders: "Do you want to be a leader? If you want to be a leader, here's what it takes. Here are the obligations you have and what it takes to be great. If you want to do that, awesome, get into it, but if you don't, don't kid yourself that you're a great leader because you're not." Those are tough words, but to sit in the big chair means we've got to deal with big responsibilities.

Let's be honest: Not every leader deserves to be where they are. We've got people woefully unprepared for the level of responsibility and accountability that quality leadership requires. Heck, maybe Bill Belichick wasn't ready for it when he coached the Cleveland Browns. We learn, we try, and we sometimes fail. That's the process for the kind of success that comes from inside the organization rather than through superficial means.

Using the Work Well Together framework, we can break account-ability down into five easily digestible bites so we may taste what it's truly like when practiced.

1: Deeds Match Words

What we say and what we do have to connect. If our teams even get a whiff of the disconnect between the two wafting off of us, the culture of trust can be timed with an egg timer.

They're going to stop trusting our actions if they can't trust our words. It's really as simple as that. The players in New England might not have always liked what Coach Belichick had to say to them, but they always knew it was coming from a desire to win, not an ego's wish for dominance. If a player didn't like it, they could leave. Belichick wasn't there to be liked. Martin agrees, "It's about habits and disciplines and doing what needs to be done, when it needs to be done, because it's right. It's about overcoming your fear of not being liked. It's about focusing on things that are potentially going to make you unpopular."

2: An Open Book (to the Right Pages)

We have to be transparent with our teams, but we can't let them see everything. Leaders who overshare about the challenges and pressure coming from above aren't leading. Part of our job is to eat pressure so that our teams are free to do their work. On the other hand, transparency about strategy is not only useful but also required. One of the hallmarks of Bill Belichick's teams was their preparedness. Not a single player could ask the question, "Why are we doing it this way?" because their coach told them exactly what they needed to do: their job. That's it. It's that balance of knowledge and instinct that allows teams to thrive under pressure. Preparation is transparent because it relaxes the whole team's natural workplace anxieties. Martin told me, "They knew that I was relaxed because I trusted them, because I had spent a lot of time selecting, grooming, mentoring, trusting, pushing, and stretching these guys who worked for me. I had confidence. I knew what their limits were."

3: Don't Shift the Blame

Bill Belichick always got hammered by the media for his taciturn press conferences that were, to borrow a word, devoid of bullshit. That was only because he refused to participate in their gossip gotcha games. He was known to wax loquacious about football history and obscure special-teams plays he'd never forgotten. Forget Chatty Cathy, meet Bubbly Bill. One thing Belichick always did was own failures and losses. He never threw people under the bus, and the buck perpetually stopped with him. His players could trust him because he wouldn't sell them out in the media to take the spotlight off himself. That takes a supreme amount of confidence that most leaders just don't possess. But, for Martin, it's pretty simple: "It's about not compromising. It's about taking accountability for what you do."

4: Be Consistent

Accountability may be simple, but it doesn't mean it's easy. It has to be practiced every day. Bill Belichick knew the importance of practice.

His players (many of whom have podcasts now) describe practices as more intense and direct than the games themselves. It can come in a bunch of small ways, none of which require us to completely turn the ship of our organizations. We can't be afraid to ask some hard questions of ourselves and our teams. We just have to make sure that we're conveying the why. Even if we don't say what it is, if we're going to practice accountability, then it has to be backed by something real. It can't just be random. Consistency comes from listening. As a senior leader, I used to rely on being able to see the smallest changes in facial expression when I was having serious conversations with the people who worked for me. Then I'd be able to say, 'That looks like that hit a raw nerve for you. Can you tell me what's going on for you? You seem proud of that achievement. Tell me about it.' To be able to say those little nuances in body language and facial expression are incredibly valuable in the communication quality that we have.

5: Grace Under Pressure

"A lot of people think they're good under pressure. I don't mean they can put their game face on so that they don't collapse in front of their teams. I'm talking about that deep, consistent, grace under pressure, and the complete consistency between what you say, think, and what's in your heart," Martin told me. Accountability gives us ways to practice our resilience. Many times, we work harder because we're avoiding being accountable. We don't want to face conflict that challenges our coherence. If we let go of that anxiety, accountability becomes a natural curiosity. We're no longer emotionally attached to results. We're simply trying to get the ease of performance. Like Tom Brady, who Martin brought up to me, "You look at a guy like Tom Brady. He runs out for his first offensive set in the Super Bowl for the Tampa Bay Buccaneers. I reckon his pulse rate wasn't above fifty-five. That guy went out there. He could have been playing a pickup game in his backyard with his son. He was so relaxed and in control and in command of that situation. That's grace under pressure. Because you don't get overwrought, hassled, or thrown off by the circumstances that you find yourself in."

Thanks to Bill Belichick, Tom Brady, and Martin Moore, we now know how to practice the kind of authentic accountability that builds resilient cultures. If we want that for our teams, then we've got five ways to check and discover how to do it.

And that's no bullshit.

THE RE-CULTURE CURIOSITY QUESTIONS

1. How can you ensure your actions consistently match your words to build and maintain trust within your teams?
2. What steps can you take to foster a culture of accountability where failure is owned collectively rather than blamed on your people?
3. In what ways can you practice and demonstrate grace under pressure to inspire confidence and resilience in your teams?

NICE VS. KIND

"People often silence themselves, or "agree to disagree" without fully exploring the actual nature of the disagreement, for the sake of protecting a relationship and maintaining connection. But when we avoid certain conversations, and never fully learn how the other person feels about all of the issues, we sometimes end up making assumptions that not only perpetuate but deepen misunderstandings, and that can generate resentment."

—Brené Brown

Alright, c'mere. Sit down. You look like you could use this. Just take the coffee, wouldja?

It's from the Greek diner down the block. Stavros makes it just the way you need it. None of that artisanal, fair-trade, tastes-like-weak-tea nonsense. This is coffee that you could float a rusty nail in, coffee that gets the job done and clears away the cobwebs.

Just like the conversation we're about to have.

You know I'm from New York. From Queens. We talk straight and fast without a lot of fluff about feelings. We're into facts where I'm from. So, you know I'm not here to blow smoke. I'm here to talk about one of the most dangerous, culture-killing diseases in the modern workplace. And no, it's not burnout. Not even close.

It's the epidemic of being nice instead of being kind.

People use those words like they're synonyms. They are not. They are opposites in action that attract vastly different outcomes. Let me break it down for you with a story.

Picture this: You're on the side of the Long Island Expressway (God help you) with a flat tire. You're standing there, suit rain-ruined, hopeless. A guy pulls over. He gets out, rolls up his sleeves, and says, "What? Nobody taught you how to change a flat tire? Jeez. Alright, move over. Let me show you." He's grumpy. He's not coddling you. He might even call you a schmuck under his breath. But he's getting his hands dirty. He's solving the problem. He's not nice. But he's kind.

Now, scenario two. Same flat tire. A different driver slows down their luxury vehicle on their way out to their Hamptons manse, gives you a sympathetic, pitying look, and drives off thinking, "Hmmm. Somebody should really help that nice person with their flat." That's nice. They acknowledged the problem. They may have even felt bad about it. But they did nothing. They avoided the conflict, the inconvenience, the mess. Nice. But not kind.

You see the difference? Nice is about appearance. It's about avoiding discomfort, yours and theirs. Kind is about action. It's about telling the truth and doing what's right, even when it's uncomfortable. Even when it creates a little friction.

And that friction, my friend, is the very engine of a healthy culture. Creative conflict builds culture, while avoiding conflict will smother culture in the crib.

Let that troubling vision sink in: A slow, quiet, polite death.

I've seen this up close. I worked with a massive health system in the South. Wonderful people. Salt of the earth. And they were raised, culturally, to be polite. To not make waves. To not offend. If you have a problem with someone, you smile, you nod, and you talk about it with everyone except that person. And someone will, I guarantee you, say, "Bless their heart." Which is the nice way of saying, "What an idiot."

Sounds harmonious, right? Feels good in the room. But the data told a different story. Their internal surveys were a five-alarm fire. Communication was broken. Trust in leadership was in the toilet. Innovation was stagnant. Why? Because no one was being kind. They were all being nice.

An employee would see a leader heading in the wrong direction on a project or passive-aggressively bullying their team. The nice thing to do? "Oh, I'm sure they'll figure it out. I don't want to hurt their feelings. They're trying so hard." So, they say nothing. Six months later, the project is a catastrophic failure, the employee is humiliated and probably looking for a new job, and the team has lost all faith in a leader who can't/won't lead. That's what "nice" gets you. A disaster wrapped in a smile.

What is the kind thing for that leader to do? To sit down with that employee and hear the words, "Look, I see what you're doing. I see the effort. And I need to be straight with you: you're heading off a cliff. Let's talk about why, and let's get you back on track. I've got your back." That's tough. It's uncomfortable. For a minute, it might not feel "nice." But it is profoundly, deeply kind. It's an act of service. It builds trust. It builds resilience.

This isn't just a theory. This is the bedrock of the transformations we lead. Look at the work we did with Zimmer Biomet, a Fortune 500 titan with eighteen thousand souls across the globe. Their engagement data was a wake-up call. Bottom quartile. Why? Lack of trust. Lack of well-being. A culture that was, I'd bet, too nice. Too conflict-avoidant.

We didn't go in and teach them to be nicer. We taught them to be kinder. To have the tough conversations. To build the resilience to handle creative conflict without falling apart. To borrow from the '90s MTV reality show: We gave them a shared language and the tools to stop being polite and start getting real.

It wasn't a soft, cuddly program that we introduced to their leaders. It was about building the muscle to face reality, together. And the result? They didn't just improve. They rocketed from the bottom 25 percent in engagement to the top 10 percent. That's a seismic shift. That's what happens when you trade the suffocating blanket of "nice" for the empowering, sometimes messy, work of "kind."

When leaders stop driving past the flat tires in their organization and start getting their hands dirty, everything changes. Trust isn't built by avoiding problems; it's forged in the fire of solving them together. The work we do together, when it's going well, is a gift. And I'm not talking about a gift of pleasantries. I'm talking about the gift of truth. The gift of Re-Culture is an organization that can finally breathe, argue, ideate, and excel because it is built on the solid foundation of kindness, not the fragile façade of nice.

So, as you finish this coffee, which, I'll be honest, is probably cold by now, I want you to take this with you. The next time you're in a meeting and see the elephant in the room, the next time you have feedback you're afraid to give, the next time you're tempted to smile and nod when you should lean in and speak up. I want you to hear my voice from this park bench in Queens.

If you have a choice, choose being kind over being nice.

RENEW YOUR WORDS AND ACTIONS

"Accountability is the glue that ties commitment to results."

—Will Craig

There's a common saying in sports that "availability" is an athlete's most important ability. A player might be a physical genius, but if they can't stay healthy, then they're of no use to the team.

It's an unfortunate reminder of the ruthlessness of professional sports. If you're not in the game, you can't help us.

For my money, my most important ability in Re-Culture is accountability. Being accountable is about being subject to one another. That's not about submitting and being subservient. Re-Culture isn't a pushover. Rather, every great team is full of individuals who give their best to the people on their team and expect the same from their teammates. Every great culture worth emulating is based on one idea: You submit your ego to the will of the group. That's how collective culture spreads and takes root in our organizations. Without it, we may get results for a time, but they will not be sustainable.

When our actions match our words, we are accountable. If I say to someone, "I'll have this task completed for you by Friday." Then, when Friday comes, and the task isn't done, I'm not being accountable. Conversely, if I say to my team that I'm going to have their backs, and then, when they get into a challenging spot where, maybe they need to work from home for a few days, reset, and get their mental health right, and I say, "I don't care. You be at your desk tomorrow ready to rock and roll," then I'm not being accountable to them.

We rise (and fall) to the level of our expectations of one another.

Accountability is a cornerstone of effective leadership and personal growth. It's about owning our actions, decisions, and their outcomes without making excuses. You know, it's easy to fall into the trap of blaming external circumstances or other people when things don't go as planned. But true accountability requires us to look inward and ask ourselves, "What could I have done better?"

In my conversations with leaders and teams, I've often emphasized that accountability isn't about pointing fingers and assigning blame; it's about creating a culture of trust and transparency.

It starts at the top. Accountability starts with leadership setting the example.

Marshall Goldsmith writes in his book, *The Earned Life*, about leading with accountability, about the Ford Motor Company turning their culture around with accountability.

In 2006, when Allan Mulally became Ford's CEO, the company was hemorrhaging $17 billion every year. The culture at the company had executives hiding problems to avoid blame, for fear that they'd be fired. Or worse.

When he took the helm, Mulally introduced weekly "Business Plan Review" meetings where leaders rated projects green (good), yellow (caution), or red (trouble).

At the first meeting, every executive reported green. Mulally paused and said, "We're losing billions. Someone's area has to be red."

One brave VP finally admitted his division was red. Rather than punishing the man, Mulally applauded him, creating the shift that would save the company. Over time, accountability became the norm, enabling Ford to avoid bankruptcy, unlike the other Detroit auto companies.

Or we can consider the case of Howard Schultz at Starbucks, in a story that's become one of the hallmarks of leadership accountability.

When Schultz returned as Starbucks CEO in 2008, the company was deep in the red. They'd scaled with too many stores too quickly, diluting the brand's quality. Team members were cut off from Starbucks' cultural mission of human connection through coffee. Somewhat radically, Schultz didn't blame anyone but himself. He admitted to the organization that under his earlier leadership, the company had prized growth above the customer experience.

Taking instant, bold, and ultimately costly action, Schultz owned the problem and closed over seven thousand stores for a day to retrain the many thousands of baristas on the basics of the Starbucks experience, which cost Starbucks millions in lost revenue. He said, "We lost sight of our purpose. That's on me. I'm responsible for the problem, and I'm responsible for the solution." He put his money where his mouth was by cutting his salary to $10,000 until performance improved.

And it did. Morale and loyalty bounced-forward, and Starbucks won back its cultural reputation because Howard Schultz owned his failure, modeled accountability, and rebuilt trust.

> If we want Re-Culture, we can start by:
>
> Work—Taking personal responsibility for strategic missteps.
>
> Well—Paying a tangible price to dovetail apologies and actions.
>
> Together—Model the accountability we want in our organizational culture.

When we hold ourselves accountable, we set a powerful example for others to follow. It encourages open communication and fosters an environment where people feel safe to take risks and learn from their mistakes.

One of the key aspects of accountability is the willingness to reset when things aren't working as well as they could. It's about having those honest conversations where we can say, "Let's create an agreement going forward that helps us work more effectively together." This kind of dialogue can lead to deeper understanding and stronger relationships within teams.

QUESTIONS FOR LEADERS: RESPONSIBILITIES VS. COMMITMENTS

If we're truly accountable and our actions share our values, we don't have to choose between culture and the bottom line. We can achieve both if we ask ourselves these three questions:

Do the Work: Take Ownership

1—"How have I recently taken ownership of a strategic misstep or failure, and what tangible steps have I taken to address it?"

Possible Steps

- Resetting priorities
- Reallocating resources
- Publicly apologizing

When we model vulnerability by naming problems (even when costly), we create a culture where everyone has permission to audit their actions, not just intentions.

Do the Work Well: Actions Match Values

2—"When was the last time I sacrificed a personal or organizational 'win' to uphold a commitment to my team's well-being or values?"

Show Your Sacrifice

- Revenue
- Efficiency
- Reputation

Sometimes leaders have to sacrifice short-term gains for resilient cultural health so their people can see them address the trade-off between results and humanity. If the leader chooses values over self-interest, trust increases, and culture grows.

Do the Work Well Together: Collective Accountability

3—"How am I creating systems where accountability is shared so that together we can own our culture?"

Shared Accountability

- Peer Feedback
- Transparent KPIs
- Radical honesty

As leaders, when we find our personal accountability rituals for our teams, we shift accountability from "my responsibility" to "our commitment."

Accountability isn't a solo act—it's a chorus. Are we singing alone, or are we harmonizing with our team?

Re-Culture leaders—

—WORK: Own their role in failures with a purpose and for a reason.

—WELL: Make sure sacrifices are in line with transparent values.

—TOGETHER: Embed accountability as a cultural practice, not a top-down mandate.

THE RE-CULTURE CURIOSITY QUESTIONS

1. How might you publicly own a recent strategic misstep and turn it into a teachable moment for your team, demonstrating that accountability starts with you?
2. What tangible steps could you take today to show that owning failure is the first step toward rebuilding trust?
3. Can you think of three moments where you chose to decline revenue, efficiency, or reputation in the moment? What was the result? Did it strengthen long-term loyalty?
4. How are you redesigning systems to make accountability a daily ritual?
5. What would it look like if you shifted from top-down blame to collective ownership, where your team feels empowered to flag risks and celebrate corrections?

RE-CULTURE FEEDBACK

"The other thing about giving feedback is that you don't do it all day, every day. It's got to be in small doses at the right moment."

—David Ross

Real communication and feedback, when integrated into our "Work, Well, Together" framework, fosters a culture where team members feel valued. When that happens, teams thrive. Then, the combination of those two leads to sustainable success. Why? Because everyone feels a sense of ownership about their work.

What's a feedback loop? It's a mechanism for guiding our systems to be self-regulating and intrinsically motivated, two key ingredients in resilient organizational cultures.

Feedback loops are fascinating because they're about refining something through repeated input and adjustment. They're inherently iterative, and if you use the Work, Well, Together framework, they can become a cornerstone of a healthy workplace culture.

RE-CULTURE LOOP 1: BUILD SIMPLE SOLUTIONS

Identify what needs to be fixed. Simplicity is key. In a workplace, we often overcomplicate things. Maybe it's because we're trying to look smart, or maybe it's because we think big solutions are more impressive. But big solutions take time, and time is precious when culture is already strained.

What would a simple solution look like? Maybe it's as straightforward as a weekly "pulse check." A five-minute survey, no frills, where employees can anonymously rate their stress levels or workload balance. Simple. Fast. It's Work because it answers the question, "Why are we here?"

In any organization, we're here to create an environment where people can thrive and do their best work.

But why start so simply? Well, if the problems seem too big for us, we won't attempt to solve them because complexity creates inertia. The more moving parts a solution has, the harder it is to implement and the more fragile it becomes. Simplicity isn't just about ease; it's about resilience, too.

RE-CULTURE LOOP 2: OVERLOOKED PROBLEMS

What are the problems that aren't obvious but undermine workplace culture? Maybe it's something like how meetings run. Everyone grumbles about meetings, but they rarely get addressed because they're so embedded in the workflow. Or maybe it's the way performance reviews focus only on numbers and neglect personal growth.

Here's the thing: overlooked problems often hide in plain sight. They're the ones that people have just learned to live with. That's dangerous because it breeds resentment and disengagement over time. Addressing these makes us Work WELL because it asks, "How can we be better?" We're looking for those subtle friction points that drain energy and morale and make it impossible to get ahead of the game.

How does this relate to feedback loops?

Overlooked problems only surface if we have a mechanism to reveal them. This is why a simple solution like the pulse check is critical. A quick five-minute check-in creates a channel for our people to voice what they might be keeping inside.

RE-CULTURE LOOP 3: SOLVE THE PROBLEMS THAT NEED TO BE SOLVED

This one is tricky. Not all problems are worth solving. Some are just noise. How do we decide what matters? It all comes down to impact. Does solving this problem improve how people work and how they feel about their work?

Let's take an example. Say you find out through a pulse check that people feel micromanaged. That's a huge problem. It impacts productivity, morale, and trust. Contrast that with a minor annoyance like people wanting better coffee in the break room. Sure, better coffee would be nice, but it's not a cultural game-changer, is it?

So maybe the question isn't just, "What needs to be solved?" but also, "What, if solved, will have the greatest ripple effect?" This is where prioritization comes in, and it's hard. We have to listen, sift through feedback, and make judgment calls.

But the payoff is huge when we get it right.

RE-CULTURE LOOP 4: DELIVER THEM AS INFORMALLY AS POSSIBLE

Formality kills momentum. If we spend weeks crafting a polished solution, we might miss the window of opportunity. Informal delivery is about speed and approachability. It's saying, "Here's a rough idea. What do you think?" rather than, "Here's the final product. Take it or leave it."

There's an old saying from Catholic school dances: "Leave room for the holy spirit." That, supposedly, kept boys and girls from getting too close on school property.

We have to leave room for our teams to bring themselves.

Culture is collaborative. If we present a solution as a finished product, our people might feel excluded. But if we say, "Hey, we're trying this out," it invites participation. It creates a sense of shared ownership, which is critical for buy-in.

Say we're dealing with a micromanagement issue. Instead of rolling out a company-wide training program, we could start with something informal like a weekly reminder email with tips for managers on fostering autonomy.

It's low-key, but it gets the ball rolling.

RE-CULTURE LOOP 5: START WITH A CRUDE VERSION FIRST

This is where things get interesting. Crudeness feels counterintuitive. We're taught to polish everything before presenting it. But in a feedback loop, starting rough is an advantage. Why? Because it invites improvement.

A crude version is like saying, "We're not married to this idea. Help us make it better." It lowers the stakes and encourages honest feedback.

Imagine rolling out a new performance review format. Instead of redesigning the whole system, we pilot it with one department. It's messy, but that's okay.

The goal is to learn, not to be perfect.

Starting crude is doing the work without overthinking. It's about progress, not perfection.

Failing faster makes us grow better.

RE-CULTURE LOOP 6: ITERATE RAPIDLY

Iteration is the heart of feedback loops. It's where we take what we've learned and make it better. Rapid iteration shows that we're listening, which builds trust. It's also energizing. People see their feedback shaping the culture in real time, and that's incredibly motivating.

For example, after piloting the new performance review in one department, we gathered feedback and made adjustments before expanding it to the whole company.

Maybe we learn that the new format is too time-consuming. Fine. We'll tweak it—and then tweak it again.

The point is to keep improving faster and faster.

Growth and collaboration are essential to our work. Everyone has a role in making the culture better.

Feedback loops are a way to embed accountability into culture. They're not just about solving problems—they're about creating a dynamic system where culture evolves through continuous input and refinement.

Focus on what matters. Start simple.

Address overlooked issues. Prioritize growth and improvement.

Deliver informally. Iterate rapidly. Involve everyone.

This isn't a one-and-done process. It's a mindset. It's a commitment to keep asking, "How can we work well together?" and never being satisfied with the first answer. That's how we build a healthy workplace culture: Step by step, feedback loop by feedback loop.

THE RE-CULTURE CURIOSITY QUESTIONS

1. How might you start your meetings with a simple, low-stakes feedback tool to uncover hidden cultural friction points, and how might addressing them free your team to focus on what truly matters?
2. How could you prioritize solving one overlooked problem that, if fixed, would free your team's energy for high-leverage work? How do you turn resentment into momentum?
3. What feedback process could you test this week to invite your team's input and accelerate culture-building through conscious iteration?

COHERENCE MAKES RESILIENCE

"The unlike is joined together, and from differences results the most beautiful harmony."

—Heraclitus

During the pandemic, organizations all over the world had to pivot quickly to a less hierarchical system. Many didn't. Their leaders, stuck in the old way of extracting product from their people, couldn't adapt. The best leaders didn't just focus on productivity; they prioritized connection. They learned that coherence begins with empathy, flexibility, and trust.

Remember the daily rituals that emerged in remote work settings? Virtual coffee breaks, wellness check-ins, or simply giving people the freedom to work asynchronously to meet the demands of home life. These practices weren't just Band-Aid solutions; they were outer manifestations of an inner coherence. Just by acknowledging the human side of work, the reality that we're all more than our job descriptions, they created harmony amongst their teams.

However, coherence can only describe the visible part of our lives. In one way, it's the melodic line of our organizations; it exists on the surface as part of the song. It's the tune we whistle while we work together. A great melody sticks in the mind. It's unforgettable. That's what great teams do: they sing the same tune. That's why if we're working well, togetherness is easy. If we're not, it may as well be impossible.

Re-Culture asks us to go deeper. If we're going to operate at the level of cultural regeneration, we need to listen deeper than the melody, to the bass line, the rhythm that drives and supports the song. Think of a great song like U2's "With or Without You" that has Bono's soaring voice, reaching for the redemption promised by The Edge's electronic echoes. Those are what make us remember the song. But what makes the song iconic is the insistent, humming bass line and the heartbeat pounding of the drums.

That's where coherence creates culture.

WHAT IS COHERENCE?

The basic definition is as follows: "Coherence refers to the quality of being logical, consistent, and orderly in thought, expression, or understanding." We've all sat through interminable PowerPoint presentations at meetings that we'd probably describe as "incoherent." A nice way to say it would be that the subject matter and the presentation don't relate to one another. It might be competently delivered and articulated, but something just feels…off. That's because all the clarity and logical flow of the work isn't connected meaningfully.

It's the same as this sentence you're reading in a chapter on "coherence" in a book about resilient culture in the workplace. Hopefully, it's unified and logically structured with clear connections between ideas, paragraphs, and chapters. I want you to understand my intent. If you don't, that's not your fault; it's mine.

Once we start looking for coherence, we start to see that it's in alarmingly short supply. An hour of work isn't an hour of work anymore. A dollar doesn't buy what a dollar used to buy. What our media tells us isn't what our eyes and ears see and hear every day.

Silos are a dangerous concept in workplace culture because they represent the fragmentation and isolation of teams, departments, or individuals within an organization. In a siloed workplace, teams operate independently, with little communication, collaboration, or sharing of information across boundaries. This creates barriers that make Re-Culture impossible.

That's why for any culture to be resilient, it has to be coherent. If trust is the binding agent for the stones of our Re-Culture tenets, then coherence is what makes them meaningful.

No matter how complex our organizations are, they have to be coherent so that every member of our team can understand them.

> Global coherence demands a permanent strategic cooperation culture at all levels.
>
> —Antonio Guterres

Coherence in workplace culture isn't accidental. It requires intentional effort and a foundation of shared values. It's not outside-in; it has to come from the inside-out through these four building blocks. For a real connection, we must build relationships that go beyond transactional interactions. It's about fostering genuine human bonds and ensuring that everyone feels seen, heard, and valued. Embracing change as a constant rather than a disruption. Coherence thrives when individuals and organizations stay flexible, ready to pivot when circumstances shift. This means cultivating a culture where experimentation and risk-taking are not just accepted but celebrated.

When minds, hearts, and efforts are pointed in the same direction, collaboration can be frictionless. But it has to be rooted in mutual respect and trust for differences of talent and temperament. Anchoring everything in a shared sense of meaning, purpose provides the "why" that keeps individuals and teams motivated, even when the road ahead is often hard to see.

These are the expectations we deliver when we bring new members onto our teams. Every organization is different—how they run their meetings, how feedback is given, how communication works, and what platforms they utilize. These are all conventions—even dress codes.

A coherent workplace culture relies on shared conventions that everyone understands and follows. For example, if we value being on time, then employees know to arrive at least five minutes early for meetings. Clear and consistently applied, conventions reduce confusion and make our working days fair and predictable. Think of George Steinbrenner and his list of rules regarding the appearance of his Yankees players.

But be wary: In toxic organizational cultures, conventions can become an object of fixation, and middle managers sweat endlessly over the small stuff. That's a recipe for burnout and stifled creativity.

Consistency is what we mean when we do exactly what we say, and our actions correspond to our stated values, ensuring that our decisions and our messages are reliable over time. Trust is an outgrowth of consistency.

Re-Culture requires consistency in our behavior as leaders. If we say we are a transparent organization, then we must regularly share updates and keep our people involved in decisions.

But be wary: If we promote teamwork but continually encourage Darwinian competition amongst our team members, then we undermine our message.

We're seeking a sense of unity and connection amongst our teams. That's cohesion that emanates from coherence. At every level, Re-Culture is about shared goals and mutual respect. Once we achieve a feeling of belonging, our people aren't just working well, they're working well together.

A cohesive workplace culture fosters collaboration and teamwork. Employees feel connected to the organization's mission and each other. For example, team-building activities, open communication channels, and inclusive practices can strengthen cohesion.

But be wary: Sometimes we try to force cohesion in ways that are inorganic to the dynamic nature of our teams. Team-building activities can be a substitute for the more difficult practice of recognizing that our team members are human beings with lives separate from their jobs. We don't need everyone to be best friends. We need a shared commitment to our values.

In Re-Culture, we have to love the process more than we love results. When I work with organizations with broken cultures, one of the complaints

I hear most often from team members is that the new hires are often left to fend for themselves. A recent Gallup study found that only 12 percent of new hires were satisfied with the onboarding process. This limits retention and productivity by 70 percent. Done correctly, onboarding new employees should follow a clear sequence: orientation, training, and gradual integration into teams. When processes are illogical or chaotic, team members end up wasting time and energy trying to navigate their tasks and their confusion.

But be wary: Like conventions, processes can become the little gods we end up serving rather than the people. Process without people is a dead culture. Process without people keeps us unproductive and stagnant. Empower your people through a process that works with them. The results will follow.

A coherent culture ensures that team members can understand the "why" behind our decisions and actions. For example, if our organizations have to change their strategy, then it is we who should explain the reasoning behind it so employees can understand our new direction. Without allowing for the "why," our people start to make incorrect assumptions, leading to disengagement or resistance.

Our communication must be as constant as change.

But be wary: If we share our "why" decisions and actions more than is necessary, then we're asking our teams to do our jobs and theirs as well. We mustn't overburden our people with the shifting winds of change. We're there to protect their possibilities and their work.

Too much concern and we're micromanaging our people through the Whys that we wrestle with.

In many ways, creating a coherent culture is like building a house. Conventions and consistency lay a strong foundation for fairness. Those predictable structures make it possible for our organizational culture to flourish and grow upward. Coherence fosters the collaboration that is the walls, beams, and struts that protect us from the winds of mistrust. Process is the electrical and plumbing systems that tie the whole place together and make it livable.

And the Why, well, that's the roof that protects us from the stormy winds of change.

Through the storm we reach the shore, we'll give it all, but we want more, and we're waiting for you.

THE RE-CULTURE CURIOSITY QUESTIONS

1. How might your organization redesign corporate conventions (e.g., meetings, feedback loops) as adaptive rather than rigid scripts? How can you make space for your teams to improvise within a shared cultural structure?
2. If "consistency" is the heartbeat of trust, what weekly rituals could transform coherence from a compliance checklist into a values pulse-check that dovetails with your organizational Why?
3. How might you manufacture situations where creative tension and momentary discomfort are the goal to help teams get comfortable being uncomfortable?
4. How is your comfort connected to your organizational incoherence?

FORGET JOHN AND PAUL, FIND YOUR RINGO

"I didn't play drums to make money. I played drums because I loved them."

—Ringo Starr

If we want coherence in our organization, we have to look beyond the A players and search for the people who provide the chemistry that bonds it all together.

During the holiday season of 2021, my family and I got to watch a fascinating documentary series that was released on the Disney+ streaming platform. It was called *Get Back,* and it was directed by Academy Award-winner Peter Jackson (*The Lord of the Rings*), one of the biggest Beatles fans of all time.

Jackson was originally going to work with Apple Corps (the Beatles organization, not the Steve Jobs one) on an augmented reality project about the band. But then they expressed interest in a new, extended documentary about the making of the *Let It Be* album, infamous in that the original documentary of the same name showed the world the infighting that tore the band asunder.

Initially, Jackson wanted no part of documenting the downfall of his favorite band. But when he watched some of the sixty hours of footage, he didn't see the bitterness and backbiting that defined the end of the Beatles. Instead, he saw a band reckoning with the end of the road, yes, but coming together with the joy of creating something with people you love.

For me, the real joy of the series is that it shows the true secret of artistic collaboration: work.

For twenty-one days (give or take), these fabulous four musicians show up every day to pick up their instruments and negotiate their way to a place none of them could ever get to on their own. It's not a magical mystery tour; it's just the day-to-day routine of cups of tea, slices of toast, and the greatest of all creative pleasures: screwing around.

They just show up every day (mostly) and get to work. That's why, on one occasion when Paul McCartney is waiting around for John Lennon to show up, we watch, in real time, as he creates the melody that would become the hit single "Get Back" seemingly off the cuff.

What comes alive is the notion that their culture, even though the band is on the verge of breaking up, is resilient to the very end. You feel that they care for one another. After all, they were all shot into the stratosphere at the same time, and it gets lonely up there where the air is thin. But even after all they've been through, they're constantly working together to make something beautiful.

John, Paul, George, and Ringo embody all the elements of Re-Culture. They play, they harmonize, they're accountable, they have rigorous standards, they never stop learning or trying, they're comfortable being uncomfortable, they make art out of mistakes, and they, at the end of it all, trust one another.

***

But for me, the secret hero of the documentary is Ringo Starr. I'd go further and say he was the secret hero of the band. And when we're coherently renewing our culture, we can't forget to look for our Ringo.

In human resources terms, the quote most attributed to Steve Jobs is, "A players attract A players. B players attract C players." That's a business truism that means that the best attracts the best, and your whole team should be built out of the best.

But it's more complicated than that.

Let's look at the Beatles. The A players are obvious: John and Paul. Watching them interact is like watching two schoolboys banter barbs and melodies and impressions and voices. In another world, they'd be a Monty Python-type group, making sketches and films that stuck a thumb in the eye of the establishment.

John and Paul—they're the ones who drive the band, who create the culture, who wrestle for control (at one point, each of them insisting that the other one is the boss of the band), and they're the shrewd businessmen who decide who gets what and when.

George Harrison is the B player. But only because that's the role to which John and Paul admit that they've consigned him. George is an A player (as his triple album of songs, *All Things Must Pass*, would attest). During the making of "Get Back," though, George is fed up with being the "little brother" of the band. He's a genius in his own right, with so many songs inside him bursting to get out. And will they!

Now we get to our C player: Ringo.

Over the years, many of us likely thought that Ringo was carried by the other three members of the band. He was the charming rogue, sometimes actor, and generally a lovable mop-headed goofball. He came late to the band as a replacement when the culture was already forming, and Ringo felt it keenly. "I was the new boy. It was like joining a new class at school where everybody knows everybody else but me." We've all felt like that. For years, rumors have swirled about the Beatles sending Ringo out for a meal and then Paul recording the drum parts while he was gone. And it's true. Ringo wasn't even the best drummer in his band.

But here's the thing: None of that matters. In the documentary, Ringo doesn't act like the new boy. He's the glue that holds the whole band together. He's always there. On time. When Paul, John, or George are starting to riff, he's always at the drums or with some percussive instrument. Even if they're just noodling around, he's always supporting, being silly, but most of all, he's just…there.

When George says, "I think I'm leaving the band," and things get screwed to the sticking post, and the band is teetering on the edge of collapse, where did they meet to hash things out?

You guessed it. Ringo's house. Well, his estate. Let's not forget: these boys were fantastically wealthy.

What Peter Jackson revealed in *Get Back* was that an organization's culture isn't just made by the geniuses; it's bonded together by the team members who are just happy to be there. Their presence (like a goat bunking in with a racehorse) makes everyone want to be there.

In sports terms, these people are called "chemistry" players. It's like the notorious culture builder Jerry "The Shark" Tarkanian said, "The secret is to have 8 great players and 4 others who will cheer like crazy."

The hiring process, at least as it's practiced today, is we're heeding the clarion call of Steve Jobs and trying to fill out our roster with A players.

But that's like trying to fill a basketball team with twelve Michael Jordans. I believe that team would lose to the 1996 Chicago Bulls, because to win a championship, you need your Bill Wenningtons and your Judd Buechlers.

If we want Re-Culture, a renewed culture built for the long-term, we need to populate our organizations with the people who make the work possible by making it feel like they're not working.

(Media question to Beatles during first US Tour, 1964)
"How do you find America?"
"Turn left at Greenland."

—Ringo Starr

THE RE-CULTURE CURIOSITY QUESTIONS

1. How might you and your organization redefine talent to value cultural catalysts whose superpower is harmonizing conflict, not just individual brilliance, and what hiring practices could help you find and elevate these often-overlooked traits?
2. What if teams allocated "glue roles" explicitly, designating Ringo-like stewards to safeguard psychological safety? How might your onboarding shift to prepare these unsung heroes to build culture around them?

3. How could KPIs track resilience dividends from chemistry builders, for example, reduced meeting toxicity or faster conflict resolution? Is there a data set that proves their impact beyond traditional productivity benchmarks?
4. What if leadership pipelines prioritized "orchestrators" over soloists, training visionaries to spot, protect, and amplify the cultural Ringos who turn their sparks into a bonfire?

RE-CULTURE IS NOT FRIENDSHIP

"You can take my factories, burn up my buildings, but give me my people and I'll build the business right back again."

—Henry Ford

One of the main notions we have to disabuse ourselves of is that culture equates to friendship. Everyone gets along. A resilient culture keeps everyone where they can do the most good for themselves and the organization. A work role with clearly defined and defended boundaries and expectations is the number one predictor of employee engagement, even above payment structure and work relationships. Those help, no doubt, but everyone doesn't have to be friends to make the organization work well together. A healthy culture is rooted in a healthy respect for the time, talents, and boundaries of everyone in the organization.

But Re-Culture starts at the top, with our leadership.

FOCUS ON RESPECT, NOT POPULARITY

A healthy workplace culture emphasizes respect and professionalism over barbecues and ball games. I have deep professional relationships with some people, and I know almost nothing about their personal lives. Respect allows us to see beneath our egos to witness what makes people tick, what gives them purpose and meaning. We're not always going to be liked. That's why we're in leadership. We have to make hard choices. At our level, relationships are built on mutual trust and accountability, not personal likability.

> "Respect is how to treat everyone, not just those you want to impress."
>
> —Richard Branson

RE-COMPARTMENTALIZATION

Professional cultures have to maintain clear boundaries between work and personal life. We have to bring ourselves to our work, but that means leaving personal problems at the door. That shows respect for other people and our problems. "Leave your problems at work at work and your problems at home at home. You will have one problem to solve at a time," writes Ruskin Kwofie.

We've all had the experience of letting a problem at home bring us down at work and unburdening ourselves on a co-worker. That's fine. It can happen. But it can't be a habit. We bring our whole selves to work well, but to be able to do it together, we have to leave room for the best part of us. The problems will be there. But it's not fair to expect friendship from the people with whom we work. Friendships can exist, but they have to take a backseat to achieving goals and ensuring everyone is treated fairly.

> "Trust is knowing that when a team member does push you, they're doing it because they care about the team."
>
> —Patrick Lencioni

FEEDBACK MUST BE CREATIVE

In a strong culture, we seek honest feedback over avoiding difficult conversations to preserve relationships. That doesn't mean we go out of our way to be creatively cruel. But many times, leaders get locked in the prison of their minds. I do this sometimes when I get overloaded with my podcast, Work Well Labs, running assessments, family responsibilities, and just the churn of the world. I feel like I've fallen off my surfboard, and the ocean is just turning and tossing me like human laundry. If I have to give feedback in that over-cooked state, it's going to come out direct and maybe a little harsh. In my mind, I think that I don't have time to consider my team's feelings, that they should just get over it. But that's not creative, cultural leadership. It's lazy and only takes one set of feelings into the equation: my own.

As leaders, we've got to get better at giving good feedback. If it's all negative all the time, then no wonder we feel negative all the time.

But we also can't avoid giving feedback either. That's the same problem, only from the opposite side of the coin. It's that toxic positivity I spoke of earlier. We can't just operate on good vibes only and hope for excellent results.

"Feedback is the breakfast of champions."

—Ken Blanchard

BEWARE OF CLIQUES

Collaboration in teams and tribes is good. Very good. But we have to be careful that cliques don't form. We see this sometimes, where the A players hang with A's and B players hang with the B's, and so on. We don't want that. A healthy workplace culture means cross-pollination among our teams. Get people with different skills working together. We never know what surprises they have in store for us. Heck, they'll surprise themselves. If we rotate groups, teams, and interactions, we'll get more from everyone. But we can't do it every day or even every week. One rotation per quarter will serve. Collaboration begins with mutual understanding, not shared lunch breaks.

It's not friendswork; it's teamwork.

"There is nothing more difficult to take in hand, more perilous to conduct, or more uncertain in its success, than to take the lead in the introduction of a new order of things."

—Niccolo Machiavelli

LEADERS AREN'T LIKED

A strong culture is about clarity and moving in the same direction. It's not about our comfort and how our people feel about us. Everybody wants to be liked. Leadership requires that, plus the respect that comes from knowing that we have their backs. We can't do that if we're out partying with them. We need a comfortable distance.

If our teams know that we can decide if they rise or fall within the organization, then we can never truly be their friend. Something will always stand in the way. Fine. Let it.

Instead, let's dig in to finding out what motivates our teams and letting them know, with clarity, when they're on the right path and bringing them back when they're not.

"A community is like a ship; everyone ought to be prepared to take the helm."

—Henrik Johan Ibsen

Coherent leadership means everyone can understand us when we speak and when we act. If they're confused, then we're not doing our jobs correctly, and our culture will suffer.

THE RE-CULTURE CURIOSITY QUESTIONS

1. How might your organization identify respect as a measurable data point, to ensure it transcends personal relationships and becomes a nonnegotiable feature of culture?

2. What if feedback cycles were redesigned as "creative collisions," where you might create anonymous peer reviews across departments, where every negative comment must be balanced with a positive affirmation? How can you make your feedback more than just individual improvement?

3. How could you embed "boundary guardians" in your teams? How might they function as role-rotating stewards to surgically disrupt cliques and create comfort with criticism?

4. What rituals would allow you to model approachable leadership?

5. Compartmentalization can be armor for your culture, so how might you create transition rituals at the top and bottom of each workday to help team members solidify work-home boundaries?

DESIGN FOR CULTURE: THE 60-30-10 RULE FOR BUILDING RESILIENT TEAMS

"Design is not just what it looks like and feels like. Design is how it works."

—Steve Jobs

You wouldn't design a room without thinking about color, balance, and feel. So why do we so often throw a team together without the same intention? We hire for resumes, for skills, for "culture fit," a term I often find means "people who think and act like I do." That's not design. That's the default. Designers don't throw things at the wall and hope for the best. That's what my grandchildren do.

That's why, if you want to build a resilient, high-performing culture, you have to design for it. And one of the most powerful, timeless design principles we can borrow is the 60-30-10 rule.

In interior design, it works like this:

Sixty percent of a room is a dominant, grounding color (like the walls).

Thirty percent is a secondary color that provides support and interest (like the furniture).

Ten percent is an accent color that adds pop and personality (like throw pillows or art).

This formula creates harmony, balance, and visual interest. It prevents any one element from overwhelming the space and creates a space that feels good, even if you're not conscious of exactly how that is.

Now, let's apply this to our teams. Think of them not as a list of names, but as a living, breathing ecosystem we are intentionally designing.

THE 60 PERCENT: YOUR CULTURAL FOUNDATION

This is the core of our team, the 60 percent who embody our company's core values and operational rhythms. These are our steady, reliable, high-trust players. They are the "walls" of our culture. They don't just know how we do things around here; they live it.

These are our seasoned veterans, our cultural carriers. They provide stability, mentorship, and consistent execution. They keep the team moving in the direction we established when we set out on the journey together. Essentially, these are the people who could run the company if it came down to it, but who are happy where they are. Without the strong 60 percent, our culture has no foundation. It becomes volatile, shifting with every new hire or market trend. Think of them as insulation because they provide the psychological safety and continuity that allows for risk-taking and innovation elsewhere. Feed them recognition and stability, and they'll live forever. But take them for granted and watch culture scores plummet.

THE 30 PERCENT: YOUR GROWTH ENGINE

This is the secondary color, the 30 percent who are the dynamic supporters and enablers. They are deeply competent and aligned with the mission, but they bring new skills, new perspectives, and a healthy restlessness. They are the "furniture," functional, vital, and shaping how people interact within the space, but they require space to do it. The "30 percenters" are the high-potential leaders, specialists from adjacent industries, and internal promotions who are brought in to shake things up. It's not that they don't care about the mission; they just have their own way of getting there. In the right scenarios, they challenge the status quo in constructive ways.

The 30 percent prevents cultural stagnation. They ask, "Why do we do it this way?" and bring fresh energy that keeps the 60 percent sharp and evolving. They are the bridge between a solid foundation and the transformative accents that make the organization feel alive.

THE 10 PERCENT: YOUR CATALYSTS FOR CHANGE

That brings us to the accents, the 10 percent who are the wild cards. They think differently, act differently, and often make the rest of the team slightly uncomfortable. Think of them like Kramer from *Seinfeld*: They'll say the thing no one else has the courage to say. They are the "art" on the wall that sparks conversation. They don't just play the game differently; they question the point of the game itself. They're necessary for every team. More than likely, they're the unconventional hire from a completely different industry. The provocateur. The creative genius. The entrepreneur-in-residence. They'd be just as happy on their own as in a group.

They're the Dennis Rodman of the '90s Chicago Bulls. They're the trickster that shows us new ways to think, believe, and act. This 10 percent is our antidote to complacency and groupthink. They are the source of our most disruptive ideas and breakthrough innovations. They force the entire team to see the world with fresh eyes. Without them, our culture becomes an echo chamber. But a warning: without the strong 60 percent foundation, the 10 percent will cause chaos, not progress. Also, they need a direct line to leadership. Without it, they'll feel constrained and shackled, and then they'll lead a revolt.

THE RE-CULTURE CURIOSITY QUESTIONS

1. Look at your core team right now. Who are your undeniable 60 percent, the people who are the very walls of your culture? Now, be brutally honest: Are you taking them for granted, or are you

actively feeding them the recognition and stability that will make them never want to leave?

2. Who's in your 30 percent asking the uncomfortable "why" questions? And when they challenge the status quo, does your culture treat them as a threat to be managed or as the essential "furniture" that keeps your foundation from becoming a prison?

3. When was the last time someone in your 10 percent, your wild card, your catalyst, made you and the rest of the team genuinely uncomfortable? If you can't remember, that's your red flag. What are you doing to actively recruit and protect these indispensable disruptors before your culture becomes an echo chamber?

MIND MOVIES

"The only thing more unthinkable than leaving was staying; the only thing more impossible than staying was leaving. I didn't want to destroy anything or anybody. I just wanted to slip quietly out the back door, without causing any fuss or consequences, and then not stop running until I reached Greenland."

—Elizabeth Gilbert

Re-Culture is work, and work is impossible without failure. In this book, we're spilling a lot of ink talking about workplace culture. But there are other cultures too—like a relationship. In ways both conscious and unconscious, Randi and I have used the tenets of Re-Culture for our entire relationship to work well together as a couple. We've been tremendously lucky, but, as the old saw says, "The harder we work, the luckier we seem to get."

My friend Natalie Ledwell wasn't so lucky. Not long ago, she learned the hard way that failure can sometimes feel like a messy series of setbacks that, in retrospect, were transformational pivots that made her stronger than she could have imagined.

Natalie created a personal development company with her husband Glen, called Mind Movies, that creates customizable digital vision boards that combine affirmations, images, and music to help users visualize and manifest their goals. It's one of those ingenious ideas that seems inevitable. But we know that even inevitable ideas start from sheer force of will.

Together, Natalie and Glen built Mind Movies into a company with a huge user base. "We went from not knowing anything about the internet, from hardly being able to turn on the computer, to building a multimillion-dollar company in a few short years. We were ticking off everything on my bucket list like there was no tomorrow."

From the outside, they had everything: a flourishing business, a happy marriage decades in the making, and the ability to fly their family and friends anywhere in the world on a moment's notice.

But one day, after an amazing trip to New York, they walked into their San Diego apartment, and Glen handed Natalie a glass of wine and a devastating declaration: Glen had met somebody else. Their marriage was over. In that moment, Natalie had a choice: She could fight, she could flee, or she could fail.

She chose the latter and, in doing so, made the ladder of her success.

Facing up to the failure of her marriage, Natalie decided to navigate through the process with Glen, defying recrimination and rancor, and chose to experience the failure fully. But it wasn't easy: "Each morning I would get up and drag myself out of bed, and I would walk along the waterfront in San Diego. I would keep walking until I felt good enough to face the day."

But slowly, over time, Natalie regained an identity separate from her husband and forged a way forward by rigorously unpacking how she helped create the failure in which they'd found themselves. Glen did too. Then they went through the process together. And they found their way to something stronger than it was before. "Now, we're able to have this amazing relationship between the two of us of mutual respect and love. We're not in love anymore, but we still love each other very much. It's been incredible."

In a way, what Natalie learned, by experiencing one of the worst failures a human being can endure, was that there is no failure, only an infinite series of moments, like drops of water in an endless sea. Our successes and our failures only define us if we let them. Natalie, through a lot of work and introspection, found that these moments, strung together, lead us to growth.

She wasn't defined by the failure of her marriage; she redefined it as another step on her evolution as a human being. The mechanism, or pivot, to this process was Natalie owning her decisions and her choices. She didn't blame or kick up a fuss or make excuses. She would have been well within her rights to do so. Her husband stepped out on her marriage and broke their vows. Natalie chose the path few have chosen and found new territories in herself and her business.

Mind Movies is still flourishing with millions manifesting their dreams, because Natalie created a resilient culture for herself, for Glen, and for Mind Movies by taking responsibility for her part of the divorce. It's amazing, the strength that it takes to lean into failure. Letting failure be her teacher, Natalie learned the most important lesson of all: Failure is the soil that makes culture grow.

THE RE-CULTURE CURIOSITY QUESTIONS

1. How might you treat your next failure as a "plot twist" in your organization's story to highlight the lessons, not the losses? How could you turn a setback into a collective breakthrough?

2. How could you rebuild a fractured culture and pivot into collective trust? How can you prove to your team that respect outlives failure, and shared purpose transcends broken vows?

3. What daily practice could help you compost failure into cultural fertilizer to plant seeds of resilience where others see scorched earth?

FAIL LIKE AN NBA CHAMPION

"I see myself as a student. Trying to learn everything."

—Giannis Antetokounmpo

I love the NBA playoffs. And, as you all know, I'm a fan of the eternally hapless New York Knickerbockers. In spite of my favorite team's history of failure, I'm still fascinated by the crucible of pressure that is the extra month of the professional basketball season. Because of that word: failure.

A couple of seasons ago, my beloved Knicks finally gave me a glimmer of hope for a couple of rounds (only to have it cruelly snuffed out by Jimmy Butler), but, for me, the real story of those playoffs was the Greek Freak himself, Giannis Antetokounmpo. When asked if his top-seeded Milwaukee Bucks' season was a failure because they lost to the lowest-seeded Miami Heat, he said this:

> So why (did) you ask me that question? It's a wrong question. There is no failure in sports. You know, there's good days, bad days. Some days you are able to be successful, some days you are not. Some days it's your turn, some days it's not your turn. And that's what sports are about. You don't always win. This year, somebody else is gonna win. Simple as that.

The post-mortem analysis on TNT's *Inside the NBA* gave us two clear distinctions. On one hand, we had Shaquille O'Neal, who said, "When you're a great player, and they expect you to win, and you don't win, in my mind, it is a failure." And on the other, Kenny Smith, who said that Giannis's answer was "one of the most eloquent ways I've ever heard someone talk about how to be successful." To the Big Aristotle, anything less than a championship constituted failure. A two-time champion with the Houston Rockets, Kenny intuitively understood that failure is crucial to success.

You cannot win without losing.

For us, in the world of business, of course, we want to win. The measure for our stakeholders is winning. I routinely ask the business leaders I work with: "What does winning look like?" And, "What will it cost you?"

LEARNING VS. EXTRACTION

How they answer these two questions tells me whether they are a learning culture or an extraction culture.

Think of Don Draper, who says to the executives at Dow Chemical, "Even though success is a reality, its effects are temporary.... What is happiness? It's the moment before you need more happiness."

Like the former Dick Whitman, the Great White of modern capitalism, in the extraction organization, winning and success are prized above all things. The leaders of the organizations expect exponential growth with a profit line that moves upward to infinity and beyond.

The extraction organization disregards the value of learning and growth in favor of short-term, quarterly gains. It's all about getting to the next fixed outcome for these organizations, like running a car on fumes and just barely making it to your destination. Success, when it happens, masks deeper problems. An extraction organization, in turn, sees its people as expendable resources, resulting in burnout, mental health issues, and societal despair. Extract and discard. We see it every day. By perpetuating a "win at all costs" culture of extraction, we fundamentally undermine the potential for personal and collective growth and miss out on learning and development's delicious, long-term benefits. There's only one thing that maintains exponential growth: cancer.

Luckily for us, Giannis is teaching us what a learning organization looks like. Learning leaders understand that failure is like chemotherapy or a controlled burn. Sometimes it's someone else's turn. We can't win every single game. There are good days and bad days. In contrast to the extraction organization, which focuses solely on fixed outcomes and short-term gains, a learning organization understands that failure is a painful but necessary part of the process. Learning Leaders look for the data to be mined in failure to make their organizations healthy.

Now, that doesn't mean we must enjoy losing or give up our personal and professional ambitions. Like the young Indiana Jones, we don't have to like losing. Competition keeps us active and engaged in our process. It's why most of us build businesses and pivot and embrace change. But it's important to realize that many times losing forces us to confront our spiritual growth. Maybe there are things we'd rather not know. A learning organization recognizes failure as an opportunity to improve and grow. Progress and development take precedence over immediate success when the emphasis shifts from a fixed mindset to a growth mindset.

In our pursuit of success, there are bound to be setbacks, detours, and moments of retreat. How can there not be? These challenges allow us to reflect, learn, and ultimately advance the culture of our organizations. Long-term growth comes not from fleeting success but from the spiritual process of continuous learning and self-improvement.

In delivering his two-minute "TED Talk," Giannis Antetokounmpo represents a new generation of leadership that embraces a growth mindset, prioritizing continuous learning and improvement over fixed, extractive outcomes.

By any objective measure, Giannis is a success. He had to come from nothing to get to the podium, where he made his exacting speech. His family was Nigerian and immigrated to Greece, where they had to survive without work permits. He and his three brothers sold merchandise on the street to survive through the lean periods. He's made it to the pinnacle of American success: he's become a champion and provided generational wealth to his entire family. He's an example to millions already.

I'm always going to live in hope for my New York Knicks to win the title again and restore the glory of Bradley, Jackson, Reed, and Earl "The Pearl" Monroe, but I'm grateful that Giannis Antetokounmpo taught me there's no shame in losing; the only shame is not learning.

THE RE-CULTURE CURIOSITY QUESTIONS

1. How might you treat your next "playoff loss" (e.g., a missed target, failed launch) as Giannis did, mining it for lessons rather than labeling it a failure? Can you shift your focus from shame to curiosity?

2. How could you design "controlled burns" into your strategy to nurture long-term resilience?

3. What daily practice would help you model Giannis's mantra, "I see myself as a student," publicly sharing your own moments of struggle to prove learning trumps legacy?

ARE MARGINAL GAINS CULTURE?

"We had three pillars to our approach, which we called the 'podium principles.'

The first one was strategy. The second was human performance. The third principle was continuous improvement."

—Dave Brailsford

As leaders, we face immense responsibility and loneliness because every decision we make is an opportunity for failure. If the organizational health is weak, even the quest for marginal gains can result in incremental failure. If the organization doesn't empower resilience and ask the right questions in the right sequence, where the Why's set the foundation and How's drive improvement, then it's very tough sledding indeed. We have to harmonize the dynamic value between those two questions. That will determine our success and if we're truly going to be in it for the long term.

I wrote at length in my last book about Dave Brailsford, known as the king of marginal gains, who famously transformed the British cycling team's performance through the use of 1 percent daily incremental improvement. Not only was Brailsford key to the turnaround of the team's fortunes, but he also became the go-to guru for every type of organization looking for that extra edge. Marginal gains were the watch-word of everyone from politics, media, sports, and business.

Brailsford's three podium principles were strategy, analyzing demands, ruthlessly rooting out inefficiencies, while still operating from com-passion; human performance, creating environments that foster trust, accountability, and optimal performance; and continuous improvement, which is the daily practice of small, incremental changes.

So, in 2023, it made perfect sense for billionaire Jim Ratcliffe, the CEO of INEOS, who, when he purchased a 25 percent stake in Manchester United, to hire Dave Brailsford, the king of marginal gains, to work his particular magic on the football club that had fallen sharply off the mountaintop since the retirement of Sir Alex Ferguson, the most era-defining football manager of the last fifty years, in 2013.

The events that have followed are an almost real-time cultural case study of an approach applied to one of the most imposing, sprawling, global sports brands in the world.

In professional team sports, particularly European football, patience is more vice than virtue. There are billions invested—in money and people. For leaders, there's no time to build incrementally to long-term success. You have but one season to build a cathedral, maybe less.

At Manchester United, the expectations are even higher.

Here's what you need to know about English football teams: They're civic institutions. I don't mean in the sense that they're owned by the government, but in the idea that these are teams that belong to commu-nities. The fans, even a global superbrand like Man U, are the culture of these teams. They may have billions of dollars, international owners, and the glitz and glam of Posh Spice and David Beckham, but at their core, they're neighborhood teams. Historically, the local fans aren't part of the culture. They are the culture.

But in the last couple of decades, an organization like Manchester United has been a victim of its own success. The culture that Sir Alex Ferguson built won every trophy imaginable and became nearly ubiqui-tous the world over. They didn't fly too close to the sun; they landed on it.

As a result, ticket prices have squeezed everyone but the rich, profits have been dividended to hither and yon, favorite players sold, and they're asked to survive on a diet of past glories.

Gary Neville, a member of the famed Class of '92 that helped usher in the twenty-five-year period of dominance, said on his podcast, "If we [the Class of '92] had come into the club at this moment in time, in this environment, we wouldn't be successful. As talented as the group I came through with—Ryan Giggs, David Beckham, Paul Scholes—if they came into this environment today, they would be set up for failure."

For one of the most outspoken ambassadors for the club to say this with his whole chest means the culture is in an advanced state of rot.

He's a local lad, though, Gary Neville. He was born a Red, and he'll die a Red. The club means more to the communities that are the lifeblood of the club. But that blood is starting to stagnate. Twelve years have seen middling results, a parade of legendary but failed coaches, high-priced quality players playing worse when they come to United. Nothing they're trying works.

That's a sign that the culture is broken. It's marginal gains on the Titanic: You can paint the deck chairs white, but the big ship is about to snap in half. Neville was even more direct: "There is a cultural thread of negativity and toxicity that runs through this club that is not going away."

Small improvements like repainting the dressing rooms are not going to cut it here.

Neville went on to say, "It's not because of one player, or their [managerial] ability. They can all take the responsibility, the medicine, and say: 'I didn't achieve what I wanted to achieve.' But it's about cultural failure, and that's it."

What Dave Brailsford has to reckon with is that coming into an existing organization, the values, the why, those are, to some degree, already in place. Organizations are like people. They have memory.

That's what culture is: it's a bunch of people and what they remember about a company and how that makes them feel. Manchester United is a brand. The Why of its culture belongs to the world and time, and Brailsford can't undo history.

We see this with organizations all the time. Habits, ways of being, norms, and standards—they all become entrenched and, if left unattended, decay.

You don't need a book to tell you that organizational culture is only as good as its people. But in this case, it is. Neville told another story on Steven Bartlett's *Diary of a CEO* podcast about when he was a player in the early 2000s, and the team was led by the Irish pit bull, Roy Keane, who kept the standards of the club and its people high. One day, one of the PR officers would regularly have footballs for the players to sign so that they could be given away to local charities and hospitals, and many of the players walked by without signing. This had been going on for a while. The PR officer had tears in her eyes. Keane noticed, asked why, and marched right up to Ferguson's office. Once informed, the manager tore the paint off the dressing room, informing the players that this was unacceptable. Ferguson understood that the people of the community were the culture of the club. That contract was sacrosanct.

Once that contract gets broken, it's fiendishly difficult to get back. It's like rotten soil that won't grow good fruit. The Why is the soil from which the culture grows. Once it turns toxic, it won't matter what you plant; it won't grow good fruit.

We have no way of knowing if Dave Brailsford is asking the Why, but the fact is, it might be too late. If he can't evolve the club, continually asking both Why and How at the right times, then he may well be on his way out.

RE-CULTURE FAILURE

Work (Why Are We Here?)—Re-Define Your Purpose and Strategy and Rebuild Your Shared Purpose

Rediscover the Mission

Clarify the organization's reason for existing. At Manchester United, the "why" extends beyond trophies and dividends; it's about a community, tradition, and identity that have lasted for over a hundred years. That's a sacred trust. And once it's gone, it's gone forever.

Disinfect Cultural Mold

Toxicity must be named and confronted directly. When we acknowledge our failures, we recommit to our core values. When we recover together, the toxicity vanishes.

Rebuild Trust with Actions

We must demonstrate the inner relationship between words and deeds. If we're not clear on that, no one else will be. Transparency and accountability are nonnegotiable to recover from failure. No time for ego.

Well (How Can We Be Better?)—Prioritizing human performance and well-being by investing in our people and their well-being.

Be Accountable

As Gary Neville noted, standards are upheld when leaders like Roy Keane insist on integrity and discipline. Leaders must champion these behaviors and empower others to do the same so that we can all weather the storm together. Apart, we drown.

Prioritize Emotional and Physical Well-Being

We bounce back stronger when we've created environments where individuals feel supported, valued, and able to perform at their best. No organization fails to fail. It comes for us all. What happens before the failure defines how lasting and deep the failure will be.

Celebrate Collective Wins

Reinforce the idea that if success is shared, so is failure. We can't ask our people to share in failure if we've given them no piece of the success. And yes, that comes with money too. Team members always bear the brunt of failure, while CEOs sometimes escape with golden parachutes. That delivers value to shareholders but not to organizations and teams.

When we reward actions that demonstrate collaboration and effort, we are modeling the cultural values we've all agreed to.

Together (Who Do We Want to Be?)—Creating a cohesive, collaborative culture creates cultural togetherness.

Don't Go It Alone

Collect data and solicit feedback about the underlying cultural cracks before seeking how best to incrementally move forward. Culture has many authors, and most of them aren't you. From top leadership to frontline employees, everyone must have a role in defining and shaping the organizational culture.

Embed Continuous Improvement

Make cultural growth a daily practice. Use tools like feedback loops, reflection, and ongoing learning to adapt to the quickening pace of change. But don't get seduced by the curtains when the foundation is cracked and leaking.

Have Dave Brailsford and his marginal gains failed at Manchester United? The short answer is: So far, unquestionably. The long answer, however, is a bit more complicated.

As of this writing, Manchester United, the most successful English football (soccer) project the world has ever known, sits in thirteenth place in the English Premier League table, and the unthinkable threat of relegation (three teams each season are demoted to a lower league) looms larger than it ever has. Things are so bad that the current manager (who's only been on the job for a month) recently called this iteration of the Red Devils the worst Manchester United team ever.

Things are bad, no other way to say it. But something tells me that no matter how much failure he faces, Dave Brailsford is licking his chops at the opportunity to rediscover the culture that made Manchester United the Roman Empire of the football world.

We will fail, and it will change us. That's forgivable. The only unforgivable failure is when we don't change when we fail.

THE RE-CULTURE CURIOSITY QUESTIONS

1. Are you a gardener tending soil, or a landscaper hiding rot?
2. How might you shift from marginal gains to rewiring cultural systems?
3. Could a "Roy Keane audit," publicly naming and dismantling norms that erode trust, rebuild the contract your team has with its stated mission?
4. How could you turn "marginal gains" into meaningful gains?
5. What daily practices could force you to distribute ownership of failure across the organization so no one escapes accountability, from interns to the C-suite?

FAIL WELL TOGETHER

"You can no longer experience reality—you are stuck experiencing yourself."

—Michael A. Singer

Re-Culture is about asking the question that Randi always asks me when we experience professional or personal setbacks in our lives, "What's the creative opportunity?"

You can see why we've been married as long as we have. It's not through anything magic or supernatural. It's because Randi, the most pragmatic person I know, is always looking for ways to bounce forward. She has no fear of failure.

Randi's taught me that when you step back from the emotions that inevitably come with setbacks, failure is a fascinating topic because we often see it as something to avoid, something to fear, yet it's an incredibly valuable resource. Inside each opportunity, failure is the springboard for wisdom. Like a gymnast, we fall, but we bounce forward into something creative.

KNOWLEDGE+FAILURE=WISDOM.

The poet Rumi wrote, "Yesterday I was clever, so I wanted to change the world. Today I am wise, so I am changing myself." The difference between yesterday and today is failure.

When we're dealing with inner lives, it's through those failure moments, when things don't go as planned—when we lose a business deal, let someone down, or face setbacks—that we gain the important insights needed to grow as leaders and individuals. I've become a decent golfer through practice, and patience with my failures. It also helps to know that golf is really just a game of misses, until the ball goes in the hole.

Failure is the best teacher I know. If we allow it, it can guide us to make better choices in the future. Better choices become habits. Habits become resilience.

In Proverbs, it says, "When pride comes, then comes disgrace, but with humility comes wisdom." (*Proverbs 11:1 Holman Christian Standard Bible*). I often talk about the importance of embracing failure with humility. It's about eating a big slice of humble pie and carrying those lessons forward. When we are humble, we let go of our attachment to the rigid processes that lead us into the same mistakes. I know of no greater impediment to success than the obsession to be right. I know you've felt that. Maybe you're feeling it right now. Like you're one of those wind-up toys that's stuck running into the same wall over and over. I've been there too. Facing failure with fortitude and forgiveness is the pivot that creates our freedom.

That's the working well portion, but what about togetherness?

CAN WE FAIL TOGETHER?

I believe we can. Failure also plays a crucial role in innovation and success. It's the stepping stone that allows businesses and people to pivot and find new paths. When we learn from failure collaboratively, we open ourselves to new possibilities and growth. It's about having the courage to engage in the process of learning and transformation, even when it's uncomfortable.

As organizations, we're all occupied getting from one task to the other, making it through another day, another week, another quarter, to the end of the year, where maybe we take a break, unplug for maybe a week. Then the process starts all over again.

Many of us, in our jobs, as leaders, feel like we don't have time to fail. We think, "If I fail, my team will fail, and I'll lose my job. If I lose my job, I'll lose my house. If I lose my house, I'll lose my family...." And so on, until we're living at the edge of the world, eating canned beans by a fire, hugging a tattered blanket around our shoulders, and trying to stay alive.

It's a painful and endless mental cycle. Because we constantly put ourselves (physically, mentally, emotionally, and spiritually) through the worst-case scenario all the way to the end.

We die a thousand deaths before we actually die. What a waste.

In *Pivot* and *Change Proof*, I wrote about failure and how critical it is to the act of pivoting and to personal resilience. When we pivot, we have to fail as fast as we can to increase the pace of our learning. And if we want to practice resilience, then we have to use little pieces of failure every day, like a great improviser, to build up a resistance to the fear of failure. For you and your teams, we need something more. It's all well and good to deal with individual failure. That's the micro level. But with Re-Culture, we're leveling up to the organizational level.

THE POWER OF FAILURE

I've learned many times, and I hope to never stop learning that risk and failure are iterative. We have to fail over and over again. If I'm not trying to fail and fail fast, I'm not trying hard enough. Because that's where discovery lies, according to Maya Angelou, "You may encounter many defeats, but you must not be defeated. It may be necessary to encounter the defeats, so you can know who you are, what you can rise from, how you can still come out of it."

That's textbook resilience.

Every failure I encounter is a creative opportunity to discover territory I never thought possible. Because it reveals inefficiencies and gaps in my process, it inspires me to create more resilient systems for my organization.

I want my team to work proactively, learning, and building the critical thinking skills that are the hallmarks of a healthy workplace culture.

That's why the risk-taking starts at the top. Even if it leads to mistakes, we'll model for our teams the behavior that will lead them to push the boundaries for innovative solutions. Those solutions are what keep us moving onward and upward.

Agility comes from failing at faster and faster rates, so we can pivot quickly when changes come. So, if we share in failure together, we'll be able to refine our priorities and objectives.

Every failure makes the organization stronger. We need to follow the example of Muay Thai kickboxers. From early on, they train their shins to both accept and deliver lethal kicks that would snap the leg of a normal person. They do this by starting on a heavy bag filled with rice or concrete, and then they move up to kicking bamboo poles. Each kick creates micro-fractures in the tibia bones. When the cracks heal, they bond together, stronger and more resilient.

Risks, mistakes, and failure (if they're micro) can do the same thing for us and for our teams.

> "All of old. Nothing else ever. Ever tried. Ever failed. No matter. Try again. Fail again. Fail better."
>
> —Samuel Beckett

THE RE-CULTURE CURIOSITY QUESTIONS

1. How might you turn team failures into "micro-fracture workouts," designing systems that strengthen your culture's "shin bones" through collective vulnerability?
2. How could you model Rumi's pivot from "changing the world" to "changing yourself," publicly sharing one failure each week to prove wisdom grows in a healthy culture?
3. What system would ensure failures are "ours," not "yours," embedding Beckett's "Fail again. Fail better" into daily practice so risk-taking becomes a team sport?
4. How can you recalibrate your team's focus on better misses vs. trying to make every shot?

How We Get from Work to Work Well

HUMAN RESOURCES

"It is difficult to get a man to understand something when his salary depends on his not understanding it."

—Upton Sinclair

We all know that workplace culture is in crisis. But to truly understand how, we need to go back to the beginning. We need to go back to the original human resources (HR) crisis. We need to go all the way back to the Garden of Eden.

Note: I'm using this story merely as a mythological story and not an endorsement of any religion.

According to the story, the Creator (CEO) puts Adam in charge of all creation as the chief human resources officer (CHRO). He's got to name all the animals, cultivate the gardens and fields, and essentially make sure that the Garden is pleasant and tranquil for when the Creator wants to come stroll through what It has made. It's a hard job, but Adam enjoys it. Plus, he's got benefits.

Noticing that Adam's a bit lonely and overworked by his task of keeping an entire plant and animal civilization running, the Creator creates for him a companion, a woman named Eve. She's an instant value-add to the organization because now Adam doesn't have to do the Creator's bidding alone. There is trust and coherence in the structure, and everyone feels good and happy.

But elsewhere on the org chart, someone is deeply unhappy.

That someone is a, well, it's a talking serpent who doesn't like how things are being run in the Garden of Eden.

"Why am I not in charge?" he bellyaches to anyone who will listen. One day, that anyone is Eve. He begins to try to poison her against the CEO and the strategies that Adam is executing daily.

"We could run this whole Garden the way it's supposed to be. Our growth is being limited from above," he hisses.

He tells Eve that there's an off-limits tree that HR says is not to be eaten. Eve asks Adam about it.

He shakes his head, "That's a no-go area for us."

Eve isn't convinced. She believes that she and Adam, the ones who do the real work, should be able to share in the spoils, and the Creator is profiting off of their labor. The talking serpent loves the dissension he's sowing in the ranks.

One day, Eve can't take it anymore. She eats from the tree. Offers it to Adam. He takes a bite because, well, he doesn't want Eve to take the fall by herself.

Now, the CEO is descending from the C-Suite to fire everybody. Adam, Eve, and the talking serpent are sent packing in a structured lay-off, and the organization itself is shutting its gates forever.

All because of a crisis in human resources.

***

As I travel the world to work with organizations on organizational resilience in the workplace, the position I interact with the most is the chief human resources officer (CHRO). Sometimes they're called the chief people officer. In short, the CHRO/chief people officer shapes the workplace culture by focusing on its people. They give talent parameters for the hiring manager to hire talent, and they create a development structure so talent can move up, they listen for problems, and they adapt to change. They future-cast for the workforce, and if something isn't right, and a problem is coming, they're the ones who let leadership know the risks of continuing.

As we've said, culture is the soil of every organization. Then the CHRO is its gardener.

In my experience, they're dedicated people who want the best for both the organization and its team members. Their mission is that the organization's actions and its values meet in a way that protects everyone.

My good friend, Kate McCann, has been a CHRO in the health-care field for more years than she would want me to mention, and she describes her role like this: "HR is a true strategic partner with operations. You want to do X, well, what is the risk to the organization?" It's not just about administration and being what Kate calls "the No Police."

However, for HR executives like Kate, it's an unenviable role because they're the ones who make sure that the strategic vision is being carried out and that the organization's goals, outcomes, and financial targets are being met. These two goals are always in conflict.

High up in the organization, leaders often don't care how the tomatoes are grown; they just want a certain number of tomatoes to take to market. But the CHRO is the one who makes sure that the tomatoes grow healthily, without blight, and that the soil will grow tomatoes every season.

I can always sense the health of an organization by how healthy the CHRO is: If they're burned out, exhausted, and hanging on for dear life, then I can pretty much bet that everyone in the organization is. They're burned out, Kate says, because there are billions of dollars of waste related to workforce culture:

> I think the culture absolutely can affect the bottom line. When you think about the cost of first-year turnover, to see 30 and 40 percent first-year turnover rates. That's not only the cost of bringing somebody in; you've got the manager's time, you're interviewing, then you're training. And within six months, the person leaves, and you have to start all over again. And that's such a waste of money. Because if you have a culture of just promoting people and you don't have a strong sense of hiring people with the right skill sets and developing people internally

to have those skill sets, either for your organization or elsewhere, you're going to waste a lot of money.

Why are people leaving in the first year? It's not because they don't want to work. They just feel like they're being treated as robots on a spreadsheet.

To figure out how we got here, we've got to go back not to the dawn of time, but to the dawn of the twentieth century.

*****

Anyone who's been protected by their human resources (HR) department has Upton Sinclair to thank. His 1906 novel, *The Jungle*, opened a window on the tragically horrific working conditions of the immigrants and children who labored in Chicago's meatpacking industry at the beginning of the modern age.

It's a harrowing account of organizational neglect and abuse, where meat was tainted with chemicals and toxic fumes that killed most workers within a few years, and time management torture where workers were docked hourly or daily pay for minor infractions.

Sinclair told the world that the workers' lives were more disposable than the meat they prepared, as efficiency and the bottom line were cudgels that pummeled their well-being.

Sinclair's book dropped like a bomb into the culture. The subsequent public outcry led to the creation of the regulatory agency we now know as the Food and Drug Administration. But more than that, it drew attention to the exploitation of the American worker. Labor reforms would follow, with workplace safety laws, minimum wage standards, and the outlawing of child labor. To bring their organizations into compliance with these reforms, business leaders created the personnel departments that would eventually become the human resources departments that create and protect workplace culture from the transactional thinking that had defined it since the Industrial Revolution.

With the creation of these early HR departments, efficiency and workflows became standardized. Think of Henry Ford's assembly line in

Detroit automobile factories. Standardization created systems for hiring workers while increasing productivity outputs. Humans were machines to be used the same as the nuts and bolts of the factories in which they toiled.

Then, in the period before and after World War II, sociologists began to study the correlation between employee satisfaction and social dynamics and how they increased or decreased outputs. It was the first time we asked the question, "If my people feel better, will my organization do better?" People may be more human than resource.

Managers and leaders, maybe for the first time in human history, considered the psychological and social safety of the people who worked for them.

The study that cued this epiphany was Elton Mayo's Hawthorne experiment, which was originally designed to find out if industrial workers were more productive in brighter versus dimmer lighting. Like most impactful experiments, it's a mix of data and anecdotes, but the salient finding wasn't about lighting at all. What they found was that industrial workers were more productive because they were being observed.

Another subsequent study found that women in a factory, working in a relay setting, were more productive if they got to choose with whom they worked, felt valued, and were observed by someone they found sympathetic.

Oh, and they eliminated the Saturday workday.

Culture (and not working six days a week), it seemed, was important to productivity. In fact, in nearly every study, culture is the key to productivity. These early studies showed us that when trust and respect flow between management and labor, culture can flourish.

Fast-forward to the 1960s and the struggle for civil rights, and diversity in the workplace became a real possibility. The United States government passed anti-discrimination laws, and our workplaces became integrated a little bit at a time. For the next decades, integration and globalization (slow though it was) led to collaboration and innovation as the talent pool got deeper.

It wasn't until the 1990s and the rise of the internet that HR evolved from pure hiring and firing to finally becoming a part (small at first) of organizational strategy. New technologies made it possible to track employee data (attrition, development, KPIs, and retention). We could finally measure employee satisfaction.

As the new century came and went, the term "work-life balance" became part of the culture. HR was able, for the first time, to mechanize and weaponize the organization's values and goals, both in the workplace and the competitive market. Remote work was here to stay.

Then COVID-19 changed it all again. We're wrestling with hybrid work models, DEI is a flashpoint in business culture and the culture wars, and our ability to process data is being turbocharged by artificial intelligence. We have feedback loops and systems. Psychosocial safety has become yet another sign of the entropic workplace.

And now, we find ourselves at this present moment when HR departments are confronting the very real generational divide in their workforces. Gen Z is the first generation that has observed what happened to their parents in their careers. And they're not going back and repeating the same mistakes.

To understand this better, I went to one of the smartest people I know: my daughter, Eden. I asked her about the conventional wisdom that her generation is entitled and lazy. She, as is the way with all daughters, scoffed at her dear old dad. "I work a full-time agency job and oversee the digital marketing strategy for WORKWELL Labs. I advise a skincare start-up and also teach yoga. So, it's hard for me personally to put a lot of stock in comments or generalizations like that. Because I look at myself, and I think my age is the least interesting thing about me, and the year that I was born has nothing to do with how I show up in the workplace, at least not in terms of my work ethic and how much I put into my work."

Talk about putting me in my place! Eden's been working since she was thirteen, so no one from any generation could question her commitment to work.

The difference is that Eden and people like her have the proper perspective on work in that there's no point in working for an organization where they can't work and feel like they're living their lives. It's that work-life harmony that I spoke about in *Change Proof.* It's not about equal time; it's about their dynamic relationship to work.

It's not that they don't want to work; maybe they don't want to work for organizations that don't value them as people. Because a big part of respect is respecting our people when they're not working for us.

Eden said, "I've always been a hustler, so I really do hate generalizations like that. Gen Z and millennials have been lumped into this big stereotype about not working hard, but I think in reality, there's a very large difference between setting a boundary and not working hard."

And it's hard for me to argue with her logic and her example. After all, I pivoted out of toxic cultures more than once because of the impact it was having on my family and me. So, I'd like to think that in some way, my kids were nurtured by Randi and me into people with healthy boundaries.

I learned it from my own parents a long time ago when we lived in Queens. My mother was a travel agent, and my father worked for the New York City Department of Parks and Recreation. And they had a small, humble ritual that had a profound impact on my life.

Every Friday, they both took the day off. They'd catch up on errands. Go on lunch dates. Read books. It was a day just for them. This is a part of the example that Randi and I try to set for our kids and grandkids. Whatever it is, it'll be there tomorrow. Not everything is a five-alarm fire all the time. That's why younger people are putting up those boundaries: so that they don't have to answer emails after 10 p.m.

This is where I think the generational conflict rubber meets the road. If our people's boundaries cause us distress, then we've got to question what we're asking of them. Eden agrees, "I think what is true is that I have boundaries when I'm out of the office. When I am not at my computer, I am not working. Does that at all make me less productive or efficient, or available when I am on the clock? Absolutely not. It makes me more productive, more efficient, more available when I'm designated to work." This isn't quiet quitting. It's the work they've been contracted to do. When we ask for extra we should be paying them more. Period.

Eden is lucky that she works for organizations that respect these boundaries. Not everyone is so lucky.

When Eden looks around, she sees the flashing red warning lights of workplace culture decline if my generation doesn't get on board. She said, "I really do see the possibility for change, because it's not sustainable. Their idea of culture right now is, 'Let's all go to a fancy dinner once a quarter and give out fun prizes at our Christmas parties.' That's not going to keep people bought in, especially as we're having a societal, generational culture shift."

Eden describes a company she knows well that's bleeding talent for this very reason: "They just lost five or six people in their early thirties, who left to go start their own business because they were not getting what they wanted. And it doesn't matter how much money you're making at that point. So, I think that we're in this pivotal place. It's going to keep happening. People are going to keep leaving. Companies are having this aha moment of, 'Oh, people aren't really that happy here.' There's just going to be more and more turnover the younger our workforce gets."

And now, we can come full circle back to what Kate McCann said: That turnover is costing the workforce billions of dollars every year. Eden and Kate are in different generations, and yet they're saying the same things.

That's evidence that the real divide is between healthy and toxic workplace culture. The evolution of human resources over time shows us that things are trending toward the workers and their teams.

The question we need to ask ourselves is simple: What side do we want to be on?

THE RE-CULTURE CURIOSITY QUESTIONS

1. How might you redesign HR policies to act as bridges of culture rather than barriers? How can you invite open dialogue about boundaries so that everyone knows what's expected of them?

2. Could anonymous feedback or employee surveys give you the data you need to discover boundaries, and if they did, would you implement them?

3. How could you match your leadership with Gen Z's boundary-setting to reduce first-year turnover and build loyalty that outlasts quarterly reviews?

4. How can you encourage boundaries between work and home, while trusting that the work will not only get done, but employees will be more engaged while at work?

5. What steps will you take to evolve your HR from an enforcer to a strategic productivity gardener?

6. Could pairing attrition analytics with cross-generational mentorship help you spot hidden stressors before they rot your culture?

How to Work Well

"A major reason capable people fail to advance is that they don't work well with their colleagues."

—Lee Iacocca

RE-CULTURAL INTELLIGENCE

"Charisma is the result of effective leadership, not the other way around."

—Warren Bennis and Burt Nanus

"Cultural intelligence: an outsider's seemingly natural ability to interpret someone's unfamiliar and ambiguous gestures the way that person's compatriots would," wrote P. Christopher Earley and Elaine Mosakowski in a fascinating 2004 article in the *Harvard Business Review* on the need for a cultural intelligence that moves beyond the one-to-one nature of emotional intelligence.

But what is Re-Cultural intelligence?

Re-Culture intelligence is about creating an environment where resilience is not just an individual trait but a collective, operationalized strength within an organization. It's the ability to foster a culture that not only withstands adversity but uses it as a catalyst for growth and innovation. It's all well and good to say we've got each other's backs, but it's yet another thing to practice it. But that's how we create, maintain, and renew Re-Culture.

Because, at its core, it's about embedding resilience into the DNA of a workplace, through leadership, communication, and systems, so that the organization can adapt, evolve, and thrive amidst uncertainty and change. It's not about bouncing back; it's about bouncing forward, stronger, and with an authentic purpose. This kind of intelligence requires a proactive approach, where resilience is cultivated before it's urgently needed, ensuring that teams and leaders are prepared for the inevitable disruptions and changes that come their way.

A 2021 McKinsey study showed that organizations investing in cultural resilience training see 30 percent lower turnover and 20 percent faster recovery from crises.

RE-CULTURE INTELLIGENCE IS SYSTEMIC, NOT INDIVIDUAL

When we are operating at the level of organizational resilience, we have to rise beyond our self-awareness and create EQ on a systemic level, or the effects will only be short-term. As leaders, we can't depend on our emotional intelligence alone. We have to embed EQ and self-awareness into our systems. How? By empathizing with our people. Getting curious about them. Seeing who they are. And letting them do the same for each other. This is not about creating friendships. We do not need to be friends outside of our work to create culture.

We shouldn't. Leave that to teenage sleepaway campers and movie people who create temporary bonds in compressed space and time. We all need time away from work. No, this is about seeing what makes each other tick and integrating that into our systems.

"I watch your back."

"And I'll watch yours."

It's as simple as that.

According to Gallup, team members in resilient cultures are 42 percent more likely to innovate and solve complex problems.

Resilient systems create resilient results.

Re-Culture is where adversity becomes a catalyst for growth, enabling teams to bounce forward with empathy and cohesion. Together. It's not just about working together. We've done that. It's about working *well* together.

RE-CULTURE REQUIRES BUY-IN

A "Got Your Back" culture, if we commit to it, takes everyone. It takes time. It takes work. Otherwise, it doesn't work. But the time and work you save by doing it is how you get Re-Culture. Organizational resilience takes emotional literacy that creates strategies that use more than just spreadsheets and deadlines. And your productivity will increase. In 2019, Price Waterhouse Coopers showed that resilient teams contribute to three times higher revenue growth and 50 percent greater profitability compared to less resilient peers. In the six years since, those numbers have only gone up.

I love empathy. That's a strange thing to say, "I love empathy."

But it's true. I love it for building a resilience culture because it's impossible without actions. You can't be like Michael Scott and just snap your fingers, be empathic, and then everyone becomes walking empathy machines.

Empathy is when we imagine what it's like to be in someone else's situation and what they might be feeling, like Atticus Finch says in *To Kill a Mockingbird*, "You never really understand a person until you consider things from his point of view…until you climb into his skin and walk around in it."

If our teams are empathizing with one another, they're already imagining what it's like to be someone else. That can't help but translate to collaborative action, because they've already done it. Over time, we'll collect data, not hard numbers, but the soft ones.

If we know how to look for it.

Now, we're free to integrate this data into our strategies. For example, during high-stress periods, adjusting workloads so the pressure gets distributed, if not evenly, then fairly, and no one is bearing the brunt of the burdens. That's a situation where we can be proactive, seeing the weather on its way and adjusting our strategies. That creates trust, the bedrock of culture. Or maybe we notice that anxiety and stress are building. That's not the time for a team-building excursion outside the office, because it'll just be more work. Or maybe we can implement a "no-meeting Fridays" during a critical period.

To be clear, we're not advocating for a four-day workweek here. Just let go of the reins a little, and your organization can run.

Any value system has to embrace counter-intuition and paradox in order to thrive.

I was competitive at tennis in college with a bit more potential than prowess to be blunt. I loved the game, but gave it up when work and family took their proper place in my priorities. After more than twenty years of only watching the game I started back up at pace. I hired a coach to help me get my game back and a few lessons later he pointed out something that not only transformed my old two-handed backhand, but was a leadership tip, par excellence.

He told me to loosen my grip, loosen the grip I had with my dominant hand so that my non-dominant hand could do the job that was required for the stroke to succeed.

Of course, it worked in an instant. Voila, my backhand was back, but better! Hmm, where else in my business life was I holding on to control too tightly, not letting things work better by simply loosening up, I wondered?

RE-CULTURE DOESN'T TREAT EMOTIONS LIKE FRED FLINTSTONE

We all remember *The Flintstones*, even if some among us say they don't, because the cultural shadow of that '60s cartoon has stretched to the twenty-first century. It was on when I was a kid. I always loved the opening credits with that gay old song, when the Flintstone family would return from dinner and a movie. Fred would get dumped outside by the saber-toothed cat and locked out of the house while he bellowed, "WILMAAAAAAA!!"

Some of us treat emotions in the workplace like Fred Flintstone.

We lock them out and expect our people to operate as autonomous robots. Then, at the end of the day, they can reconnect with their emotions and head home.

To use a modern example, Apple TV's *Severance* literalizes this principle, where its premise is about a company that splits its employees into two distinct people. The one at work has no idea about the one at home.

In our lives, it's not science fiction; it's non-fiction: That disconnect creates a vicious cycle because the force with which we deny our emotions in the workplace is the strength of the rebound when we least expect it.

We don't seek conflict in the workplace, but we can't fear it either. David Augsburger writes, "The more we run from conflict, the more it masters us; the more we try to avoid it, the more it controls us; the less we fear conflict, the less it confuses us; the less we deny our differences, the less they divide us."

That means, if we want to create culture builders throughout our organizations, then we've got to get honest with our own emotions. We can transform conflicts into building trust without doing trust falls at an offsite.

If we check in with our people, they'll check in with each other, and the culture will create itself. That's an unbeatable combination.

RE-CULTURE USES MENTORS

There's a great moment at the end of Steven Spielberg's *The Fabelmans* when the stand-in for the young director gets himself a meeting with John Ford (played by another great director, David Lynch). The mentorship he gets is short, direct, profane, and life-changing for young Steven.

He would later say, "The delicate balance of mentoring someone is not creating them in your own image, but giving them the opportunity to create themselves." That's the lesson we have to teach our people.

They're going to have varying emotional styles, and our work is to see which groups they naturally occupy. We don't want to double up, pairing optimists with optimists and realists with realists. We want to let opposites attract to create harmony with different voices.

I like to think of creative conflict as the oyster and the pearl. A grain of sand finds its way into the shell of an oyster, forcing the irritated species to produce a lubricant to cover the sand, creating, over time, a valuable pearl. Workplace mentorship is the dynamic lubricant that creates pearls from conflict. Dynamic tension, if done correctly, is a powerful tool for our organization's long-term health.

That can only occur if leaders operate emotionally proactively to create trust and help navigate the volatile nature of the work.

I hate to repeat myself, but it's not just about working well; it's about working well together.

We can't do that if we don't take care of each other.

THE RE-CULTURE CURIOSITY QUESTIONS

1. How might you shift your organization from idolizing individual resilience to designing systems where "having each other's backs" is a part of the workplace code, turning collective empathy into a structural advantage beyond your competitors?

2. If "empathy is action," what rituals could transform your emotional literacy in your organization from a soft skill into a measurable KPI, like redistributed workloads or "no-meeting Fridays" or "manager burn-ins" that preempt burnout while fueling the innovation you need to survive?

3. How might you reframe workplace conflict not as a cultural failure, but as a diagnostic tool, using creative conflict to reveal systemic gaps in trust, communication, or resource allocation?

4. What if workplace mentorship programs intentionally paired different perspectives (optimist + realist, veteran + newcomer) to forge an "oyster/pearl" that bonds teams through tension, not just harmony?

5. Where might you loosen your grip on control and let others step up to get an even better result for the team?

PIXAR AND THE TRUST EQUATION

"If people do not believe that mathematics is simple, it is only because they do not realize how complicated life is."

—John von Neumann

The child psychologist Erik Erikson developed an important theory that outlines eight stages of how we develop throughout our lives. Each stage is marked by a specific conflict or challenge. The first stage is trust versus mistrust. It occurs during infancy, typically from birth to around eighteen months.

My wife Randi and I are the parents of four young adults. And now, we've got beautiful grandchildren who are pure magic. There's something miraculous about human beings that we created creating human beings of their very own. They're perfect packages of unconditional love that we love to spoil every chance we get.

For Erikson, the environment that nurtures either trust or mistrust sets the foundation for our worldview and our relationships to others and to our lives. Trust is how we enter into whatever culture we're born into. How? Those who land in safe, predictable homes see the world as consistent and reliable. It sets the foundation for our future relationships, our emotional well-being, and whether we'll have a positive outlook on our lives. Conversely, an environment of mistrust, where our needs aren't met consistently, fosters feelings of fear and anxiety and an inability to form close bonds later in life.

Our caregivers in those first eighteen months are our leaders. Their responsiveness, attentiveness, and emotional availability shape our sense of trust, establishing the clear base that enables us to explore the world with confidence as opposed to insecurity and fear.

To the leaders among us, doesn't this all sound very familiar?

It should. As leaders, we are the caregivers of our organizations, and while the people who make them up aren't exactly our children, we are the ones who establish an environment that's trusting and secure. Organizations with high levels of safety and trust are resilient. They've got close bonds between their people, higher levels of engagement, and significantly higher productivity.

Our ability to create a resilient workplace culture is tied to the level at which our people trust us.

So, how do organizations get trust wrong? Answer: They haven't mastered the trust equation.

In 2022, the Edelman Trust Barometer published a study on trust in the workplace. They reported that even in the face of trust erosion in nearly every institution we once held dear, the final holdout was the workplace. On nearly every metric, an overwhelming number of respondents said they trusted their employer, they felt a community with their co-workers, and they trusted their co-workers more than they trusted anyone else in their lives. Trusting employees vastly over-perform those who don't, and trusting organizations keep their employees far longer than those where mistrust and cynicism roam rampant.

Trust also over-performs at the bottom line. *Forbes* further reported that organizations with a robust culture of trust deliver, on average, 400 percent more value to shareholders.

The evidence is irrefutable that it's both the right thing to do and the right thing for your business.

Yet why, only a year later, did Gallup share the results of a study that employee trust in management was at an all-time low?

Maybe the answer can be found at Pixar.

In *Change Proof,* I wrote about Ed Catmull and his approach to imaginative resilience at Pixar, which, from the 1990s until recently, was one of the most trusted brands in the world. Customers, employees, and Disney all lined up to be a part of their culture of innovation and commitment to story over profits.

But it might not have survived were it not for Galyn Susman, who, during the creation and production of *Toy Story 2,* saved Pixar.

A year before the film was due to premiere (not that long for a computer-animated film in the 1990s), Galyn was away on maternity leave. But because of her position as supervising technical producer, she was still working from home so Pixar could meet its release date.

Then, the unthinkable happened: Somehow, the wrong series of buttons got pushed that dumped the entire movie and its backup drives into the digital ether. Gone, as though it never existed. The company went into a blind panic. An error this catastrophic could sink the fledgling movie studio.

Enter Galyn Susman, who just so happened to have the entirety of the workflow and all the files backed up on a computer at home.

Because she was trusted to work at home and because she trusted management to have her back, Galyn was able to save the day. If Pixar didn't trust her to deliver away from the office or if she didn't trust the organization to have her back with a new baby, the whole situation could have been worse.

So, great. Everyone trusts each other, and they're all still working well together, happily ever after.

Well, not so fast.

In 2024, Galyn and nearly two hundred longtime Pixar employees were unceremoniously laid off when their *Buzz Lightyear* stand-alone film tanked at the box office. This was part of a Disney-wide effort to cut $5 billion in costs and streamline the company's entertainment division.

Now, this kind of thing happens all the time. Sometimes, you have to make hard choices for the good of the company. A studio has to respond to shifting market forces. No one would disagree.

And yet.

What does it say about the overall culture of a wildly successful start-up? That it allowed its trust to get chewed up by an apex predator for more money than it knew what to do with, and that this would, some twenty years later, result in one of its original team members and the woman who possibly saved the company being fired by press release? Nothing good.

So, what is the Trust Equation?

$$\text{TRUST} = \frac{\text{COMMUNICATION (Open + Clear)} \times \text{ACCOUNTABILITY (Words + Actions)}}{\text{TIME}}$$

Simple, really. If you want trust, you need open and clear communication combined with accountability where actions and words are in accord. You take all of that and divide by time, and you get trust. Which is really just a fun mathematical way of saying that trust has to be earned with accountable communication over time.

A 2024 study found that 86 percent of all failures of workplace culture are due to poor communication. The good communicators boost productivity by 25 percent. That starts with you.

We're going to spend a whole chapter on how to create a culture of accountability, but for now, just know that the accountability crisis is upon us, with 93 percent of team members unable or unwilling to take accountability for their performance.

And time? Well, there's never enough, is there?

But think about this: Whether you've got a $1 trillion market cap or $10,000, you've still got the same number of hours in a day. How you use your time and to what end is what's going to define you and your organization.

Galyn Susman had worked for almost thirty years at Pixar. She'd earned trust in the most dramatic way possible. And then she was fired. Like Andy dropping his favorite toy for a new one.

Write this equation down on a Post-it note and put it somewhere on your desk or in your office where you can see it. You'll never go wrong if:

1. You're communicating with your people in a way that's transparent and easy to understand.
2. You're accountable to each other by meaning what you say and doing what you said you'd do.
3. You're allowing for time to build relationships and not forcing them before they're ready.

You can't walk up to a complete stranger on the street, ask them to trust you, and expect immediate dividends. You have to give them a reason to trust you. Given enough reasons and enough time, eventually that person is going to give you their trust.

But, like culture, trust is difficult to earn and easy to lose.

Just ask Galyn Susman.

THE RE-CULTURE CURIOSITY QUESTIONS

1. Time vs. Tension

    If trust is earned over time but eroded in moments, how can leaders balance urgent business decisions (like layoffs) with the long-term cultural "interest" they've built?

2. The Accountability Paradigm

    When accountability is framed as "owning outcomes," how might this clash with the human need for grace during failure? Where would you draw the line?

3. The Pixar Paradox

    Galyn Susman's story shows trust can save a company—and later be discarded. What "trust rituals" could prevent loyalty from becoming transactional, even in crisis?

4. Formula in the Wild

    The Trust Equation says Communication × Accountability ÷ Time. If you had to add one variable (e.g., Empathy, Transparency, Courage), what would turbocharge trust in your team?

5. Infant to Institution

Erikson's first stage is trust vs. mistrust. How might an organization that is stuck in "infancy" (fearful, reactive) "grow up" to a culture of secure, resilient trust?

FEEDBACK IS THE COMMUNICATION SILVER BULLET

> "The best way to find out if you can trust somebody is to trust them."
>
> —Ernest Hemingway

Organizational cultures regenerate and renew the same way an ocean does. It's a fascinating and continuous process that's both fragile and resilient.

For my part, I'm lucky to live near the ocean and to be a creature of the water still. Everything I feel about the world and my work washes away when I'm near the ocean. In fact, Randi and I have conspired together to build our lives in such a way that we spend most of our year somewhere near water. We need it. Because it's immense, it's all-consuming, awesome, and a source of healing for us.

So much of our lives comes from the sea. Heck, that's why it used to be prescribed for a variety of ailments. "Got a touch of the dropsy? Go get your body in salt water." It's healing.

I talk about the ocean a lot.

But one aspect of it that I secretly really love is that it's dark, it's scary, and so much is happening that we don't see. Because that's my experience with life. Each person I'm lucky enough to meet has an ocean of consciousness inside them. They've got hopes, dreams, fears, rage, secrets, shame, grace, and intelligence. Every single person.

That's one of the beauties of saying "I love my life" every single morning when my feet hit the floor. It's not sentimental. It means that I love the ocean that lives inside me, and that helps me love the one inside of you too.

The ocean is unknown, the way we are unknown to ourselves. That's a scary place to be. But it doesn't have to be.

Someone who shares my love for the ocean is Janine Hamner Holman. She's an internationally recognized speaker, bestselling author, and expert in organizational culture change who brings unique insights into diagnosing and solving organizational challenges.

Janine's a valued member of WORKWELL Labs and a contributing WORKWELLian, focused on conscious leadership, and for her, culture is a dynamic process: "For better or for worse, nothing is permanent, and everything changes." Janine pivoted away from following my footsteps in the legal field and into the non-profit sector. That's where she learned everything about culture because you've got to, as she puts it, "do everything that's needed to be done."

THE IMPACT OF TOXIC LEADERSHIP ON TRUST

Janine knows a lot about trust and leadership because she was the victim of a bad boss. Think Ebenezer Scrooge, but more insidious.

Janine's boss had a leadership technique that was based on giving very public praise and recognition. "Of course, that was fun. It was fun being praised like that. The problem was that you always knew that the fall was coming." Being effusive in public isn't a bad thing, unless the organization and the leader aren't cultivating a culture of trust.

This particular boss was using expressions of praise and gratitude as deposits on future mistreatment. Janine described to me how toxic things got between them.

> In my case, it wasn't just that I would fall out of grace.
> It was that I would fall underneath the outhouse. She

would publicly shame me and she would say, "Janine is an absolute effing idiot, and here are all the mistakes that she just made." Her voice would get so excited, her voice would get hard. She would do it in front of people who are accountable to me. She would do it in front of my peers. She would do it in front of my customers.

Janine spent eight and a half years with this person as her leader, and it led her to seek medical help. The culture of stress was spiking Janine's cortisol all day, every day. She was in a permanent state of flight, but she said she couldn't flee. She could only think, "Obviously, this is a form of bullying."

Studies have been done on rats and mice where they're put in a scenario where the animals are shocked, the control group at regular intervals, and the experimental group at random.

The control group adapted fairly quickly to the effects of the shock. But the randomly shocked group experienced negative impacts almost immediately: their fur fell out, their immune systems started to fail, and they experienced weight gain and general lethargy.

Cultures of mistrust like the one Janine experienced are exactly like this. She had to take a six-month leave from her job because of the way she was treated. Whether they want to admit it or not, that company's culture made it possible for Janine to be bullied. She told me she's had to step on toes with the older reaches of upper management, and they say, "This is how we've always done things here. I had to fight, and I was bullied, and I paid my dues."

There are many companies out there like this. Maybe yours is.

I'm here to tell you that it's not too late.

THE GENERATIONAL DIVIDE: BRIDGING TRUST ACROSS AGE GROUPS

By 2030, the cohort of the millennials and Gen Z will be the bulk of the workforce, and so far, the culture of mistrust has created a chasm between the older generations and their younger colleagues.

It's up to us to teach them and to create cultures of trust where people can give and receive feedback. Maybe that younger associate who says, "Why are we doing things this way?" drives you absolutely batty. Good! They should.

An organization that builds a culture of trust will build bridges between these two groups. We have a lot of knowledge to transmit to them, but they're not always going to want to hear it. And, young people, like my children, are sometimes trying to change something before they've even understood it.

The baby and the bathwater have to stay in the house. It's better for everyone.

Janine said something ominous when she used the phrase, "the Gray Tsunami," in our chat. She was referring to the coming retirement of the baby boomers and the first wave of Generation X. Almost half of the workforce is about to retire, and when they do, they're going to take with them a significant chunk of the institutional knowledge of our organizations.

Frowning, she said, "We've got to crack this code. Organizations have got to understand that this is not a phase, that this is because of how these [younger] generations were raised, often by the folks who are being pissy about what these younger folks need in the workforce. We failed to pay attention at our peril."

Janine says that the secret is trust and, if you lose it, how to get it back: "Part of how you build trust is being consistent, doing what you say, being predictable. When we are clear and when we are consistent, then people know that they can trust us."

RE-CULTURING: REBUILDING TRUST FROM WITHIN

The root cause of a lack of trust is the lack of constructive, creative, and compassionate feedback.

Cultures of trust know that predictability and consistency can only be gained through how we give and receive feedback. There's just too much expectation of mind-reading. And that's because people haven't been taught how to lead a culture that leads with trust and compassion.

If we speak the truth without compassion, then it's barbarism, it's aggressive, and it creates a culture where people are walking on eggshells. We've all been in those rooms. It's exhausting, isn't it? If we're modeling the "First In, Last Out" mode of leadership, then we're forcing our people to reckon with both their jobs and our psychology. We're making them swim upstream. No wonder one in four people in the workplace describe themselves as lonely. Janine goes further and says that leaders have to take responsibility for fostering trust. "If you are looked to as a leader and or if you manage other people, you must say, 'This is what works for me. I love it, and it's part of my identity. I am not asking you to do the same thing. What I care about is that you get your work done.'"

Janine taught me that Re-Culture is about regaining trust. The way to begin is to look in the mirror and practice radical honesty. It truly is the way to bridge the divide of mistrust.

Like the ocean, trust is dynamic, ever-changing, and covers almost everything we do.

RE-CULTURE CURIOSITY QUESTIONS

1. Toxic Tides to Trustworthy Currents

   If your culture's "waters" are polluted by fear or silence, what daily acts of feedback could act as a cleansing tide? Who needs to dive in first to model vulnerability?

2. Generational Reefs and Feedback Currents

   When older and younger teams clash like storm waves, how might feedback become the coral that bridges divides? How do you nurture growth while honoring your organization's history?

3. Calm Seas or Silent Storms?

   Is your feedback a lifeline or a hidden riptide? What "buoys" (e.g., clarity, empathy) could you anchor to ensure trust flows even in turbulent conversations? How do you model these "buoys" to your people?

RE-CULTURE WELL-BEING

"Love is not an affectionate feeling, but a steady wish
for the loved person's ultimate good as far as it can be
obtained."

—C. S. Lewis

It's impossible to work well without protecting the well-being of every-one in your organization. Healthy cultures are made by healthy people.

Are we all perfectly healthy all the time? No, that's impossible. We don't exercise as much as we should, and we don't eat as well as we might. And we don't sleep as long as we need. We work in high-pressure environments, and everything rests on our shoulders. But that's all the more reason to be consciously husbanding the well-being of our people so they don't burn out of our organization.

Do you know the origin of the word "husband"? It comes from Old Norse, where "hus" means "house" and "bondi" means "tiller of the soil." There's that word again: cultivation. Our culture, if it is to be renewed and revived, means that we need to care for and cultivate our soil. What's our soil?

Our people. In Re-Culture, their ability to bounce back allows all of us to have each other's backs.

"People are rallying around the idea that burnout is an
organizational problem, not a personal problem. People's

feelings of burnout and fatigue are validated when we all feel them together. Organizations are no longer going to make this a personal problem."

—Jennifer Moss

We may not want to hear this, but the well-being of our employees is our responsibility. Now, it's not ours to bear alone; they, too, must bear the cost and the consequences of how they manage the stress and anxiety of being alive in this day and age. But more than ever, we have to cultivate a culture that doesn't burn people out in the first place. We have to show, not just tell.

How do we do that? We have to show our people that we love them and their work. All the telling in the world ain't gonna cut it. If we don't have love, then we have to clear out everything that's blocking us from finding it. Because it is there. All the time.

"I love my life" is the refrain that's defined me since hitting the midlife crisis wall. I was a high-flying lawyer in Manhattan representing the underdog and trading elbows with people straight out of Gordon Gekko's fantasies; but even then, especially then, I was so unhappy. Oh, I was good at pretending that I was happy. I'm a positive, optimistic, and faithful person by nature. That's the gear I idle in.

I knew, though, deep down, there was more love just waiting to come out. And so, I pivoted. Extending love through our work became the business we wanted to be in. Randi and our team even named the business More Love as a reminder that inside all of us is more love than we think.

It's a queasy word, though, love. Isn't it? By itself, in our irony-poisoned age, it means everything and nothing.

That's why we have to look for other languages to truly say what we mean.

The Greeks have a word for love, the highest form of love, which is called "agape," and it means to hold someone up, higher than ourselves. But it's not a pedestal, worshipful kind of love. It's about seeing people better than they see themselves—like a great bathroom mirror with perfect light.

Early Christians (who used Greek to disseminate their spiritual texts) adopted it as emblematic of the love the Creator has for its creation, a spontaneous but constant cultivation of the spirits of the people under its charge.

It's a humbling, almost sacrificial act. Think of Jesus Christ, washing the feet of his disciples on the night he was arrested. In the moments before his darkest hour, he showed them how to lead: through service.

Or, to take a more modern example, it's akin to John F. Kennedy saying, "Ask not what your country can do for you, ask what you can do for your country."

To lead them is to love them—not through words, but through a daily practice that shows our teams our love for their well-being.

"Agape love is…profound concern for the well-being of another, without any desire to control that other, to be thanked by that other, or to enjoy the process," writes Madeleine L'Engle.

This is what we're looking for when we have Re-Culture leaders looking out for the well-being of their teams.

Let's get specific.

RE-CULTURE LEADERSHIP IS SELFLESS.

When we practice Re-Culture leadership, we put the needs and welfare of our people above our own. If we see someone who's falling behind, we don't consign them to the dustbin. We help them up and walk with them for as long as they need.

RE-CULTURE IS COMPASSION.

When we're rooted in empathy and a desire to understand where people are coming from and if they're in distress, it's our job as leaders to understand their situation. We may not succeed, but we have to try—especially if their work tasks are leading them to burnout. Even if we don't fully understand, we'll get more out of them in the long run if we simply acknowledge where they are and provide the resources to get them on their feet.

RE-CULTURE IS RESTORATIVE.

We can't hold grudges or harbor resentment if someone needs time to get their mind, body, or spirit back in alignment. We must seek to make that a part of their growth and improvement as human beings, not just a cog in a wheel. If seldom is heard an encouraging word, then the skies, I assure you, will be cloudy all day.

RE-CULTURE IS SACRIFICIAL.

When we make sacrifices for the benefit of everyone's well-being, even when it is costly or inconvenient, then we're leading from Re-Culture. We may not want to pull longer hours or push ourselves, but if we're doing it for someone else as opposed to some nebulous outcome, then we're going to end up with a resilient culture. We can't do it all the time, but we must do it to attract and keep talent.

RE-CULTURE IS PROACTIVE.

Re-Culture isn't passive. We demonstrate it daily through our actions that show others our concern and care for them. We have to check in with people before they're on the red line. It's not HR's job to show it either. We have to do it. If we've got fewer employees, it's easier, but even with thousands, we've got to try. People will notice if our support is genuine and not offered at the breaking point.

RE-CULTURE IS FAIR.

Re-Culture leadership extends to all of our people, leading with dignity and respect, even if we might not get along with them out in the world. It's like what they used to say about Vince Lombardi, "He treated us all the same. Like dogs." That's not necessarily what we're after, but at least with the Green Bay Packers legend, the players knew where they stood. That's all we want. Eliminate the mystery. Be direct. People sense fairness intuitively, and it's our job to honor it. Not everyone is going to like us, but they'll respect our decisions in the long run.

RE-CULTURE IS PATIENT.

Re-Culture leadership is a skill that we must develop and practice every day. Our people need a leader who is steadfast, enduring through challenges and difficulties without losing sight of the bigger picture. It may seem daunting at first, like wearing shoes too large for our feet, but I promise that if we practice patience, over time, we'll become perfect in our leadership.

We're going to meet all manner of challenges as leaders. Some will come from outside our organization, but most will come from within, as the organization's culture renews itself. Some will stay, some will go, and there will be the pains and losses associated with growth. Stick to your values.

It takes patience to become patient.

RE-CULTURE DOES NOT JUDGE.

Re-Culture leadership doesn't judge or condemn others but accepts mistakes and encourages growth.

When we support someone who has made poor choices, keeping them accountable to the standards we set, then we help them stay on the path with us.

We have to be watchful of the people on our teams who judge others. They're usually hiding, trying not to be judged themselves.

Left to their own devices, this kind of person is toxic to culture.

RE-CULTURE IS ENCOURAGEMENT.

Re-Culture leadership seeks to build others up, fostering their potential and self-esteem.

We can't mentor everyone all the time. There just aren't enough hours in the day. But we can create systems where our people have each other's backs. It starts at the top.

Mentoring someone to help them achieve their goals, offering genuine praise and support along the way.

RE-CULTURE IS LOYAL.

Re-Culture leadership is about committing to our people, sticking with them through good times and bad. Think about what we gain from staying loyal to a team member we've found, trained, and developed into a culture builder. If we walk through the fire with them, then our culture is enriched beyond measure. On the other hand, we betray our culture when we cut people loose at their lowest point. Re-Culture is about believing in the best possible version of the people who work for us.

"Trust is earned, respect is given, and loyalty is demonstrated. Betrayal of any one of those is to lose all three."

—Ziad K. Abdelnour

CULTURE CODE

Re-Culture Leadership is a necessary ingredient in the "Well" aspect of our Work Well Together code. Use these keys to practice leading from a consistent, selfless, generous, and humble kind of love leadership.

Think of the great leaders who've gotten the most from their teams. They all practice the Five Keys of Re-Culture Leadership:

Listening
Empathizing
Collaborating
Empowering
Own Your Mistakes

"The art of coaching is doing, thinking, and being: doing a set of actions, holding a set of beliefs, and being in a way that results in those actions leading to change."

—Elena Aguilar, *The Art of Coaching: Effective Strategies for School Transformation*

THE RE-CULTURE CURIOSITY QUESTIONS

1. How might you and your organization reimagine leadership as a stewardship practice where managers and teams act in service of everyone's well-being without recognition?
2. What if your organization's leadership included self-preservation clauses mandating leaders' rest as nonnegotiable, modeling that organizational sustainability starts at the top?
3. How could "restorative pauses" be designed into your workflows to challenge the "grind mind" and normalize recovery as an integral part of organizational productivity?
4. What if fairness were engineered through your process through the collection of employee well-being data?
5. How might mutual care be tested and renewed through "stress drills" that reveal where lip service meets lived values regarding well-being?
6. How can you contribute more love to the people who support the business you are in?

PERMISSION MISSION

"What we can do is to bring out the best in society and the best in each of us."

—Arne Sorensen

If you want an example of how Re-Culture leadership renews culture, look no further than Arne Sorenson, the late CEO of Marriott International. In 2020, when a global pandemic imprisoned us in our homes, the hospitality industry faced a near-death experience. Hotels were drowning under a wave of sickness, government mandates, and an app that made it possible to rent your home to a weary traveler. The winds were against Arne Sorensen and Marriott.

Through it all, though, like a sea captain, he led his organization to safe harbor. He kept his teams together and helped them weather the storm until their customers emerged, blinking into the light, and began to experience the world again. He exemplified care and concern for his people and their communities. He prioritized the well-being of his people over profits.

He was culture.

Like me, Sorensen was a former lawyer who found that the law wasn't his true calling, but he learned some important lessons about the big, bad business world:

"The big advantage is you get used to being attacked as a lawyer. I tried cases, hostile-takeover cases, basically.

In that context, there are brilliant lawyers on the other
side whose aim is to make you look bad, show that you
don't understand your facts or you don't understand the
law. You do that year after year for a while, you develop
a certain toughness."

I really feel every word of what he says there. That was my experience,
too. I appreciate the toughness I learned as a lawyer, but I hated seeing
other people as adversaries. It's an exhausting way to live—and it's mean.
I'm grateful that I pivoted away from that life and into one where people
weren't problems to be solved, but I could help people solve problems.

Something inside Sorensen felt the same as he worked his way up
through the Marriott Corporation, and over two decades, he earned the
trust of Mr. Bill Marriott, who, at first, wasn't so sure about grooming a
litigator to take over the family business. This is what he said:

"...litigation does not have a primary goal of making
people feel good. When I think about a litigator, I don't
see someone who is putting his arms around people,
coaching, counseling and loving them, supporting and
promoting them."

But that's what Bill Marriott saw in Arne Sorensen. Even though he
was unsure at first, taking a high-powered lawyer under his wing, he saw
something the younger man maybe didn't even see in himself.

That's one of the first lessons about Re-Culture leadership that
Sorensen learned from his mentor. In *Pivot*, I talked about the importance of mentors on our journey. In a way, they're like our parents. They
download their genetic code to us so that we may pass it on to those who
come after us. In this way, we pass down institutional wisdom.

That's the true magic of culture and how you remake it in your
image: You think about the people that made you who you are, and you
give thanks to them by making something they could be proud of.

Arne Sorenson kept Marriott above water during COVID-19, and
he kept them swimming, moving forward into the world yet to come. He

said, "I've tried to take the longer view—anticipating what's next: tomorrow, next quarter, and next year." He did it by leaning into Marriott's culture, bearing the slings and arrows, but bouncing forward from a place of foundational strength. The culture he learned and stewarded made it possible.

What Sorensen learned from Mr. Marriott was that Re-Culture leadership is about seeing people at their best. Maybe they're not where you need them to be immediately, but it's our job to look past ourselves and see what's on the other side of the mirror.

Here are a few key Re-Culture leadership lessons you can learn from Arne Sorensen.

SACRIFICE

Facing massive revenue losses in the face of a global pandemic, Sorenson gave up his salary for the year and further reduced the salaries of the executive leadership team. That takes a tremendous amount of trust and buy-in. This act ensured that more resources could be directed toward retaining as many frontline employees as possible. If employees are sacrificing, then leaders have to give them permission to do so.

"What we can do is to bring out the best in society and the best in each of us."

COMPASSION AND EMPATHY

In a heartfelt video message to employees, Sorenson candidly addressed the difficulties Marriott was facing and acknowledged the personal toll the crisis was taking on what Marriott culture called "associates." His authenticity and vulnerability resonated deeply, showing that he cared for them not just as workers but as individuals with families and struggles.

"A big part of our people-first culture is treating people with respect and transparency."

UNCONDITIONAL CARE

Sorenson worked tirelessly to implement programs that supported furloughed employees, including offering continued health benefits and access to resources. His decisions reflected a commitment to people over profit, even when the company was at the financial breaking point. His associates knew he'd be the one to fall on the axe, but he did it anyway. I don't know about you, but I'd run through a wall for someone like that.

"My guideposts have been three simple tenets of leadership: listen, empower, communicate."

GENEROSITY AND ACTIVE EXPRESSION

With Sorensen's guidance, Marriott established a relief fund to assist employees in need, supported by contributions from the leadership team. Sorenson encouraged hotel managers worldwide to repurpose unused hotel rooms to house first responders and health-care workers, showcasing a commitment to community care. Sorensen showed that companies and communities need one another to work well together. A little generosity goes a long way, but miserly corporate giving will get you haunted by three ghosts on Christmas Eve.

"For them to feel good about their work is about being compensated fairly, of course, but more than that, it's about being respected as an individual by the team. You immediately see the way this can work, and when it works well, it makes all the difference in the world."

PATIENCE AND ENDURANCE

Throughout the pandemic, Sorenson emphasized Marriott's long-term culture and the importance of maintaining relationships with employees, customers, and communities. His steady, compassionate approach helped the organization navigate change while preserving its core values. Re-Culture leadership is also about loving the company for what it is, too. That love permeates in such a way that everyone, from the C-Suite to the interns, can feel what the company means. And it's not something you show in a glossy corporate training video. It has to be from the leader, and it has to come from love.

"The first instinct has got to be to say, 'okay, let's see how it works,' as opposed to, 'why the hell did you do that?' Because it makes a difference in the way people feel ownership about their work."

Arne Sornenson died in February 2021, after bringing his organization's ship into safe harbor. His leadership left a lasting legacy, and his company is better off than when he received it. Like a steward, he didn't act as though the company was his and had always been. He knew it was his job to renew a culture capable of sailing again. His actions during a time of world crisis strengthened loyalty, reinforced Marriott's reputation as a people-first company, and inspired countless leaders with his compassion and selflessness.

Arne Sorensen's Re-Culture leadership exemplified how Re-Culture leadership can manifest in the corporate world, creating a culture of care and resilience that endures even beyond his life.

THE RE-CULTURE CURIOSITY QUESTIONS

1. How might you demonstrate sacrifice beyond financial gestures (e.g., salary cuts) to cultivate trust and solidarity during crises? In what ways can you "lead by example" to ensure your teams feel valued and protected, even when resources are scarce?

2. How can you embrace vulnerability (like Sorensen's candid video addressing Marriott's struggles) to transcend hierarchies in your organization? What risks and rewards could come with you openly sharing your uncertainties while still projecting leadership values?

3. How can you design systems or rituals that ensure your values endure beyond your tenure? What practices prevent cultural erosion when you're not around?

THE BARBIE PROBLEM OF LEADERSHIP

> "The challenge of leadership is to be strong, but not rude; be kind, but not weak; be bold, but not a bully; be thoughtful, but not lazy; be humble, but not timid; be proud, but not arrogant; have humor, but without folly."
>
> —Jim Rohn

In Re-Culture, values are verbs. They can't just be spoken of as a noun; they have to be put into action. Daily. And that starts with leadership. However, it's getting harder and harder to determine what exactly a leader is and what they do. To put it more simply, it's harder and harder to lead.

If we want to see how difficult it is to be a leader, here's a recent job posting—

"You're not just another product leader; you're a 5-for-1 talent who sees opportunities where others don't. You bring together behavioral design, gamification, AI, and global product expertise to create meaningful impact at scale.

You might be:

- An ex-product leader who understands gamification, habit formation, and global engagement.
- A neuroscientist-turned-product-builder with expertise in cognitive development, well-being, and behavior change.

- A mission-driven AI/ML product leader seeking to apply AI to storytelling and personalized health technologies to build a global maternal healing ecosystem.
- Someone who has scaled consumer apps to millions of users, harnessing vitality, network effects, and real-world impact.

This role is not for someone who wants to simply follow a roadmap. It's for a builder, a co-creator of a movement that can last for generations."

I won't say what the job posting was for, but if I told you two years ago what it was, you'd look at me like I was A) a time-traveller from the future, or B) insane. There are likely a few thousand, or maybe only hundreds of people who fit a profile this specific. It's an almost impossible bar for one human being to clear to be a product leader for a company designed for something for which there probably isn't even a market.

No wonder we're all wondering how to become better leaders.

On another level, it uses a lot of verbiage we're going to use together in this book. It looks good—on paper. But does this leader even exist? It feels like we're looking for unicorns in a world of horses.

Either way, based on this posting, we have to admit that it's harder than ever to be a leader. How hard is it?

Let's take a deep breath and paraphrase the amazing speech from the *Barbie* movie.

AS A LEADER…

You have to trust everyone, but you can't let people take advantage of your good nature. You have to let people take care of themselves, but you can't take a day for yourself. You have to get along with everyone, but people can take out their frustrations on you. You have to have values, but you can't force them on people. You have to make room for play, but you can't let people screw around. You have to embrace discomfort while making everyone around you comfortable. You have to keep an eye on growth, while others get to work through their mistakes. You have to take responsibility for failure, while protecting others from its consequences. You have to be grateful, but the gratitude is never returned. You have to believe, but you constantly have to prove your worth. You can't be too tough, but you can't be too weak. You have to have standards, but you have to ask everyone's opinion. You have to care about the bottom line, but your people have to come first. You have to make sure everyone's on board, but you'll be alone if it goes sideways. You have to exceed expectations, but you can't hog the credit. You have to care a lot, but you can't care too much. You have to know where you are going, but everyone gets a turn at the wheel. The buck stops with you, but so does the axe. You have to be the one who knows, but you can't explain yourself. You have to be big, but you have to stay small. You have to run fast, but you've got to make sure everyone can keep up. You have to have vision, but you have to make bifocals for everyone else.

Trying to make sense of all the paradoxes and contradictions. It's nearly impossible!

Okay. We all got that out of our system? Good.

Know what? As they say, "Pressure is a privilege." We want to sit in the big chair, then no matter how uneasy our heads are, we're the ones who have to wear the heavy crown.

The sooner we get over the fact that, as leaders, we're probably going to do it wrong and that many people are going to be unhappy with what we do, the sooner we can get in the business of doing it right and being happy with whatever comes next.

Because it is coming.

Our next leadership job might not even exist. Yet.

THE RE-CULTURE CURIOSITY QUESTIONS

1. How might you embrace the tension between being "strong but not rude" and "humble but not timid" to transform that paradox into a dynamic adaptability practice rather than a burden of perfection?

2. If "values are verbs," what rituals or systems could you co-create with your people to help them act their values when contradictory demands collide (e.g., prioritizing growth vs. protecting the organization from failure)?

3. As roles evolve toward "5-for-1 unicorn" expectations, how might we redefine leadership not as a solo act of impossible mastery, but as a collective dance, where admitting "I don't know" becomes the first step in orchestrating the diverse expertise of our people?

THE GREAT ESCAPE

"Pleasure in the job puts perfection in the work."

—Aristotle

Is your organizational culture a living promise that keeps people from seeking escape, or a broken one driving them to safer ground?

The sense of smell, they say, is the most evocative sense for memory due to how our brains have evolved and protected us since we were animals. You see, back when we were just barely human, living tribally, smelling what food was healthy and what food was toxic meant that our brains had to process that information through the amygdala (the almond-shaped nugget in our brains that tells us to fight or flee). So, as we grew from tribes to towns, towns to cities, and as our civilization grew, our sense of smell became tied to our emotional processing. When you get right down to it, smell makes us feel a memory.

That's why certain scents, like, say, freshly baked chocolate chip cookies, remind us of our mothers. Hence, realtors often will light a candle with that scent or bake cookies in a for-sale kitchen before an open house. Create a familiar smell, trigger a memory, create a bond, and maybe sell a house. That's the theory anyway.

THE UNIVERSAL SUBSTANCE

One specific odor that's been unchanged for decades and is instantly familiar to all who encounter it is WD-40. It smells of a car mechanic's workspace, a father's tool shed, or a wood-shop class.

WD-40 is one of those magical substances with a myriad of uses: It prevents rust, acts as a lubricant, degreaser, and solvent. It can clean power tools, grimy headlights, glue, and stains, and it can even unstick stubborn zippers.

If you walk into any shop, house, warehouse, oil rig, military base, school, or manufacturing plant in the world, a can of WD-40 will be somewhere close to hand. It's always there for exactly what you need, even if you don't know that you need it.

GARRY RIDGE: THE HUMBLE CEO

There's no one who knows that better than Garry Ridge, who went to work for WD-40 in 1987, and within ten years, he was CEO. I've had the pleasure of knowing Garry for years now, as he's also an adjunct professor near me at the University of San Diego. Moreover, he's the co-author of an empowering book on organizational culture with the fantastic title, *Helping People Win at Work: A Business Philosophy Called "Don't Mark My Paper, Help Me Get an A."* (Garry and I both share an affinity for our titles being our theses.)

Garry, true to his nature as a native Australian, describes himself as a "consciously incompetent, probably wrong, and roughly right former Chairman and CEO of the WD-40 Company." And, along with being one of the humblest, down-to-earth CEOs I've ever known, he's taught me a vital lesson about how to lead from values.

His values are distilled into a phrase that provides the title of this section: "Leadership fails when ego eats empathy instead of empathy eating ego." Above all, Garry prizes psychological safety, compassion, and understanding. Add those up, and you get empathy, Garry's north star that helped him navigate WD-40 through the days of 2020 when our entire global system was upended. Garry told me that uncertainty is just "a series of events that may or may not occur. Most of them don't occur." These two simple statements provide the DNA strands of a leadership approach that can work in any organization: empathy and humility.

For Garry and WD-40, the way that these two strands become systemic rather than individual is through a hierarchy—but not the kind you think.

MASLOW'S CULTURE

In a beautifully written article published on LinkedIn, Garry made his case for the kind of hierarchy that works for him: Maslow's hierarchy of needs, a five-tier model of human motivation and needs. Human beings have to fulfill basic physical needs (food, water, shelter) before moving up the pyramid to more complex, emotional, psychological, and ultimately, spiritual needs.

At WD-40, the hierarchy pointed toward the possibility that an organization could fulfill a person's needs more than just, "I work, you pay me for my time, so I can eat and put a roof over my head."

Garry knew, through his experience of the world of work, that the third tier, the sense of belonging, was where culture was forged. Rather than the word team, WD-40 uses the word "tribe" to delineate their working groups. "Tribe ticked all the boxes. Tribes is about contributing to the whole, not individually winning and losing at all costs. Any role you can think of within an indigenous tribe has a counterpart in the corporate community. Warriors. Teachers. Nurturers. Learners. Scouts. Hunters. They can all be found inside a company structure."

A tribe isn't just a loose collective of interests, like we have now; it's a mutually interdependent group where each member bears responsibility not only for themselves but also for the health of the collective.

And that's what Re-Culture is: collective action where we grow together, endure challenges together, bounce forward together, and have each other's backs.

But it's not just words at WD-40. They've got the numbers to back it up. Garry told me, "During COVID-19, there was research done by the ADP Research Group that showed that employee engagement globally dropped down to 16 percent. Ours is 93 percent."

I asked Garry. How? How was this possible? During a global pandemic the world hadn't seen for a century, where organizations faced staggering attritions, what did WD-40 do differently? I needed to know.

Laughing, Garry said, "We did a little digging, and we wanted to find out why. What came back very clearly was that we are living our tribal promise of a group of people that come together and protect each other. We feel safe in this environment, and if we can get through this together, we can get through anything together." I love that phrase, "The tribal promise of a group of people," because it's a Re-Culture phrase that's about working well together.

THE GREAT ESCAPE

WD-40 didn't work some kind of magic. They didn't spend millions hiring a big consulting firm to come in and reorganize their hierarchy. They didn't put a bunch of fancy slogans on the wall. They just made the people in their organization feel like someone had their back. It sounds almost absurd to write those words.

Yet, think about how often you feel that about your leaders? Do your team members (your tribe) feel that way about you? In an era where the conventional wisdom says, over and over again, "Nobody wants to work anymore." So much so that this era has been called "The Great Resignation," but Garry Ridge and WD-40 have nailed the problem and given it a better name:

> It's not the Great Resignation. Here's what it is. It's the Great Escape. People are escaping from organizations where they don't feel they belong. They're not treated with respect and dignity. They don't go to work each day knowing they're making a contribution to something bigger than themselves. They're not learning. They're

not being protected and set free by a compelling set of values, and they're not going home happy. It's not the Great Resignation. Anybody I talk to who's moving from one organization to another said, "I've had it. I just can't put up with this toxic environment anymore, and this has proven to me there must be something better." This is a great escape. That's what it is.

There's that word again. Values. If people feel as though they are valued members of the tribe, then they don't need another tribe. Coherence between what we say, what we do, and how that makes our people feel, that's our values.

At WD-40, they start with honesty, with trust, and all other values flow from there. In his article, Garry wrote them down for us:

- We value creating positive, lasting memories in all our relationships.
- We value making it better than it is today.
- We value succeeding as a tribe while excelling as individuals.
- We value owning it and passionately acting on it.
- We value sustaining the WD-40 Company economy.

Using these five WD-40 values, write your values down right now. See what you come up with. Don't think. Just write. Even the effort of writing, you're using your empathy and placing its value on your organization. How many of us have ever done that? Empathized with our bricks, walls, spreadsheets, pay schedules, supply chains, and the people that make all these resources human.

COLLISION ZONES

Now, sure, organizations are doing phenomenally well, maybe better than they've ever done before. The numbers back this up. However, these organizations are like Formula One racing teams: They're flying around the track at speeds that have never been seen before. But they're doing it on bald tires. High speeds and bald tires will lead your organization into a ditch, or worse.

That's why you not only need values, but you also have to demonstrate them. The companies that state them, practice them, and protect them will be resilient.

I was lucky enough to visit WD-40 and see their values in action. They didn't just put them up in the break room, taped to a wall. They built the walls with their values. Designed into the architecture of the entire WD-40 offices are areas called "collision zones" where members of the tribe can meet, discuss challenges, share insights, and brainstorm solutions. I didn't just see it with my own eyes; I heard the sound of a resilient organization where everyone felt like they were exactly where they belonged.

It reminded me that WD-40 is a universal substance, useful everywhere, always recognizable by that unique smell.

It smells like values.

VALUES REFLECTIONS

Replace transactional "teams" with an interdependent tribe where every member contributes to the collective, shares responsibility, and embodies their own leadership.

"Tribes thrive when individuals win together, not at each other's expense."

Codify and live organizational values daily. No slogans, but behavioral blueprints. Use them to guide hiring, problem-solving, and conflict resolution.

"Values are the organizational smell: If they're absent, everyone notices."

Build environments where mistakes are learning moments. Welcome dissent.

"Fear stifles innovation; safety fuels it."

Create spaces for cross-tribal collaboration. Encourage spontaneous "idea collisions" to solve challenges and spark innovation.

"Break silos before they break your culture."

Prioritize servant leadership: remove barriers, amplify voices, and measure success by how your tribe thrives, not just profits.

"When leaders eat ego for breakfast, empathy becomes the tribe's oxygen."

Re-Culture isn't a program; it's a promise. Honor it, and people won't seek an escape hatch. The "Great Escape" isn't about laziness. It's a flight from cultures that fail to honor humanity.

WD-40's tribal ethos and empathy-first leadership offer a blueprint for retaining talent in turbulent times.

WD-40's slogan is "Repair it, Don't Replace it." So, if you repair your values, rather than replacing them, you won't have to replace your people.

THE RE-CULTURE CURIOSITY QUESTIONS

1. How can we shift from transactional "teams" to interdependent tribes where everyone shares responsibility for the collective?

    "Are we winning together? Or at each other's expense?"

2. Do our core values actively guide daily decisions, or are they just words on a wall?

    "What would our organization smell like if values were absent?"

3. Are we fostering environments where mistakes become learning moments, dissent is safe, and empathy silences ego?

    "Does fear of failure stifle innovation here?"

4. Where can we design intentional spaces for cross-tribal collisions of ideas and perspectives?

    "Are silos quietly eroding our culture?"

5. How might leaders prioritize serving their tribe's growth over personal agendas?

    "Is empathy the oxygen our tribe breathes? Or is ego choking it?"

    Is your organizational culture a living promise that keeps people from seeking escape, or a broken one driving them out?

BOUNDARIES, NOT BARRIERS

"If I could sit high, how much greater I'd be! What a king! I'd be ruler of all I could see!"

—Yertle the Turtle

It's quite an old story, we've all heard before,
About this old turtle who wanted much more:
To sit his old butt at the top of the heap
But he couldn't ascend without using his peeps
In a tall turtle stack where they bore all the weight
He made them feel small so he could be great.

That's my little rhyme for you, but I'll stop there, because you get the idea. *Yertle the Turtle* is Dr. Seuss's 1958 story of a hierarchical org chart of turtles and the toxic leader who stacked and climbed them so he could be master of all he surveyed. It's a cautionary tale about the dangers of, well, being a turtle who uses other turtles for your gain without caring about the value of the tower of turtles beneath you. It's not "Got Your Back" culture; it's "On Your Back" culture, and it's got a lesson for us in how organizational culture values those at the top of the tower.

If we go back to the earliest human societies, we didn't need hierarchies because we existed in relatively small, stable, and egalitarian groups. We hunted, gathered, and shared. Those were our values. But as we evolved, spread out, and populated the world, things got more complicated. Now, other values were opposed to ours. What to do?

We dealt with this by creating rulers who used hierarchies like armies to dominate, control, and scale the world. In a complicated and growing world, knowing where you are in the stack of turtles keeps things simple, and it keeps power concentrated at the top. By the time it makes it down to the bottom, it's so diluted as to be nonexistent. Kings, lords, knights, earls, and peasants. Easy. Everyone knows their place.

But as the world grew and people started to take their own divine rights by the sword or the pen, hierarchies became more common in their situation. Like the military, the Vatican, or the Mongol tribes. We spread our values through the hierarchies of submission. Join or die. Again, it was all about power.

That's why hierarchies were and still are a ruthlessly efficient way to distribute authority and resources from the top down. In a hierarchical system, authority plus resources equals values.

For instance, the armies that invaded Normandy and pushed east to Berlin had to solve logistical labyrinths that would make our heads spin. So, it's good to know who's in charge, what orders to follow, and who's going to carry them out. Hierarchies flourish in simple, stable environments. Wars, chaotic though they may be, are fairly simple enterprises: We're over here and want to be over there. They're over there and want to be over here. In the whole history of work since the Industrial Revolution, we've borrowed our industrial hierarchies from the military. Which, as we've seen, helps a company grow from a single twenty-six-horsepower automobile into the Ford Motor Company, the defining corporation of the twentieth century.

In 2025, when it comes to workplace culture, hierarchies are mostly considered barriers to a healthy, thriving work environment. If we aim to work well together, then our historical attachment to hierarchies is no longer necessary. It was useful for a time, but now hierarchies can be replaced by a healthy culture, as Brian Chesky writes, "The stronger the culture, the less corporate process a company needs. When the culture is strong, you can trust everyone to do the right thing." The values way of saying this is from Roy Disney, "It's not hard to make decisions when you know what your values are."

Based on the accounts I hear from a surprising number of team members I speak to, hierarchies now only seem to exist to protect themselves, not the people at the bottom of the stack, as it were. They tell me that org charts serve to silo teams off from one another, making communication a minefield to navigate. Without clear communication, trust erodes, and all of a sudden, our hierarchies are walls too high for culture to climb. Research shows that when people feel like they matter, when their contributions are valued, and their well-being is prioritized, they're more engaged, productive, and fulfilled. On the flip side, feeling disrespected or undervalued can lead to stress, burnout, and even physical health issues.

That's why, whether we want a flat or a matrix organizational structure, we've got to value creating boundaries, not barriers. Boundaries are like our good fences. Barriers, if you see the poem another way, are also good fences. The question we're asking in Re-Culture is: "What do we want to choose?"

***

Setting a boundary is not a one-and-done deal. It's an ongoing process that requires reinforcement and adjustment. People will test your boundaries, sometimes unintentionally, and it's up to you to hold the line. This can be exhausting at times, but it's necessary. Think of boundaries like a garden—you have to tend to them regularly to keep them healthy and effective. Neglecting them can lead to confusion or erosion of trust.

Boundaries—not barriers—are essential in resilient organizational cultures, but they come with some hard truths we need to hear. Let's dive into a few of those truths, because understanding them can help us navigate the complexities of creating a healthy, thriving work environment.

• Boundaries Require Clarity and Courage

At the personal and the collaborative level, boundaries aren't a passive act. They require clarity about our needs and values, and the inner courage to communicate them effectively. But when we do, or even when we're gearing up to try, we feel that cold, clammy feeling on our hands and in our stomachs. It's uncomfortable setting boundaries. Everything in us wants to run—especially in workplace cultures where we feel overworked or hounded by constant vibrations of our inboxes. The truth we all have to face is this: If you don't define your boundaries, someone else will define them for you. That's where we get to burnout, resentment, and feeling our organization doesn't see our value. In Re-Culture, "No" is complete sentence, and boundaries are about saying, "This is what I need to be my best self and do my best work," and that takes guts. That's the work.

The way we do it well? Well, it's our responsibility to set our boundaries, but it's our organization's responsibility to protect them. This might be an extreme example, but it's something akin to when a player in a sport suffers a head injury. It wasn't always this way, but now, the team and the leagues take the decision out of the player's hands to protect them from themselves. That's what we need to do for our teams. Boundaries are one thing, but if they're not respected, then we attack the self-worth of our people. There's a quote from Lorraine Nilon, "The more you value yourself, the healthier your boundaries are." That's so true, but it's even more true at the organizational culture level. If we truly value our organization, then boundaries needn't be feared; they should be welcomed.

But...

• What if Boundaries Are Not Always Welcomed?

Here's a tough one: Not everyone will appreciate or respect our boundaries, especially in cultures that reward taxing team members to the max or where leadership's emotional intelligence is in the single digits. Some people might see our boundaries as resistance or even laziness, which can create tension at best and retribution at worst. I've heard countless stories of leaders badgering their people with accusations of all kinds. But the reality is, boundaries are not about pleasing others— they're about protecting your energy and ensuring you can contribute sustainably. It's not your job to make everyone comfortable with your boundaries; it's your job to uphold them with consistency and integrity.

As leaders, we have to model the same. Our boundaries are our values. Trust is the pivot that keeps our team's boundaries and our cultural values in a dynamic relationship. Again, it's not about balance. That's impossible. There will always be power imbalances in every company. We use ours responsibly when we protect boundaries. When we do that, we create Re-Culture, a resilient organization that's together, pulling in the same direction.

• Boundaries Are Not Barriers—But They Can Feel Like It

In our research, we've found that one of the biggest misconceptions about boundaries is that they're walls meant to keep people out. In truth, boundaries are bridges—they define where we end and where others begin, creating a foundation for mutual respect and trust. That said, when we introduce our boundaries into a workplace that lacks them, they can feel like barriers to those higher up the hierarchy (especially those in the middle) who are used to unlimited access and control of those beneath them. That's why it's crucially important for us to communicate the "why" behind our boundaries. If we frame them as tools for collaboration (and productivity) rather than obstacles, then we're operating in that zone of trust we were talking about. We might say something like, "I've noticed that I've been feeling overwhelmed lately, and I realized it's because I'm not giving myself enough time to recharge after work. To be at my best, I need to set a boundary around after-hours communication. I'd like to agree on a system where non-urgent matters can wait until the next workday. How does that sound to you?" Framing the boundary as a way to improve performance allows our leaders to participate in the process rather than the zero-sum game of boundaries. Then, as leaders and team members, we're seeing the same thing, the same way, speaking the same language. That's where culture thrives.

• Boundaries Can Expose Cultural Weaknesses

This one is purely for the leaders among us because there's a hard pill we have to swallow if we want to lead with cultural intelligence: When our people start setting boundaries, we might (if we're aware and open) notice fault lines within our workplace culture.

My family and I have lived in Southern California for years, so we're quite aware of the fault lines in our great Golden State. We're used to earthquake drills and what to do when the earth's core shakes us to our feet, but how many organizations can say the same for theirs?

If we fear that boundaries will make us weak, then we are weak.

For example, if we, or leaders who work for us, meet boundaries around work-life balance with resistance, then that's a blinking red warning light that our culture prioritizes output over well-being. Don't be disheartened by this. It's an opportunity to renew and refresh your organization's culture. If we let them, boundaries can serve as a mirror, reflecting the health, or lack thereof, of our organizational culture.

In the end, boundaries are a value proposition in our organizations. They're about fostering a culture where people can thrive as individuals while conspiring in a shared mission. It's not always easy, and it's not always comfortable, but it's always worth it.

> *Then, a turtle named Mack, at the bottom, he huffed,*
> *"We turtles are tired, we've just had enough!"*
> *So he burped out a boundary, Yertle fell with a smack*
> *Back into the pond, back into the pack,*
> *And swam with the turtles in all sorts of weather*
> *No hierarchies here, just Working Together*

BOUNDARY BOUNDARIES

Get Clear on Your Boundaries (Know Your Why):

"I need to disconnect from work after 6 p.m. to recharge and be effective during the day."

Communicate Boundaries with Clarity and Compassion:

"I'd like to work with you on this so that we can work better together."

Anticipate Pushback and Stay Firm:

"I understand that this is a shift, but I've found that I'm more productive and focused when I have time to recharge. I'm committed to delivering my best work, and this boundary helps me do that."

Model the Behavior You Want to See:

"Thanks for your message. I'll take a look at this first thing tomorrow."

Know When to Escalate or Exit (if All Else Fails):

"My health and well-being are too important to risk on this or any job. Another opportunity will open up for me elsewhere where I'm valued."

THE RE-CULTURE CURIOSITY QUESTIONS

1. How might organizations dismantle hierarchies by redesigning authority as a network of clear, mutually respected boundaries rather than overall, top-down control?

2. What rituals could normalize boundary-setting, embedding it into your daily organizational practice, rather than treating it as a one-on-one confrontation?

3. If boundaries are "bridges, not barriers," how might your teams co-create visual or tactile systems to make boundaries more tangible and actionable?

4. When employee boundaries expose cultural fault lines (e.g., resistance to work-life harmony), how might you reframe these moments as invitations to renegotiate values, not defend outdated norms (the "I had to deal with it" defense)?

5. What if mentorship programs paired "Yertles" (hierarchy-dependent leaders) with "Macks" (boundary advocates) to model how power shared through boundaries fuels resilience better than through rank-and-file hierarchies?

MICROMANAGEMENT BUILDS MICRO ORGANIZATIONS

"Micromanagement fails because no one person can control multiple people executing a vast number of actions in a dynamic environment, where changes in the situation occur rapidly and with unpredictability. It also inhibits the growth of subordinates: when people become accustomed to being told what to do, they begin to await direction. Initiative fades and eventually dies."

—Jocko Willink

Let's be honest. We've all had a boss or a manager who was a micromanager—constantly critical, forever finicky, and always antagonistic. No sooner have they assigned a task than they're either doing it themselves or drawing lines so narrow that you can't help but step outside them. Micromanagers can never be clear in their instructions, but they're always clear about your failures. Which they seem to take as a personal affront. When you encounter them, you feel cold in the pit of your stomach, with clammy palms. You're on edge and on guard seemingly all the time. They're exhausted and exhausting.

For some of us, they conjure painful memories of cruel teachers or guardians, or bullies.

Micromanagers don't realize that they're stifling creativity and innovation. They try to steer the ship by controlling every single wave and gust of wind rather than setting a course and trusting the crew to navigate themselves home to safety.

Micromanagers are like rabbits: They breed more micromanagers—lots of them. They teach their teams how to lead, so that when everyone moves up a peg, the micromanagement stays firmly in place.

But here's the good news: micromanagers are rarely conscious of what they're doing.

You may be reading this, feeling stung by these words, thinking, "I only have the best intentions. Someone has to ensure quality and efficiency. We must be perfect. Or I'll lose my job."

Maybe that's true: Maybe you see yourself climbing a huge mountain, with base camp a distant memory. Maybe it's just that your standards are high, and you're pushing your team to join you where the air is thin and where the view seems to go on forever.

Maybe people don't want to work as hard as you do. Maybe your perfectionism will never be appreciated in its time.

But maybe isn't *must be*. To build a culture of resilience in our organizations, we must be better. Sometimes getting better is letting go.

Let's get real: Micromanagement violates the one tenet of Re-Culture that we can't afford to violate—trust. When we lose autonomy, trust follows, and both are crucial for a thriving work culture.

I've worked with thousands of businesses now, and I've seen firsthand time and again how micromanagement can create a culture of dependency, where team members feel they can't make decisions on their own. This not only hampers their growth but also limits the potential of the organization as a whole.

A garden that's pruned down to the nub, that's not allowed to grow, will be just small enough to fit on your desk, but it won't flourish on your land. You can admire it, but it won't bear the fruit that creates lasting bonds.

A great leader knows when to step back and let their team take the reins. It's about creating a space where people feel empowered to contribute their unique perspectives and skills. That's what you hired them for. This doesn't mean abdicating oversight but rather fostering an environment of trust and collaboration. When people feel trusted, they're more likely to take ownership of their work and positively push boundaries.

If you want to micromanage, then fire everyone and go it alone. I guarantee you won't get very far.

> "If you want to go fast, go alone. If you want to go far, go together."
>
> —Anonymous

Using Work Well Together, let's break down how micromanagement can saw off each leg of the Re-Culture stool and see if, due respect to Jeff Foxworthy, "You might be a micromanager."

WORK

Are you changing values, goals, or nonnegotiables without consultation?

Are you overly involved across every department?

Do team members suppress surprise when you join their meetings?

Do you insist on being involved in every detail of a project, even if you're not even close to the weeds, let alone in them, with every department?

Are you second-guessing everything your teams bring you?

Do your employees bring you increasingly minor fixes and decisions for your approval?

Then you might be a micromanager...

Are you using technology or apps that track employee productivity and attention, even if they're working from home?

Do you require frequent check-ins throughout the day?

Do you ask for status updates before the previous status update?

Are you asking for reviews that disrupt workflow?

Have you stopped receiving outcomes and are negotiating over minutiae?

Are you only sweating small stuff?

Then you might be a micromanager…

Have you stopped delegating?

Are you holding more information than you can keep straight?

Are you assigning more blame than tasks?

Are your team members being forced to help one another, delaying important tasks?

Are you staying later and later every day?

Do you have team members working weekends?

Have you stopped trusting your team members?

Then you might be a micromanager…

Are you noticing that team members are taking sick days?

Is there a lack of confidence amongst your team?

Are you struggling to find motivational tactics?

Did the pizza party seem glum and forced?

Are you redoing work or giving extensive notes on already completed tasks?

Are you starting to feel burned out?

Then you might be a micromanager….

Have you begun seeing fewer mistakes of innovation and more mistakes of inattention?

Is your team's work starting to look the same?

Do you feel less creative?

Does the work you're creating feel less exciting and energizing?

Have you felt your mind wandering during meetings?

Then you might be a micromanager…

Are you talking more in meetings?

Has your team stopped speaking out during meetings?

Is your team always agreeing in a perfunctory way?

Are you losing talented team members to other companies, for the same or less money?

Has your team stopped taking ownership and pride in their work?

Does every project feel like a Frankenstein? Stitched together rather than holistic?

Is work coming back incomplete or without attention?

Are your teams asking you more questions at every stage?

Have your teams stopped collaborating?

Then you might be a micromanager…

***

Now we know that micromanagement in your workplace will manifest in myriad ways, leading to a violation of our Work Well Together ethos. They'll be overworked, unable to work well, and, well, they won't be together very long, because attrition will grow exponentially.

But what does this look like? What if we created a case study in micromanagement? That might help us examine the roots and causes and offer some solutions if you, or someone on your team, is a micromanager.

Imagine…

A mid-sized start-up, buzzing with potential and a ready-made market, but at present, they're bogged down by inefficiencies and redundancies in leadership. There's a lack of clarity in roles and expectations, and so growth, for the moment, has plateaued.

A high-priced executive search company (more on them later) brings in a new team leader as a part of a mini-reorganization.

Enter Sonny, a team leader with a reputation for being "hands-on."

His last role was heading up an ambitious team of developers, designers, and product managers, building to a high-stakes app launch that hit the market to great fanfare.

Once the onboarding process is complete, everything seems to be going swimmingly. Sonny has an excellent track record, and his presence kicks everyone into gear almost immediately. Where things were blocked, now they're clear. Sonny's ruthlessly efficient with workflows and team tasks.

But then things take a turn…

Sonny insists on attending every team meeting, approving every decision, and even reviewing design tweaks. His justification? "I want to ensure quality."

But it goes even further…

Not only does Sonny rewrite code himself (not using the company standard), but he also dictates color schemes and questions why tasks weren't being done to his exacting specifications.

Team members are regularly brought up for minor offenses. Not only are they berated during the day, but they're also barraged with emails at all hours of the night.

One day, during a critical sprint planning meeting, Sonny interrupts to make a "small adjustment" to a developer's task list. This one small thing creates a ripple effect, causing the entire timeline to shift, making the deadlines impossible. When a product manager speaks up, suggesting they stick to the original plan, Sonny hand-waves this concern, saying, "Trust me, I've been doing this for years."

Before long, the team is deflated and defeated. Developers stop sharing innovative ideas that will make the product stand out even more, knowing they'll be overruled by Sonny, who's mistrustful of any idea that doesn't originate between his ears.

The designers start end-running Sonny, funneling everything through the product manager, taking them to the brink of exhaustion and burnout. At last, the product manager is forced to take medical leave. Sonny takes over their position as well. You, the CEO, know nothing of this, as Sonny's begun to cover his tracks and falsify results. Complaints die at his door.

Productivity tanks, and morale hits an all-time low.

Things come to a head when the product launch is delayed due to confusion over some last-minute changes Sonny introduced. You intervene and hold a team-wide feedback session. When asked what could improve the workflow, one developer bravely states, "We need space to work without constant changes and second-guessing." The room goes silent, but their eyes blaze with agreement.

You meet with Sonny in your office. You give him time to vent. And he does, blaming everyone and everything for his missteps. But you know better.

You realize that Sonny's micromanagement isn't about ensuring quality—it stems from a fear of failure and lack of trust in his team. He's never led a team of strangers before. On his last launch, he was a part of a team but not the leader.

You choose to keep Sonny, knowing that he has the potential to be a good leader.

Your first order of business is to gather the team together again so that Sonny can own his failures in public. The team, impressed by his vulnerability, decides to continue on.

You work with Sonny to help him delegate effectively and focus on strategic oversight rather than daily minutiae.

With Sonny stepping back, the team thrives. They deliver a polished product on the revised timeline, earning rave reviews. More importantly, the workplace culture began to heal, proving that letting go can be more powerful than holding on.

THE RE-CULTURE CURIOSITY QUESTIONS

1. How might you reframe your fear of failure into a catalyst for empowering teams? What practices could help you relinquish control? How can you foster accountability and innovation while ensuring that "quality" emerges from deep trust?

2. What organizational structures can you implement that create autonomy and prevent micromanagement from becoming culturally "contagious"? How can your teams sustain momentum without top-down intervention?

3. When you publicly own your micromanagement mistakes, how does this act of vulnerability reshape your team's psychology? What rituals or processes can turn such moments into lasting cultural repair rather than temporary fixes?

HOW TO ADDRESS MICROMANAGEMENT (AND NOT HAVE TO FIRE ANYONE)

WORK

If you took high school English in the United States sometime in the twentieth century, then you likely studied Robert Frost's "Mending Wall," specifically the prophetic phrase, "Good fences make good neighbors."

Our teacher always asked us: Was Frost being sincere? Do good, clean, well-maintained boundaries keep our society civil? Or was he being ironic? Do fences only serve to divide us from one another, so that the only time we see each other is when we mend our fences?

That's a topic for a different book, but I do believe that healthy boundaries in the workplace are a sign, symptom, and solution for culture. Good fences may make good neighbors, but good boundaries make for healthy organizations. You've got clear lines between managers and team members. Responsibilities are clearly defined so that decisions are framed correctly, and team members can make changes independently without approval. Throw away the tracking apps that only serve to make your culture feel Orwellian.

Instead, be a WORKWELLian.

WELL

Instead of daily check-ins, make them weekly. Free up time for work and take less time for meetings. Use your tools to measure outputs and products rather than your team members' processes. If the outcomes are good, then you can leave people alone. If they aren't, then you've got to intervene. But let solutions come from below. Don't dictate.

Reframe your mindset with open-ended questions. So instead of asking, "Is the project on schedule?" ask, "What progress have you made on the project so far, and what challenges are you facing?" This gets people talking. It expresses your curiosity and keeps your team member encouraged and engaged. Then you can see where they need support and then target that area.

When there are successes, micromanagers tend to let the opportunity go by. Instead of recognizing good work, the good work becomes just another day, and motivation plateaus. Bill Belichick can get away with "Do your job," but you can't. Why not? Because he's probably the best and most successful coach in the history of the NFL. Due respect, you're not Bill Belichick.

And that's okay. You don't have to be. Don't copy the greatest; it'll only make you feel more insecure about yourself.

There's a great leader inside each of us. If I didn't believe that, I wouldn't be in this business. But your great leadership is specific to you and only you. Once you get right with your authentic leadership style, then you'll be more confident, and that confidence will spread, like good news, and all of a sudden, you'll have creative, constructive feedback to give.

You'll feel better, and you'll be more productive. And so will your teams. If you create actionable steps at each stage of the process, people will blossom. In truth, it'll make you feel like you're not doing anything. That's where things get fun.

TOGETHER

Togetherness results in psychological safety, where feedback is open but still challenging and competitive. Maybe you've created a "no-blame culture" where mistakes can be shared without the anxiety of recrimination. It'll seem like it'll take more time than you have, and it might—at first. Over time, however, it'll save you time and maximize results.

You'll start to create innovation challenges where team members can propose and test ideas without fear of failure. In Re-Culture, a good idea can come from anywhere.

Or, if things go well, you'll be able to provide time within the working week for team members to explore creative projects outside their regular tasks. Let's call it "business Montessori." And it might seem ridiculous. Who knows? Maybe it is. Whatever fosters a culture where failure isn't the enemy but a friend will lead you to Re-Culture.

But you've got to get there together. That's where the magic is.

If you promote open dialogue between teams and are transparent with who you are, then you open up all sorts of avenues for team members to contribute. You're no longer subtracting, you're multiplying. You're doing it together rather than hierarchically and siloed. Re-Culture is about creating a coherent structure where everyone is speaking the same language. Now, you're not dominating meetings, but you're listening actively.

MICRO-MENTORING: BORDER COLLIES

There's a dog breed out there, beautiful dogs, that come mostly from the British Isles called border collies. They're sheep-herding dogs made famous in the stories of James Herriot, the vet-turned-author.

Border collies are working dogs. They want to herd sheep. It's in their genetic code. If they can't herd a sheep, they'll herd most anything. Starting with you.

Now, a dog like that, if you take it into an environment with zero work and maximum boredom, that dog will go insane, literally, from inactivity.

I think of micromanagers the same way. They desperately want to do the best work possible. They are perfectionists. But they're letting the perfect be the enemy of the good.

They're sitting on a welter of insecurity and ego. That's normal. I get a big kick out of it when they finally realize what they've been doing.

So, when I'm working with micromanagers (the ones willing to own it), a common reframe I like to make with them is to see themselves as "micro-mentors" instead. That does two things: It changes a pejorative into a positive. And it gives them something to do. It gets them curious about their teams and their members, and less on tasks and outcomes. Focusing only on tasks and outcomes will kill resilience in your culture. We get them curious about the people. Once they do that, outcomes follow. Once they begin the effort of getting to learn more about their people and how they need to be supported, the team feels that. They come alive. They've established trust, and they can feel that their leaders see them.

In the Re-Culture way of micro-mentoring, we're about providing guidance and support and allowing for freedom and surprise. Add those together, and you get growth and abundance.

Micromanagement is a symptom of deep cultural issues—inside the organization and the person—of a lack of trust, fear of failure, and the absence of management development. If you put people in important positions before they're seasoned, then the dish, I promise you, will come out tasting foul.

Once you empower your people with clarity and purpose, you'll begin to see a healthier, more collaborative, and resilient culture.

And you won't have to fire anyone. Starting with you.

THE RE-CULTURE CURIOSITY QUESTIONS

1. How would you design boundaries that empower your team to turn fences into frameworks for ownership rather than control?
2. What rituals or tools could you create that would replace micromanagement with trust? Can you measure outcomes instead of

hours? Can weekly check-ins be focused on progress rather than compliance?

3. How could you redirect your perfectionist energy from overseeing tasks to mentoring growth? Do you have it within you to ask, "What support do you need?" instead of "Why isn't this done?" to unlock unexpected potential in your team?

4. Where might your "border collie" instinct to "herd" become curiosity about your team's unique strengths, creating space for them to surprise you?

5. What practices could you adopt to create psychological safety for your team to experiment and innovate without fearing your reaction?

6. How might you publicly celebrate how a mistake was made (e.g., bold thinking, collaboration) to signal that learning trumps blame?

7. Where's the place between your "perfect" and the organization's "possible"?

LEARN TO GROW BETTER TEAMS

"If learning was something you understand one time, and you don't need to go back, maybe the role of the coach is not important. The coach, my job, is to make sure the players do it, not just to understand it. To make sure the players do what is needed for the team. Always. Always that."

—Pep Guardiola

When I have folks on my podcast, after I've given an introduction of the basics of their bio, I like to ask, "What's something that's not in your bio that you would love for people to know about you?" That question always fast-forwards the interview past all the small talk and chitchat. It drops us right into a real place where my guests are a little outside their comfort zone right off the bat. It gets us breathing together in a really fun way.

Not long ago, I had a guest on named Andy Clement, an executive with Kimberly-Clark, a multinational corporation that creates and distributes paper-based products. I went through the usual spiel that I get from publicists and asked my usual back-footed question, and Andy said, "My daughter was diagnosed with diabetes on her first birthday. If you want to talk about resilience, then it's what I've witnessed her go through over the past years and being with her [through that process]."

Wow, talk about getting real right from the jump.

Watching our children go through medical challenges and setbacks is one of the worst things a parent can experience. We'd gladly, in a heartbeat, trade places with them. But that's not how it works, does it?

I was floored by his honesty and the family resilience he was modeling to me. Andy and his family had to hang together through a lot of ups and downs, but they kept growing outward, participating in charity work and bringing attention to juvenile diabetes. Spiritually, they drew strength from their church and rebuilt themselves every Sunday.

I asked Andy to give me his version of resilience. Again, with simple, honest directness, he answered, "It's quite simply the ability to recover quickly from challenges, day in and day out. They happen at work and at home. In simplistic terms, that's how I think about it."

For Andy, at Kimberly-Clark, growth is the way they learn resilience, which is a lovely little inversion of the way we usually think about how resilience needs to come first. But Andy describes their growth mindset a little differently: "We've been promoting that a lot in Kimberly-Clark, which is accepting challenges, not running away from them, learning from them, and being okay with failure. As I think about the history of Kimberly-Clark and myself, that growth mindset has helped us be around for a while and does tie to our culture."

For them, if they're operating from a growth mindset, resilience follows naturally. And I think they're right. The mistake film producers most often make says legendary filmmaker Jean Renoir is simple, "They struggle for perfection instead of personality. They hire a dozen writers and director thinking the result will be more perfect. They're right. It will be more perfect. But it will be less interesting." Film producers are the leaders and managers of show business so our organizations can take a lesson from them. When we seek this e mythical, airless kind of perfection, it chokes us off from the oxygen of innovation.

In a growth mindset, we're learning, not perfecting. Andy told me, "If you're going to have challenges, it's how you act when you get them. You view them as opportunities for business improvement or self-improvement, versus shutting down and saying, 'I've been successful. We're just going to do it my way.'"

Whereas, in an extraction mindset, we're focused purely on short-term, marginal gains over long-term resilience. This is the number one affliction of every unhealthy culture. Produce more, produce faster, and push all margins are the rallying cries. No one talks about how that more has to come from less. No wonder we're burned out.

Many of our organizations are training and extraction cultures. We're going to train you for this one specific job, and we're going to squeeze as much out of you as we can until you likely leave for another job, and then we'll do it again with a new hire. Churning through the same cycle—train, extract, train extract. Meanwhile, as we've seen, each new hire has to be trained, and that costs money.

At Kimberly-Clark, they practice growth feedback with their sales-people, who face more rejection than all the other professions put together. Rather than punishing their sales team for the loss of business, they use these moments as learning opportunities. "These types of losses or problems can be gold if they're not ignored. It also means, 'You missed your quota. You didn't get these four or five sales that we expected you to. That's okay, but how do we make sure that we make you better in the future?' That's a growth mindset from a sales manager's perspective versus, 'I'm going to have to put you in a plan.'"

There's nothing worse in sales than to be told we're going to be put on a plan. Because what's next is usually the exit.

Instead, K-C applies the three questions for learning organizations:

1—"What's working for me? What worked in this situation?"
Is followed by the question,
2—"What didn't work in this situation that we're talking about?"
Finally—
3—"What could be done differently?"

These three questions correspond with Work, Well, and Together because they start positively. It's been said a million times, but starting feedback on a positive note tells our people that we're not just looking for the negative. That's often the default. Growth is impossible if we sit in the negativity of failure.

Then we're ready for getting well with some honesty statements like, "How can we make sure this never happens again?"

We finish off together with the collaborative opportunity to imagine and decide what the growth opportunities are.

Kimberly-Clark has made this kind of feedback pervasive throughout every level of the organization. "That happens at a senior level and a junior level. When you get into that routine of doing it, you begin to build your growth mindset."

Extraction organizations ask three versions of "Who's to blame?" They attack and replace. That creates a culture of fear, risk-avoidance, and zero-sum competition. It's this kind of transactional, bottom-line thinking that corrupts the source code of culture. It doesn't matter what code you write on top if the underlying code is toxic.

Andy's seen firsthand how an organization like Kimberly-Clark has survived for over 150 years and has survived the business and organizational changes since 2020:

> I've been amazed at how certain people in our organization have been able to pivot and be successful with it. Quite frankly, there are certain people that I would not have thought of initially, then other people that were outstanding sellers that our previous model had taken more time to get there. They weren't as change-proof. They thought that they would all go back to the way it was. As you said, it's not going back to the way it is. It's hard to predict necessarily how people are going to react to that and whether they've got that growth mindset or not.

Not only does Andy get my previous two book titles in that quote, but he's also given us a simply powerful lesson in the kind of growth and resilience that he learned from his daughter:

Accept the challenges, learn from them, and grow together.

THE RE-CULTURE CURIOSITY QUESTIONS

1. How can we turn this challenge into a shared opportunity to innovate and strengthen our team's resilience?
2. What unique strengths or perspectives can each of us contribute to bridge gaps and elevate our outcomes?
3. How can we build psychological safety so that risks and "messy" ideas are welcomed as part of our growth process?

CONFIRMATION BIAS

"People believe what they want to believe and then look
for reasons to reinforce their beliefs."

—Abhaidev, *The Meaninglessness of Meaning*

Let's do an exercise. Get out a pen and paper, and without thinking, write down what your strengths are—the things you believe you're good at and the things you think the ones who know you best would say you're good at. Set a timer for two minutes and don't stop writing until you hear the alarm.

Nice work.

Look at your list. Chances are pretty good that you came up with a healthy list. Of course you did. You should be proud of it.

Now. Let's put the shoe on the other foot. Take a new piece of paper and a fresh THREE minutes to write down your weaknesses, your blind spots, and the areas that need improvement. Be specific and ruthless with yourself. Three minutes. Go.

Welcome back.

Now put your two lists side by side and compare. I'll bet all the money in my pocket against all the money in yours that your first list is not only longer by a little but by a lot.

That's because, as leaders, our default setting for self-awareness is low. How low? Try 15 percent. A basic restaurant tip is all that covers the leaders who measure up as truly self-aware. That means nearly all of you reading this sentence are thinking that you're not in the 85 percent.

We want to be self-aware so badly that we have convinced ourselves that we are. We confirm our own bias.

Let me give you an example of what I mean:

Often, I'm invited to develop and train with an organization at something called an "offsite," which is a way to release their teams from the pressure and familiarity of the workspace. It's great because in this new environment, with a new voice (mine), they can begin the process of stepping back and seeing their business from above the proverbial forest.

One such occasion, we were at a really lovely spot with a whole bunch of activities and entertainment, including a mentalist. He was a pretty famous guy from across the pond, with some television specials, and it was such a treat. But the part I found fascinating was that at each stage of his set, he told exactly what kinds of tricks and mental games he was going to do and how he was going to do them. Each illusion, each mental trick was remarkable because even though we knew what was coming, we still couldn't figure out how he did it. He had the skill and confidence to let us into his secret world, and yet we were all fooled. We were fooled because we wanted to be.

It dawned on me that part of why that works is the fact that this mentalist was banking on our lack of awareness. If we had greater awareness, perception, and insight, maybe we would not be fooled at all. This is magic, after all, not the miracle of turning water into wine.

In our lives and in our businesses, what we're seeing or what we think we're seeing is not actually what we're seeing. That's the whole point of it. Our lack of awareness is part and parcel of and crucial to the success of his craft of magic.

This off-site mentalist showed me that in our organizations, self-awareness is one of the most powerful forces, and, if harnessed correctly, it can pay lasting dividends.

However, we can't forget that our strengths are yin to our weaknesses' yang. We have to work on the things we do well because that's what makes us who we are, and it's the foundation of our organizational culture.

But in the Re-Culture renewal that we're seeking, to have profitable organizations that last, it's vital to become more aware of areas where we are weak and where we have blind spots. That's where we grow.

True self-awareness comes from an honest accounting of our weaknesses.

THE RE-CULTURE CURIOSITY QUESTIONS

1. How might you intentionally seek out feedback that disrupts your self-perceived strengths?
2. How might you confront your leadership narrative with the reality of how your employees experience it?
3. What processes could you create to actively disprove your black-box decision-making?
4. When you confront uncomfortable truths in yourself, how do you experience them in your body?
5. How could you turn your weaknesses into strengths?

How We Get from Work Well to Work Well Together: The Code of Culture

WHAT IS THE CODE OF CULTURE?

"Talk is cheap. Show me the code."

—Linus Torvalds

From *Pivot* to *Change Proof* to *Re-Culture*, the golden thread that ties all three books together is something I call the Code of Conduct, and it's been a part of my daily ritual for nearly my entire life. I've performed this ritual more times than I've done anything else.

I adapted my Code of Conduct from Ben Franklin's list of thirteen virtues that he used to keep himself calm and resilient during a time of epochal change in world history.

They're as relevant today as they were more than two hundred years ago when he wrote *The Autobiography of Benjamin Franklin*:

TEMPERANCE. Eat not to dullness; drink not to elevation.

SILENCE. Speak not but what may benefit others or your-self; avoid trifling conversation.

ORDER. Let all your things have their places; let each part of your business have its time.

RESOLUTION. Resolve to perform what you ought; per-form without fail what you resolve.

FRUGALITY. Make no expense but to do good to others or yourself; i.e., waste nothing.

INDUSTRY. Lose no time; be always employ'd in something useful; cut off all unnecessary actions.

SINCERITY. Use no hurtful deceit; think innocently and justly, and, if you speak, speak accordingly.

JUSTICE. Wrong none by doing injuries or omitting the benefits that are your duty.

MODERATION. Avoid extremes; forbear resenting injuries so much as you think they deserve.

CLEANLINESS. Tolerate no uncleanliness in body, cloaths, or habitation.

TRANQUILLITY. Be not disturbed at trifles, or at accidents common or unavoidable.

CHASTITY. Rarely use venery but for health or offspring, never to dulness, weakness, or the injury of your own or another's peace or reputation.

HUMILITY. Imitate Jesus and Socrates.

Even though it's a little archaic, it's a really good list of virtues, many of which we've forgotten about in our modern, irony-poisoned culture.

In creating my Code of Conduct, I created a list of experiences that I desire for myself every single day, a way to both pose and answer the question: how do I want to experience myself being today? For me, they're not virtues so much as they are me casting my lure into the stream of the day to catch the states that will make me the best "Adam Markel" that I can be. It's a list of my priorities, with the knowledge that though perfection is a goal, it's not a reality. It's the striving that makes this code work because it's about setting the intention and then being open to receiving whatever the world throws at me. It calibrates my nervous system, my emotions, and my thoughts in a way that allows me to convey these experiences to the people in my life. Taking the architect's strategem, my code becomes a blueprint for what I wish to build each day.

I experience gratitude today.

I experience a positive and harmonious attitude today.

I experience myself adding value to other people's lives today.

I experience creating from relaxed focus today.

I experience myself living by a higher standard today.

I experience living in absolute integrity and kindness today.

I experience harmony in everyone and everything today.

I experience creating empowering solutions today.

I experience living with a fearless heart today.

I experience myself feeling the presence of unconditional love today.

I experience myself being healthy, wealthy, and wise today.

I experience, receive, and manifest miracles today.

I experience forgiveness today.

Then, before I close my eyes for sleep, I go over the Code of Conduct one more time and ask myself, as honestly as I'm able, "Did I experience these thirteen states today?" I've done this ritual so many times now that it's a habit and a part of who I am.

Even now, when I read this list of states that I want to experience, the feeling I get is something akin to feeding a punch card into the computer of my whole self. The Code of Conduct is a program that governs every system of my body, my mind, my heart, and my spirit. It's not random but designed—just like a genetic, computer, or legal code.

For me, the Code of Conduct sets the program for how I'd like to experience my day. It's a simple but essential process to reverse-engineer my attitude so that no matter what the world throws up in front of me, I'm already prepared to experience in a way that's intentional, proactive, and resilient. Starting the day with a comprehensive set of intentions keeps me accountable to no one but myself. Sometimes I read them in stillness, but more often I declare them softly aloud, and am reminded of these words too:

> *So shall my word be that goeth forth out of my mouth; it shall not return unto me void, but it shall accomplish that which I please, and it shall prosper in the thing whereto I sent it (Isaiah 55:11 Holman Christian Standard Bible).*

Since *Change Proof* came out, I've heard many reports from folks who've adopted the Code of Conduct, and they say that it feels strange at first, but the more they practice it, the Code becomes an indispensable guide for how they conduct themselves in every moment of their day.

Nowadays, everything in our lives is measured on computers. Maybe you're reading this book on a Kindle with a million times more power than the room-sized computer terminals of my early youth. They made us all feel like we were about to enter a future beyond the science-fiction fantasies promised at the 1964 World's Fair. We thought the year 2000 would look much like *The Jetsons*, with robots and computers doing all the mundane tasks, freeing us humans to be more self-actualized and evolved than our forebears.

Back then, the computer programmer would write the code on coding sheets, then, on the computer card ("Do not fold, spindle or mutilate"), they'd punch holes out of it by hand, feed it into a computer, which would then read the holes through light, converting the light into visual data.

However, those early computers had more in common with sewing looms than with the devices we carry around in our pockets in 2025—all connected to the cloud, and containing data points more infinite than the stars in the sky.

In a few hundred years, rudimentary analytical machines have given way to FORTRAN, which gave us C++ and Python, and now we've climbed to the foothills of tangible artificial intelligence, where we design code for computers to write code for themselves.

And yet.

For all their processing power, even Jensen Huang and NVIDIA's most supercharged supercomputer still pales in comparison to a single human brain—even a brain like mine, that sometimes needs a cup of coffee in the morning to get going.

The human brain's built-in coding system is a miracle of design. If we compare every moment our brains experience to a computer, the overall sensory input would be roughly equivalent to 11,200,000 bytes per second.

Then, if we further break that number down, our eyes take in the vast majority at 10,000,000, our skin 1,000,000, our ears and nose 100,000, and our tongue takes in the least at 1,000 bytes per second.

Does anyone want to hazard a guess at how many bytes per second we're consciously aware of?

Fewer than fifty bytes per second. That tiny fraction is all we can perceive at any given moment. The rest is filtered through our brain's amazing, efficient compression code so that we don't fall to pieces from experiencing too much of the world all at once.

Some believe that taking psychedelics or having near-death experiences, when our brains are flooded with neurochemicals, is when the brain stops compressing and we fully experience the totality of everything our reality has to offer.

Maybe that's what heaven looks like.

But here on earth, as we walk through our daily lives, the programming of our brains is constantly filtering and dumping vast amounts of information we may never be aware of. It's a masterpiece of code.

It's no wonder then that our species evolved to create computers.

But codes weren't invented with modern-day computers. We've had codes almost from the beginning of human intelligence—the Code of Hammurabi, the Ten Commandments, the Golden Rule, the Tang Code, the Five Pillars of Islam, and the Bushido Code, just to name a few.

They're legal codes, systems that govern our behavior, define how a society should be governed, and how we should work together.

The oldest surviving code we have is the Code of Ur-Nammu, an ancient Mesopotamian legal text that follows the "if/then" formula. For instance, "If a man commits a robbery, then he will be killed." Okay. Stick with me, because all this history will be really interesting in a moment.

Fast-forward to today, where we have vast human resources departments that lay out codes of conduct that define the ethical and behavioral expectations the organization sets for its employees, leaders, and stakeholders. But it's not just a list of rules. It's a reflection of an organization's culture, values, and commitment to a common sense of purpose. It's the DNA of an organization's identity that offers protection, empowerment, and trust, and creates a workplace culture where people want to thrive.

These codes <u>are</u> culture.

"When you are finished changing, you're finished."

—Benjamin Franklin

FROM CODE OF CONDUCT TO CODE OF CULTURE

The thirteen states or experiences of the Code of Conduct are how I build the algorithm of my day at the individual level. It's the programming that changes my software in ways that are specific to me and my experience. But, given the state of the world, we have to move from the inner world to change the outer world.

To paraphrase a James Bond title, "The Inner World Is Not Enough."

With the foundation of Work Well Labs and our mission of spreading organizational resilience and culture, I began to wonder if it was possible to transmute the singular properties of the Code of Conduct into a collective culture: Could the Code of Conduct re-code an organization?

Maybe it's as Paulo Coelho writes in *The Alchemist*, "When we strive to become better than we are, everything around us becomes better, too." He's talking about something called "transmutation," which is the transformation of one solid form into another. It's not like how water transforms from solid to liquid to gas. What we're talking about is alchemy, when a solid like lead or metal turns into gold. If transmutation is an inner process to an outer one, then would it be possible to change the inner core of a team or an organization?

I asked myself, "Can the Code of Conduct spread from an individual and transmute that change into a collaborative, resilient, got-your-back culture?"

What if there were a code of virtues that could be fed into an organization's workplace to produce a renewed and regenerated culture?

Culture, I thought, needed a code.

There it was: An easy swap of "conduct" for "culture" and I had a name. *The Code of Culture.*

But every code is more than just the name. At a fundamental level, the Code of Culture is a shift from rules and rituals designed to guide personal growth to a set of collective principles that shape how we, as a team or organization, thrive together and build a culture that helps us work well together.

Just as the Code of Conduct serves as an individual algorithm for navigating each day with intention, the Code of Culture goes further, amplifying our practice by taking the same core ideas and expanding them into a collaborative framework that guides teams as we interact, lead, and build together.

The Code of Culture is about groups that Work Well Together.

That's the equation.

When we strive to work well together, we transform personal resilience into organizational resilience. And an organization that's resilient is one that has a healthy, thriving culture. We can't have one without the other.

So, what is the Code of Culture?

I fed the thirteen experiences of the Code of Conduct through the pivotal mechanism of Work Well Together, and out came the ten non-negotiable attributes that every great culture possesses. These are the ten bricks every organization must have to build its cultural foundation.

My ten cultural virtues are as follows.

Trust
Values
Coherence
Well-Being
Accountability
Play
Growth
Failure
Gratitude
Optimism

Now, I know that there are those out there who might be screaming, "What about X?" or "You've forgotten Y!" And that's fine. No program is perfectly comprehensive. Like it or lump it, these are my ten virtues that, if we harvest and husband them, will help us create a real and lasting culture for our organizations.

But ten cultural virtues aren't yet a code because a code is a set of instructions that are fed into a computer to ask it to perform a given task. We need something more…instructive.

We're back to the Code of Ur-Nammu and its "if/then" way of describing its laws. Our very early attempts at governing ourselves used the same formulation that programmers use when creating the source code for the computers on which we are all so dependent.

An "if, then" instruction (commonly called an "if statement") is a fundamental programming construct that allows a program to make decisions by executing specific code only when a condition is met. When the "if statement" is true, then the program executes a specific task. We can see this in how pilots fly a plane: If the altitude is at such and such a level, then the pilot executes a task based on that altitude.

The way to think about the instructions of the Code of Culture is to say, "If I'm doing the FIRST PART, then culture will follow."

The Ten Instructions for the Code of Culture are these:

Trust—

If we prioritize integrity and nurture open communication in every interaction, then trust deepens, and collective purpose flourishes in the culture we build together.

Values—

If we anchor our choices in purpose rather than cheap convenience, then our decisions will be clear, and our culture will have lasting value.

Coherence—

If we replace rigid barriers with strong boundaries that honor both autonomy and interdependence, then collaboration becomes a dance of trust, where collective culture thrives without sacrificing the individual.

Well-Being—

If we treat the mental, physical, and emotional health of our people as the sacred fuel of our organization's engine, then our culture becomes renewable, our resilience contagious, and our shared potential unstoppable.

Accountability—

If we hold ourselves accountable for the ripples our actions create in the lives of others and the integrity of our mission, then trust becomes a shared currency, a culture that evolves, not as a fragile ideal, but as a living, breathing force.

Play—

If we make space for delight as our co-pilot and curiosity as our compass, then culture transforms into a playground, where friction fuels creativity, and failure becomes fertilizer for growth.

Growth—

If we chase progress with open minds, letting go of perfection, then we cultivate an ecosystem of resilience, where experimentation thrives and even stumbling becomes the soil of our culture.

Failure—

If we build missteps into our culture, treating them with reflection, not regret, then failure becomes the foundation for growth, wisdom, and resilience.

Gratitude—

If we let gratitude magnify every collaboration, no matter how trivial or small, then our organization transforms from ordinary work into a culture of belonging.

Optimism—

If we code with an eye for the future, with one eye on today and one on tomorrow, then our culture becomes agile, where every constraint is an invitation for reinvention.

The Code of Culture contains everything we need to renew our organizations and make our leadership worth following. It's what happens between us any time two or more people are gathered to work together.

This is the code to get you there.

"You may be able to 'buy' a person's back with a pay-check, position, power, or fear, but a human being's genius, passion, loyalty, and tenacious creativity are volunteered only."

—L. David Marquet

THE RE-CULTURE CURIOSITY QUESTIONS

1. How can we transform silence or assumptions into conversations that deepen trust?
2. Where have we traded long-term cultural value for short-term gain? Can we course-correct?
3. What outdated rules can we reimagine as flexible guardrails to empower collaboration without chaos?
4. How can we redesign workflows to prioritize renewal, not just relentless output?
5. What rituals can we create to regularly ask, "How did our decisions impact others this week?
6. What "serious" problem could we approach with playful experimentation instead of a rigid strategy?
7. What imperfect experiment are we avoiding out of fear, and how might it catalyze growth?
8. How can we celebrate "intelligent failures" as milestones, not mistakes?
9. What small act of appreciation could we institutionalize to make belonging tangible?
10. What constraint feels like a dead end, and how might it become a launchpad for reinvention?
11. How will we, as a team, commit to one virtue this quarter to rewrite our cultural code? And what will we stop tolerating to make it real?

How to Work Well Together

"Coming together is a beginning, staying together is progress, and working together is a success."

—Henry Ford

PLAYTIME

"The truth is that play seems to be one of the most advanced methods nature has invented to allow a complex brain to create itself."

—Stuart Brown

At its core, play isn't just about having fun; it's creative learning.

I'm blessed to be a grandfather of three beautiful, perfect children, so I'm in a very play-filled time in my life. Some days, it's all play from waking up to bedtime. Like it's a job they don't want to leave. That's the great thing about kids: Everything to them is an opportunity to create and dance with the universe without any of the self-consciousness we acquire as we age.

It's natural, then, that these three play machines living with pure, fearless hearts got me thinking about culture. To learn about how play impacts organizations, I went to one of our WORKWELLians, Elaine Chung, to see how exactly we can use play to renew and regenerate our culture.

Elaine is a play expert, corporate consultant, and the founder of My Play Type, a company dedicated to reviving workplace culture by integrating it with organizational dynamics. And it's not just all for giggles. She believes that work that combines play increases productivity too. Her clients not only include the PTA but also Fortune 500 companies.

Elaine's work begins with the premise that "when kids are little, and they have all the parents and grandparents around, we create a very nurturing environment to invite low-risk-taking exploration together. As we get to be adults and get into the work environment, societal norms start shaping how we react. I've seen firsthand how it closes down." Play is work for kids—the same way herding sheep is for some dog breeds. They're doing what they would naturally do if no one were around to tell them what to do and how to be. Work is fun.

However, an overwhelming number of the organizations I visit aren't having any fun. They're not playing. When I ask people if they'd like to enjoy their work more, they answer, "Change every aspect of my job and then maybe I'll enjoy it." That's a dangerous place for us to be. As we've noted already, a crash is coming for workplace culture if we don't act fast. Now, that might be a bit grim if we want to play, but Elaine says that play is serious business.

That's because play begins with leadership. We may think that play is something we do every so often when things get grim. Like a camp counselor, we have to try to entertain sullen campers on a rainy day. Sometimes we get a marker and a whiteboard and say, "Let's brainstorm together," but it's not enough, she says, if leaders don't create a safe space for teams to offer up out-of-the-blue ideas.

You can't "blue sky" if you don't clear the airspace of anti-idea guns ready to shoot innovation out of the sky.

Elaine agrees, "If we don't have a true connection, it won't feel safe. It won't feel safe to offer the idea. It won't feel safe to iterate on the idea. Therefore, you won't have deep collaboration and consistent collaboration."

Some of us might read the words "safe space" and roll our eyes. There's a lot of talk about safe spaces these days and how we're just coddling people who don't want to work. It isn't true that they don't, but if the words make our skin crawl, think about this: A study from Ragan Communications found that productivity went up 50 percent and team member engagement went up 75 percent when they felt psychologically safe in the space in which they work. Safe spaces, it seems, do work.

So, we can thumb our nose at a phrase, or we can create real wins for our organizations. It's not a binary choice: We can have culture and productivity—as long as they're in harmony with one another. They're never going to be balanced or equal. They're dynamically related. If they're not in harmony, communicating coherently, maybe we need to look inward.

If you can help your employees discover where they thrive, especially in the toughest times, you can create a strong bond with them that can get you through challenges with a tad more joy.

I don't want to do psychotherapy here (that's a whole other book), but part of our unwillingness to create these environments is related to our fear of standing out, getting it wrong, and being made fun of by our peers. Or maybe a hard-driving adult who wouldn't allow failure cloaked us in an anxiety we can't seem to shrug off, no matter how successful we become.

I remember the feeling I had in the third grade when I didn't have the right answer and was praying my little heart out that I wouldn't have to answer for it. There was no safety in that environment.

That's why we leaders have to lead with play, says Elaine. "The starting point is to start within. You, as a leader, are you at your best? Because that can set the tone of how you're leading the group, looking at your team, and understanding their play type at work. You can see that by asking, 'What do you get excited about?' when you're doing your one-on-one. Be genuinely curious about the work that they're doing and what they're achieving, and what they do and don't like. I've seen one-on-ones too many times, and it's just a checklist."

A key component of play is learning. If we really get to know our teams on a one-on-one basis and learn what makes their engines fire, then we can make sure that everyone's in a role where their engagement remains high. It's not always going to be in the black, but it doesn't have to be in the red either.

In Elaine's work on play, it's all about finding out where people thrive, where they can be at their best. That's why it's just as important for team members to communicate where they feel what Elaine calls the "flow state," which happens when we are working on something and time seems to fly by. Is this possible every day? Of course not.

We're looking for small moments of play, every day, but it's not just whimsy. This is really about a learning model that flows from curiosity and not being afraid of making mistakes.

Before you plan your next team event, read this next bit from Elaine and save yourself some of your budget: "You don't just create it once. You have to keep embedding that in daily practice. It's the same thing because an organization is made up of people, each person. It can't just be an annual event. What do your leaders do daily, every week, in each interaction they have with their employees? Does that link up with the type of culture that you want to build? If you don't have that, it won't happen."

We might be frustrated thinking that we've done something wrong, but we only need to look at how children process failure. When I watch my grandchildren who are learning to walk, they don't get emotional when they fall. As long as they're not hungry or tired, they don't let it ruin their day or anyone else's day. They simply try again. Try again. Fail better. The bravery to try, according to Elaine, removes the judgment.

We see it everywhere, across the board, with all the changes and uncertainties flying around like monkeys from Oz trying to keep us from building sustainable cultures. Belt tightening constricts everything and means we're driving our teams harder for less money and almost zero meaning. We can have money without meaning, but we won't have it for very long, because we'll burn through our teams faster than we can make new ones.

Elaine worked with a team that was going through something like this. And she had the teams break up into smaller units that would work together throughout the week and then report back to the larger team. This created trust and psychological safety where they could look at each other and say, "You've got my back." People get meaning from one another.

That's not a huge swing for the fences. It's something small that pays huge dividends down the road.

We don't have to win; we just have to be willing to play the game.

"Anybody with ability can play in the big leagues. But to be able to trick people year in and year out the way I did, I think that was a much greater feat."

—Bob Uecker

THE RE-CULTURE CURIOSITY QUESTIONS

1. What barriers exist in my team/organization that prevent people from sharing "messy" ideas or admitting mistakes? How can I dismantle these to foster a culture of experimentation?
2. As a leader, how can my daily actions reflect a commitment to play and psychological safety?
3. Where am I prioritizing efficiency over learning?
4. What small, repeatable practices could I introduce to infuse moments of play (e.g., brainstorming without judgment, celebrating "failures" as learning) into our daily workflows?

EVEN JEFF BEZOS SAYS INEFFICIENCY IS THE NEW EFFICIENCY

"His [Thomas Edison] method was inefficient in the extreme, for an immense ground had to be covered to get anything at all unless blind chance intervened and, at first, I was almost a sorry witness of his doings, knowing that just a little theory and calculation would have saved him 90 per cent of the labor. But he had a veritable contempt for book learning and mathematical knowledge, trusting himself entirely to his inventor's instinct and practical American sense. In view of this, the truly prodigious amount of his actual accomplishments is little short of a miracle."

—Nikola Tesla

Some of you might be familiar with the concept of "tithing," which is a Christian tradition of giving 10 percent of our income to the church. "Tithe" comes from the Hebrew word for tenth, and the tradition predates Mosaic law with the story of Cain and Abel, who each offered the fruits of their labor to a Creator with whom they had a direct, personal relationship. As early farming societies evolved, the landowner would mark out a tenth of their field for spiritual wanderers to harvest and use for themselves.

As the kids say these days, it's giving charity.

So, what does this have to do with workplace culture? Well, if we're instructed to play to keep our culture resilient, a little inefficiency can go a long way.

Since Michael Lewis's *Moneyball* landed in the culture, the tsunami of data analytics has washed over not only baseball but also almost every aspect of our lives. We're beset on all sides by the relentless press of efficiency experts trying to get every last bit of our productivity.

We're not working well because we've constructed an Orwellian system where any flare-up of inefficiency must be stamped out immediately, so we're maximizing shareholder value.

I don't know if you've heard of the panopticon before, but it's an invention by eighteenth-century philosopher Jeremy Bentham, who created a hypothetical prison in which a single guard could watch every prisoner. This was possible because the cells were arranged around a guard tower, and the prisoners would never know whether they were being watched.

Even then, the panopticon was seen as a kind of torture device, but now, with monolithic online retail services observing every second of their warehouses and their delivery drivers, organizations with keystroke spyware on home laptops, and workflow app monitoring, our workplace culture has made the old new again. It's efficient, yes, but it's neither ethical nor creative.

Speaking of monolithic online retail services.... Let's hear from Amazon's Jeff Bezos, who, contrary to the way his company is run, has some salient thoughts about inefficiency. But he calls it "wandering."

"Wandering is so important because wandering is a kind of humility," Jeff Bezos begins. "Wandering sounds so inefficient, but the only way to go straight to your destination is if you know where you're going."

Jeff continues:

> "Sometimes you know where you're going. But sometimes you don't. And wandering is the acknowledgement

that—in life, business, invention, and building a company—a lot of the time you can see the mountain top, but you can't see the trail. So you have to explore and wander. It may feel very inefficient. But it's actually very valuable."

Ultimately, Jeff explains, you need to balance execution and exploration:

"When you know where you're going, yes, you should be very efficient.… You just need to do both [exploration and determined execution]. And they actually do feed each other. It's the things that come out of the execution that give you new data and ideas about what the next steps should be in your exploration. The two things don't work against each other. They work together."

THE 10 PERCENT RULE

To take Jeff's words to heart, I've taken the concept of the tithe and created a way to generate a small dose of inefficiency by willfully giving away a tenth of our productivity each day.

The idea is to deliberately set aside a small percentage of time, resources, and energy that aren't focused on immediate productivity. It's not wasted time but an investment in experimentation. It could be anything. It doesn't even necessarily need to benefit the organization directly. Renewing culture is about pursuing and nurturing something greater.

Think about it this way: The workday is eight hours. That's 480 minutes total. Ten percent of that is only forty-eight minutes. That's less than ten minutes per hour that our team members can do work outside their daily deliverables. This does not include their lunch hour.

The next step, if we're able, is to set aside 10 percent of our annual budget to fund experimental projects, pilot programs, or R&D. It's not about immediate returns but finding innovative ways to explore new directions. Who knows what may result? The point is that by taking the pressure off, we give space for real creative thinking.

The 10 percent rule doesn't necessarily apply to time. We can borrow from our failure commandment and institute a 10 percent failure rate. If our teams aren't failing, then they're not trying. That doesn't mean that we flail about failing at will. But a designed and controlled amount of failure is good for everyone. Learning and growth require a certain amount of failure.

How about meetings? We all hate unstructured, inefficient meetings where managers are using the group to think out loud. The 10 percent rule says, Take ten minutes, no more or less, at the end of each meeting to creatively brainstorm and share ideas not on the agenda. This will break down silos and lead to insights out of the blue.

Or the 10 percent rule can apply to cross-pollination between departments, where team members get exposure to work and ideas that they wouldn't normally get in an efficient working system. Opening up to new ways of thinking can spark new ways of thinking.

We can always use a 10 percent rotation system where 10 percent of the working day, one day a month, is spent shadowing a member of another team in another corner of the organization. This allows the learning of new skills and engages curiosity in a real way.

Reserve 10 percent of annual time for employees to participate in workshops, courses, or creative sessions that aren't directly tied to their daily work. By investing in broad-based learning, we help spark innovation that can be applied back in their roles.

When planning projects, build in a 10 percent "time slush fund" for unforeseen ideas, iterations, or improvements. This not only reduces pressure, but it also provides time to assimilate discoveries made along the way.

Or we can establish a recognition system that celebrates teams or individuals who have taken creative risks. Not all risks will lead to wins. That's fine. But sharing "inefficiency wins" with the whole organization reinforces the idea that efficiency, even if those efforts don't lead to immediate wins. Publicly sharing stories about "productive inefficiency" reinforces the notion that not every effort needs to be hyper-efficient to be valuable to the whole team.

Just as the tithe once set aside a sacred fraction for nurturing the soul, so too does our 10 percent rule offer a deliberate pause to rekindle innovation, challenge the relentless drive for hyper-efficiency, and reclaim our collective curiosity.

When we purposefully surrender a tiny fraction of our time, resources, and even our occasional failures, we not only break the yoke of efficiency but also invite a renewed sense of purpose into our organizations.

Ten percent at a time.

THE RE-CULTURE CURIOSITY QUESTIONS

1. How might you intentionally "waste" 10 percent of your team's time on curiosity-driven projects? Where would you find that 10 percent?

2. How could you implement a "time slush fund" for shadowing colleagues, brainstorming wild ideas, or tinkering with "useless" prototypes to ignite the kind of play that inflames innovation?

3. How could you reframe failure as a "10 percent tithe" for learning?

4. What daily, weekly, monthly, quarterly, and yearly rituals could you create with your team that would signal that inefficiency isn't laziness, but the soil from which culture grows?

5. What guardrails could you dismantle to free your team to tithe their energy to experiments that feel inefficient but build resilience?

6. How might cross-departmental "inefficiency swaps" (e.g., engineers attending marketing creative sessions) foster collaboration and understanding?

HOW TO FAKE LIKE YOU CARE: ZEN AND THE ART OF CURIOSITY

"Curiosity is an everlasting flame that burns in everyone's mind. It makes me get out of bed in the morning and wonder what surprises life will throw at me that day. Curiosity is such a powerful force. Without it, we wouldn't be who we are today. Curiosity is the passion that drives us through our everyday lives. We have become explorers and scientists with our need to ask questions and to wonder."

—Clara Ma (the twelve-year-old who
named the Mars Rover called "Curiosity")

Curiosity is one of the most powerful tools we have—not just as individuals, but as leaders, teams, and organizations. It's the spark that ignites the blue paper of growth, innovation, and connection. When we harness the power of our curiosity, we step outside of ourselves, ask questions, explore the unknown, and challenge assumptions. Without curiosity, we stagnate. With it, we grow into something we never could have imagined. If empathy is the garden of our cultural values, then curiosity is the soil from which it grows.

> "We do not believe in ourselves until someone reveals that deep inside us something is valuable, worth listening to, worthy of our trust, sacred to our touch. Once we believe in ourselves we can risk curiosity, wonder, spontaneous delight or any experience that reveals the human spirit."
>
> —E. E. Cummings

Now, imagine you're alone on a distant planet, wandering from place to place, exploring the farthest reaches of a world that's never felt human feet upon soil where nothing grows. Maybe it did once, a million years ago. But now it's an arid desert full of rocks and canyons cut by the wind. Powered by the heat from decaying plutonium, your mission is just that: exploration. No goal. No outcome. No stock price. Just pure exploration to find out if the planet Mars was ever home to life and if it ever might be. That's the Mars Curiosity Rover, named and autographed by a sixth grader from Kansas, Clara Ma.

I love that name. It has the wonderful possibility of exploration.

In my work, I often talk about the importance of creating a culture of curiosity within organizations. This means fostering an environment where people feel safe to ask questions, experiment, and even fail. It's not about having all the answers—it's about being willing to explore the questions. Curiosity allows us to approach challenges with a beginner's mind, free from the constraints of "we've always done it this way." It's the antidote to complacency.

If anything, the years since 2020 have shown us that an old world is dying. The way we've always done it, the status quo, the guardrails are all gone. This is the time to get radical with our curiosity and leave no stone unturned in our exploration for new, better ways to create our cultures. That's the Code.

That's why what I find particularly fascinating is how curiosity connects to resilience. When we're curious, we're more adaptable. We see setbacks not as dead ends but as opportunities to learn and grow. Curiosity helps us lean into discomfort and uncertainty, which are often the breeding grounds for transformation. It's like water—it flows around obstacles, finds new paths, and nourishes everything it touches.

Curiosity is what keeps my life vibrant and meaningful. It's what drives me to seek out new experiences, to connect with others on a deeper level, and to continually evolve my own culture. There's no ceiling on our growth. That's why I believe that when we approach life with genuine curiosity, we not only expand our horizons but also inspire those around us to do the same.

> "The important thing is not to stop questioning. Curiosity has its own reason for existing."
>
> —Albert Einstein

My good friend and a part of our Work Well Labs is April Beyer, who is, to my mind, the expert on curiosity and how it can lead us to leadership literacy, which is another way of saying, "Read the room." A skill, according to April, that many leaders don't possess, so they're looking for the "curiosity hack" that will help them engage with their people.

"Oftentimes, when I'm coaching people, they'll say, 'Tell me what questions to ask.' I find that fascinating. Because I can give you the questions, but I'm essentially painting them on you in a robotic fashion. If you don't know why you're asking them, if you don't know the value in the ask, then I don't know what to tell you." There is no curiosity hack.

April believes it's difficult but not impossible to teach someone how to be curious. When she says it, you know that she knows, because she's a matchmaker with a relationship success rate (the couples she sets up who stay together) that would make Ted Williams as green as the Monster in Fenway's left field.

April told me, "So, how I can teach it is to give them the reason. We begin by asking, 'What are your core values, and how do you want to feel when you're leading? What would you like the result to be?'"

True to form, April has perfectly described that Work Well Together key we've been crafting for our culture.

1. What are your core values? That's the work.
2. What do you want to feel when you're leading? That's working well.
3. What would you like the result to be? That's togetherness.

But let's drill down into that second bit there. That's the part that fascinates me, because it's a genius way to get inside the person we want to be. It's almost as if we're having empathy for a leader that might not even exist yet. That leader is inside all of us. Of course, we may want to be curious, but that's not enough. We have to, in some way, at first, at least, pretend to be. It sounds silly to say, but fake it until you make it. You put yourself in the position of a leader whom you would follow. It's not out of a book. Not even this one.

We have to practice curiosity, even if it doesn't come naturally to us, according to April, because "I have to tell you, I'm gonna, I'm gonna say that 90 percent of the people I meet in my day-to-day life and my business life are lacking a higher level of curiosity."

If we want curiosity, we can go to an amazing text for leaders who want to get their ego out of the way and start getting curious. It's *Zen Mind, Beginner's Mind* by Shunryu Suzuki, and it's a classic Zen Buddhist text that profoundly but simply explores the principles of mindfulness, presence, and approaching life with a fresh, open perspective. And it doesn't use the word curiosity once.

Let's look at a few quotes from the book and see what they tell us about how you can practice curiosity.

> "In the beginner's mind, there are many possibilities; in the expert's mind, there are few."

One of the qualities of leadership we're most lacking is the idea of considering even more than a single possibility. We get locked into our preconceptions, judgments, and expertise. But if we're renewing our culture to bring it up to code, then it's about seeing our organizations with fresh eyes, the way an outsider would. Be our consultants. We'll save time, effort, and money doing an emotional audit of our organizations and our people. That's the strategic opportunity.

If we approach each day with fresh eyes, we're open to new possibilities. Now, that doesn't mean we go walking around looking at flowers and clouds and letting bliss clean our minds out. A truly curious mind is one that's quite rigorous. It's exhausting work constantly setting our egos aside. Most leaders can't or won't do that.

Stay open to learning. Don't act like the answers are ready-made. See people where they are.

> "When you do something, you should do it with your whole body and mind."

All leaders have pressure to produce outcomes. The bottom line looms over all. That's always been true. Curiosity isn't about forgoing all attachments and going to live in the hills somewhere. If we truly focus on process and engage with exploration in our work, new possibilities won't be hard to find. They'll be seeking us. The results are there; they're not going away. If we fixate on them at the expense of everything else, then we won't be seeing people; we'll only be looking at our reflection.

When I'm engaged with my whole self, no matter what I'm doing, for the first few days of the practice, I'm exhausted. This is where most of us quit. But when I keep at it, I find I have more energy than ever before.

> "In the beginner's mind, there is no thought, 'I have attained something.'"

Truly great leaders never arrive. Culture isn't cement. We don't set it and forget it. Culture, as we've seen, is the soil from which our organization grows. It needs tending. Because there is no end goal. No matter how much I think I know, I'm constantly surprised at what the world throws up in front of me. Kierkegaard writes, "Life must be lived forwards, but can only be understood backwards.

> "To study ourselves is to forget ourselves."

At an organizational level, this is about asking, "Why are we doing things this way?" We've all used the Five Whys technique to get deeper than our closely held assumptions.

Let's try to ask Five Whys to see why we should be asking why:

Why should we use curiosity to create a workplace culture?

Curiosity encourages teams to ask questions, seek knowledge, and explore new ideas.

Why is it important for employees to ask questions and seek knowledge?

Learning fosters growth, enabling us to develop collaborative solutions to challenges.

Why is growth critical in the workplace?

Growth allows us to adapt to change and uncertainty to foster resilience.

Why is adaptability crucial for an organization?

Without adaptability, we risk stagnation in fast-changing markets.

Why does curiosity specifically enhance adaptability?

Curious teams proactively identify trends, experiment with new approaches, and embrace change, building organizational resilience.

By the time we've reached the end, we've gone deeper than ourselves and to the root of the question. That's a place where we can work well together.

Thanks to April Beyer and a Japanese Zen Master, we've seen how a healthy curiosity doesn't kill cats; it builds and renews our culture. And like most things in this book, it costs us nothing but our egos, our assumptions, and our stagnant beliefs.

> "The strategic opportunity in leadership literacy that allows us to get our egos out of the way so that we can read our people."

THE RE-CULTURE CURIOSITY QUESTIONS

1. How might you approach every challenge with a "beginner's mind," setting aside your hard-won expertise to ask, "What if?" and unearth possibilities your team may have overlooked?
2. Could you pause before decisions to ask, "What does this look like to someone seeing it for the first time?" to help you spot assumptions that stifle curiosity?
3. What daily ritual could help you "forget yourself" long enough to truly study your team's unspoken needs, turning ego into fuel for questions, not answers?
4. How can you weaponize the Five Whys not just to solve problems, but to dismantle your leadership ego to reveal where your need for control smothers your team's curiosity?

LISTENING WITH INTENT

"When did I realize I was God? Well, I was praying and
I suddenly realized I was talking to myself."

—Peter O'Toole

The title of the great English actor Peter O'Toole's memoir is *Loitering
with Intent*, a phrase he cheekily borrowed from an old English law
that refers to a criminally minded type hanging around waiting to do
some crimes. So, I've borrowed it from him to talk about how to use
play and curiosity to listen better. Communication is the cornerstone
of culture, and open communication isn't possible if we're merely just
hearing the words. It demands our presence. Once we start listening with
intent, really doing it, we learn pretty quickly how little listening we were
doing before.

When our people sense they are heard without judgment, trust
deepens, paving the way for the kinds of collaborative problem-solving
and shared understanding that make for effective leadership. Listening
is the bridge we build to allow our people to travel to where we want
them to go.

Active listening is one of the most powerful skills we can develop—
not just in the workplace, but in every area of life. It's about being fully
present, not just hearing the words someone is saying, but truly understanding their message, their emotions, and their intent. It's a skill that

builds trust, strengthens relationships, and fosters collaboration. But, like any skill, it takes practice and intention.

To learn more about listening, I listened to my old buddy Reed Diamond, who's been a guest on my podcast and appeared in *Change Proof*. Reed's been acting professionally for more than forty years, so you know he's not just resilient, he's a model for resilience in the face of uncertainty.

- Be Fully Present

For Reed, active listening starts with presence. In acting terms, that means "getting present" with the person opposite us. Presence is about letting go of our preconceived notions and reading the other person like a book. Some can do this naturally, and some have to work at it, but it all comes down to noticing the subtle cues most people miss.

That means putting down the phone, closing the laptop, and giving the other person our undivided attention. It's about showing, through our body language and focus, that we're there for them.

Presence is a gift, and in today's world, it's one of the most valuable things you can offer.

- Listen to Understand, Not to Respond

Reed told me that when to really listen, we have to "listen with our blood."

One of the biggest barriers to active listening is the tendency to think about what we're going to say next while the other person is still speaking. Instead, focus entirely on their words, tone, and body language. To help us do that, there's an acting exercise that Reed borrows from Sanford Meisner, the famed acting teacher, who developed something called the "Repetition Game" to get us out of our heads and into someone else's.

According to Reed, the basics of the game are just one person offering up a basic observation about the other person, let's say, "You're wearing a red sweatshirt." Then they'd say back to the first person, "I'm wearing a red sweatshirt." And they do this back and forth until something naturally happens, and then they're repeating something else, like, "You're smiling." And "I'm smiling." Repetition is the key that unlocks deeper conversations.

I might feel strange to do at first, but to Reed, active listening is just a form of play: "I always think about it as passing the ball, right? That's what the repetition exercise is. You pass the ball back and forth, but as you're passing it, things shift. And then you adjust to that, and then you throw it in a different way. The math of acting is one plus one equals infinity. Because if I'm playing off of you, and you're in, you're kind enough to play off of me, and we're playing together, we're gonna get somewhere." That somewhere is something deeper than just the words people say.

So, when we're meeting with our teams, in one-on-one settings, we ask ourselves, "What are they really trying to communicate?" And then repeating and rephrasing it back to them so they feel heard. This shift from listening to answer to listening with intent can transform the quality of our conversations.

- Don't Just Plan

Something odd has happened in the world of customer service. I've noticed that when I'm on the phone with a corporate call center, and I'm expressing frustration with something related to their product, I hear the same phrases: "I'm sorry to hear that, that must be very hard, and I'm here to help." Sounds good, right? Finally! Someone's listening to me. But that's not how it comes across, does it? It sounds as though they're reading some canned script. The "listening" is a designed plan to keep us from freaking out. The words don't match or create a feeling other than ick.

That's because communication is about more than just words.

Listening with intent, the way an actor like Reed does, means we pay attention to tone of voice, facial expressions, and body language. These nonverbal cues can provide valuable insight into emotions and intentions. Even on the phone, we can tell when someone's not really listening to us.

That's why we've got to let go of plans and control. Reed told me that actors do it too, most times to the detriment of the truth of the scene they're playing. "Sometimes I'll go, 'Oh, this doesn't feel right. I'm gonna bail.' And 99.9 percent of the time, that's my best take. And the reason I wanted to bail was that it wasn't going to plan. This doesn't feel right. I'm not in control. And that's essential to great work. Putting yourself out there." We might not want to put ourselves out there with our teams, but if we do, we're creating a culture of transparent communication. Sometimes there will be mistakes.

But we can mitigate these mistakes by borrowing from actors like Reed. And Robert DeNiro. Reed learned a powerful lesson from someone who worked with the great actor. His less experienced scene partner was making things a little more complicated than they needed to be, so DeNiro asked if they could just talk and listen, Reed recounted. And that's Acting 101. Because most people just want to talk. And listening is everything. It's essential in your work as an actor, and it's essential in your work as a human.

It's easy to jump to conclusions or make assumptions about what someone is saying, especially if we think we know where they're going. But assumptions can lead to misunderstandings. Instead, we need to approach our conversations with curiosity and an open mind. If we're unsure about something, ask for clarification rather than filling in the blanks ourselves.

Because we don't want to fill in the blanks with our biases, assumptions, and plans.

Finally, active listening requires self-awareness. Pay attention to your own biases, emotions, and reactions during the conversation. Are you getting defensive? Are you tuning out because you disagree? Recognizing these tendencies allows you to course-correct and stay fully engaged.

Active listening is a practice—it's not something we master overnight. But the more we commit to it, the more we'll see its impact on our relationships, our leadership, and our ability to connect with others on a deeper level. It's about creating a space where people feel valued, respected, and understood.

All we have to do is listen.

> "Of all the skills of leadership, listening is the most valuable—and one of the least understood. Most captains of industry listen only sometimes, and they remain ordinary leaders. But a few, the great ones, never stop listening. That's how they get word before anyone else of unseen problems and opportunities."
>
> —Peter Nulty

THE RE-CULTURE CURIOSITY QUESTIONS

1. How might incorporating the "Repetition Game" technique, inspired by acting exercises, help you move beyond passive hearing to actively mirror emotions and intentions in your conversations?
2. How could approaching that moment with curiosity, instead of a plan, have altered the dynamic and outcome?
3. What internal barriers most often disrupt your ability to listen fully?
4. How can you borrow an actor's mindset of embracing imperfection to turn these moments into opportunities for trust-building?

HOW LEADERSHIP TEAMS GET STUCK

I want to tell you a story about a company I worked with that we'll call LUNX. On the outside, they were winning. They had a strong, competent CEO and a team of leaders who were, individually, very good at their jobs. But on the inside, their crew was misfiring. The entire executive leadership team (ELT) knew it. In fact, when I asked them to rate their own team's effectiveness, they gave themselves a four or five out of ten.

Let that sink in. The people steering the ship knew it was barely seaworthy.

When I work with organizations like LUNX, I don't look for villains. I look for patterns. And the pattern at LUNX was a textbook example of a culture that had grown faster than its container. The talent was there, but the trust, clarity, and alignment were not. When I look for Re-Culture moments, this is what I'm talking about, because it means that, from the outside, the results are enviable, but from the inside, the culture is hardly worth envying.

When I dug into their private responses, I found the true source of the cultural malaise: the CEO. She was a force: extremely competent, driven, but worryingly central to every major decision. Her strength had become their weakness. By bypassing the chain of command and micromanaging, she unintentionally created a culture of dependency. Her team of capable leaders was waiting for instructions instead of owning their outcomes. They were frustrated, disempowered, and afraid to speak up and risk her wrath.

Sounds familiar, doesn't it?

In Re-Culture, leadership isn't about being the smartest person in the room. It's about creating more leaders who can steer the ship when the storms come.

When we centralize control, we don't get efficiency. We get a bottleneck. We get a team that avoids ownership because they know it will be taken from them.

As a result of this leadership bottleneck, the energy of communication had nowhere to go. The finance department wasn't putting out timely guidelines. HR would roll out training without telling department heads what the training modules were for. This wasn't a technology problem; it was a people problem. The LUNX leadership team lacked the basic protocols and, more importantly, the safety for candid, timely dialogue.

Like many companies, they were polite, but they weren't honest.

To renew organizational culture, we have to create structures for brave conversations. Without a forum where leaders (and rank-and-file employees) can say, "This isn't working," without fear, you get a polished surface hiding a rotten foundation. The goal isn't to avoid conflict, it's to make conflict productive.

At LUNX, their people were struggling because they didn't know who was supposed to do what. Roles were blurry. Key positions were understaffed.

The result? Middle management was described as "beat down." They were the ones caught between an unclear executive vision and the day-to-day demands of the business. We can't hold people accountable for a game when the rules and positions are constantly shifting.

The quickest way to kill our culture is ambiguity. That's what we need to get brutally clear on roles, responsibilities, and who owns what outcomes. When people know the boundaries of their lane, they can run faster in it.

At LUNX and many other companies, the culture is split between the "old guard" and new leaders. This creates an "us vs. them" energy that breeds complacency and a lack of urgency.

They were meeting their shareholder metrics, but the underlying culture was one of fear. Fear of making a mistake, fear of the CEO's disapproval, the list is endless. Fear spreads through a culture like a virus. Fear-based cultures are low-energy cultures. Rather than innovating, they're locked in a cycle of comply and go along.

Every organization is always in a cultural transition. The question is, is it intentional or accidental? If we don't consciously define the culture we want, we will by default reinforce the culture we have, even if it's not working.

This is the simple, direct approach that I took with their leaders.

I told them that our work wasn't about fixing broken people. It was about fixing the broken connections between them.

We held up a mirror. We showed them the data: "You rate yourselves a four out of ten. Communication is your number one issue." They couldn't argue with the numbers. That's why the work we did together was anchored on trust, not teamwork. The time for trust falls was well in the past.

Instead, we did structured exercises that put them all into a state of discomfort. I often find that when people are put under pressure, they're at their most vulnerable and are more honest. To get them there, I asked them a series of rapid-fire questions: "What's one win, one loss, one aspiration, and one thing you need support on?" This cut through the corporate babble and got right down to the human stuff where culture is made.

The answers were profoundly real and actually showed that, inside, the entire team wanted the same things. They just didn't know it. They all wanted to do better, to be better, but they just didn't know how. One manager described himself as a "people pleaser," so he was making decisions from a place of conflict avoidance, which is really just another way of saying he was a yes-man at LUNX. Yes-men (and -women) are dangerous to culture because they make it seem as though everything is operating at its peak, but inside, it's just treading water.

As a lifeguard, I know that a swimmer can't tread water forever. Eventually, they'll drown. They've got to make it to the shore. The leaders at LUNX were swimming in complexity, and that kept them stagnant. Re-Culture isn't complex; it's about getting back to the fundamentals of how the group actually works together.

To combat this, I introduced the ELT to a simple RACI framework to clarify decision-making. We've all seen these matrices before, and I'll admit, they're a little basic. But at the level of culture, with leadership teams that are wrestling with exponential complexity every single day, sometimes we need to be reminded that the basic building blocks of workplace culture are:

Who's Responsible?
Who's Accountable?
Who's Consulted?
Who's Informed?

When I pushed the LUNX team to publicly state their own ownership, they realized that clarity is the prime mover of the accountability they were lacking. From this, they created rituals for giving and receiving feedback without defensiveness. We all need reminding that feedback is not a critique of our past, but an investment in the future. LUNX learned that one person need not be the source of all decisions, nor is it the collective. It's the harmony between the two: The ability to lead and be led.

Within a year, LUNX's internal metrics told the story: the ELT's self-rated effectiveness score doubled from a four to an eight out of ten. The bottlenecks that once defined the CEO's leadership dissolved, and cross-departmental project completion accelerated by 40 percent as leaders stepped into clear ownership. Perhaps most tellingly, their internal survey scores measuring "psychological safety" and "role clarity" jumped from the 30th to the 85th percentile, proving that the culture was no longer operating from a place of fear, but from a renewed foundation of trust and accountability. The talent was always there; it just needed the right structure to win together.

The bottom line for LUNX, and maybe for you, is this: Your culture is your most renewable resource, but you have to be intentional about renewing it. It starts with the leadership team having the courage to look in the mirror, admit the engine is misfiring, and commit to the simple, powerful work of realignment.

You have the talent. Now build the trust.

THAT'S WHAT THE MONEY IS FOR: GRATITUDE

Gratitude isn't transactional. True gratitude acknowledges effort, creativity, and humanity, not just results.

Our team members aren't just their economic contributions to shareholder value. In Re-Culture, gratitude ensures that leaders are operating from humility, service, and the right perspective on the work. Is what we do important? Absolutely. Otherwise, we wouldn't be doing it. But is it the most important thing? Ask anyone on their deathbed if it is.

That's why cultural leaders who practice regular gratitude inspire loyalty and foster a sense of shared purpose among every department they touch.

Great cultures use their organizational resources to build connection, not alienation.

Gratitude, when paired with generosity, creates a ripple effect of positivity and collaboration.

Gratitude is, without a doubt, one of the most transformative practices we can cultivate in our lives. It's my foundational element, not just for personal happiness, but for resilience, connection, and even our physical health. It's one of those rare things that's both profoundly simple and deeply impactful. And what's amazing is that it's accessible to all of us, no matter where we are or what we're going through.

Gratitude won't solve all our problems, but it's easiest and cheapest tool we'll use. When we do, it permeates every aspect of our lives and our culture.

For me, gratitude is the silver bullet to every challenge that awaits us. If we approach our daily lives grateful for the opportunities in front of us, there's nothing that can bring us down.

Within our teams, we so easily forget to be grateful because we're just trying to survive from one day to the next.

It's about pausing to recognize the opportunities in our work, even in the midst of challenges, asking ourselves if we want to be grateful or anxious, and then choosing gratitude. When we do that every day, as an operational philosophy, we'll feel better about every aspect of our organization.

Now, gratitude practice when we scale up to include groups of people, is not about ignoring difficulties or pretending everything is perfect. We have to choose to focus on what's good, what's working, and what we can appreciate. Then, from that perspective, turning to the areas that require our attention and work.

If we think about it, running an organization is just a way of creating problems that cost money. Solved problems create new ones. That's the harmonic way organizations function. We never arrive at some utopic ideal of cultural perfection. There's always some new leak in the walls that needs our attention. In some ways, we're like the boy at the leaking dike, with more watery holes than fingers. Some of us, right now, are thinking, "I'm up to my neck in water and losing strength. It would have been better if I never started out on this journey." And yes, in a parallel universe, if our group of people had not come together to solve this specific task, then these particular problems would not exist. That's true.

But what are we going to do? Quit? Throw in the towel?

It's easy to forget we came to drain the swamp when we're up to our asses in alligators. That's work. Get to it. But do it from a place of gratitude, and we're seeing with new eyes.

That shift in focus will change everything.

It's like flipping a switch that illuminates the beauty and abundance that's already in our teams. So many times, I work with teams that want the solution to their problems to come from outside. We want the magical McKinsey fairy to come in, charge us an arm and a leg to tell us what our problems are and how to fix them, and then we feel secure.

I'm sorry, but the solution to our problems is in our building already. If we think otherwise, we're just going to create new ones. Compound problems are worse than interest because the rate is 100 percent.

We are our solution. The way to understand that runs through gratitude.

There's also a powerful science behind gratitude. Studies have shown that groups practicing gratitude can rewire institutional networks. It strengthens neural pathways associated with positive emotions and weakens those tied to negativity and stress. It's like a workout for our teams, training them to default to appreciation rather than complaint.

The complaints and the appreciation exist in equal measure. It's a question of what we choose.

And the benefits go beyond organizational mental health. Teams that practice gratitude tend to be strong individually. They have stronger immune systems, better sleep, and even healthier hearts.

Gratitude is where the simple meets the profound.

Organizationally, it can start first thing in the morning—when we come together and express gratitude for another day working on the same thing. We ground ourselves in gratitude and let the day hold what it holds. Every moment is a gift, even the imperfect ones.

And let's be honest: Most moments of our work together are imperfect. But that's where the magic of gratitude lies. It's not about waiting for everything to be just right. It's about finding the beauty in what we are together.

Gratitude puts the Well in Working Together.

Because gratitude is the ultimate connector. When we express gratitude to others, it strengthens our relationships and builds trust. It's a way of saying, "I see you. I value you. And I appreciate what you bring to my life." Whether it's a simple thank-you or a heartfelt acknowledgment, those moments of gratitude can create ripples that extend into every aspect of our organizations.

One of the things I love about gratitude is how adaptable it is. We can practice it in so many ways, through small expressions, like notes, thoughtful gifts, and acts of service. We can say to a team member who's struggling, "Hey, take a breather. We'll cover you until you feel like yourself again."

These small, intentional acts of gratitude can have a huge impact over time.

And here's the thing: Gratitude isn't just about feeling good. It's also about our resilience. When we cultivate gratitude, we're better equipped to handle life's challenges. It helps us reframe setbacks as opportunities for growth and keeps us anchored in what truly matters.

Gratitude is the life raft that keeps us all afloat, even in the stormiest seas.

THE RE-CULTURE CURIOSITY QUESTIONS

1. How might you design gratitude practices in your organization that honor bold effort over outcomes?
2. How do you turn "Thank you for the win" into "Thank you for showing up"?
3. How will you applaud vulnerable attempts regardless of results to rewire your culture's relationship with risk and vulnerability?
4. How might spotlighting one act of quiet courage each morning shift your focus from outcomes to process?
5. How can you weaponize gratitude as a tool in times of crisis?

TOUCH IN A TOUCHLESS WORLD

"I love inside jokes. I hope to be a part of one someday."

—Michael Scott

Throughout the months of 2020, viewership on Netflix went through the moon, as it were, specifically the NBC/Universal hit sitcom, *The Office*.

Why?

Well, to me, the answer's obvious: We missed being in the office. Duh.

But we were missing more than just that. We loved watching *The Office* because the message of the show is that though they drive us crazy, our office is a family that drives just as crazy as our real families. Whether we like it or not, we spend more waking hours with them than with our real families.

Or at least we did. Once we were trapped inside our homes, unable to work, it was nice, for a time, because we hopped off the hamster wheel for a few months. But then we began to realize that we were made for more than that. We longed for a connection to the outside world. We longed for contact with a group of people making something together.

To borrow a phrase from Dunder-Mifflin's local ad that proclaimed, "Limitless paper in a paperless world," in 2020, we longed for touch in a touchless world.

Touch, whether we know it or not, is a part of how we create a culture of gratitude in our workplace, but we can't touch each other for two reasons:

- The history of the workplace (and history itself) is littered with men in powerful positions (or anywhere on the organizational ladder) creating a toxic environment for the women who work for and with them through unwanted physical advances.
- A global pandemic changed the very nature of what an office of people working together is.

Yes, we still shake hands or offer the odd high-five here or there. But until the workplace culture is cleansed of the toxicity of certain behaviors, we've got to check ourselves at the door. Not because we're worried about HR violations, but because it's the right thing to do. And it offers up a whole host of interesting opportunities when we use the touch of gratitude to build trust and to use that trust to create a culture of which we can be proud.

From our very first moments drawing breath outside of our mother's bodies, we're seeking something to trust in. The mechanism that we first use to find it—our first point of communication—is physical touch. That's why doctors and midwives suggest that mothers and fathers hold their new babies in skin-to-skin contact to bond with one another. These bonds release oxytocin, the hormone that tells our brain who and what to trust. It's the neuro-chemical feeling of security.

But safety is not just for babies.

An NIH study found that physical touch is evolution's way of keeping the group together. Thousands of years ago, if I was on my own, I was probably going to die. So, it makes sense that feeling cut off from society feels, emotionally at least, like a kind of death sentence.

The good news is that social isolation and loneliness can be curtailed through physical touch.

If you stand back and watch any gender-specific group of people, any team, or any organization working well together, you'll see a complex language of physical touch amongst the team members. I'm speaking specifically of teams that aren't co-ed. Groups of men and groups of women engaged in athletic competitions at all levels will engage in touch, free of self-consciousness or trepidation about crossing lines. They touch each other because it makes the team better.

The good teams touch one another to create the bonds that solidify the resilience they need for success. Think of a football team on offense, huddling together to call the play they're about to run, their shoulders in contact as well as their eyes. Think about when a successful play happens in soccer, where the players all rush together to pile on top of one another in a kind of ecstatic joy. We can't do that in an office setting. Even Michael Scott knows that.

All of it is a spontaneous physical expression of the spiritual culture they've built together and how they maintain it. In groups, touch is necessary to create cultural bonds. But in a workplace, as we've established, we can't touch one another, nor should we.

So, what do we do? How do we replace something we know is vital and useful to the collective while still protecting the individual?

What we've got to do is recreate the idea of physical touch in the aggregate, in remote and in-person environments by leveraging psychological, sensory, and active substitutes that can mimic (to our brains at least) the trust-building and bonding we used to get from person-to-person contact.

If we can do it, we can foster greater social bonding, thereby reducing stress and anxiety.

> "Too often we underestimate the power of a touch, a smile, a kind word, a listening ear, an honest compliment, or the smallest act of caring, all of which have the potential to turn a life around."
>
> —Leo F. Buscaglia

FIVE KEYS TO REPLACE PHYSICAL TOUCH AND STILL CREATE COLLECTIVE BONDS

I'll admit that shared rituals in a virtual office environment can seem a little corny—especially at first. So, our mileage may vary when it comes to some of these suggestions. Like everything, our leadership and how it creates our culture must feel authentic to who we are. Me, I'm the "I Love My Life" guy. I love to celebrate the people in my life and my work. It's what makes me feel alive. That might not work for everyone. The important thing is to find an empathy delivery system that feels right for the team members in our care. Because they are (in our care!).

Amplify Nonverbal Cues

At its best, touch communicates empathy and presence, but virtual offices often strip away nonverbal signals. We've all had the experience of reading an email or text and imputing a certain tone that the writer didn't intend. Hence, in the absence of physical cues, the way we communicate with one another becomes even more important.

So, use video calls whenever possible for face-to-face interaction. Look directly into the camera to simulate eye contact, and use warm, expressive tones to convey emotion. Enjoy yourself. Imagine we're the hosts of a party. We want everyone to feel included. We have to do what comes naturally to us. If we're naturally introverted, we can practice at home. Even if we fail, our teams will see the effort. A little goes a long way—like a simple smile or nod during a conversation to let your teams know you're listening and available.

Remember, just because they work for us doesn't mean we have to treat them that way.

Find a language with your heart that works for you.

Create "Sensory Engagement"

Touch activates the parasympathetic nervous system, lowering stress. Substitute with other senses. Keep meetings short. Don't waste time.

This one might be a little out there, but we can help our team members create their own environment from home. We can send textured items, like stress balls, for some tactile expressions during the virtual working hours, especially during virtual meetings.

Create natural breaks in the day. Don't expect team members to be chained to their desks for the entirety of the working day. That's a recipe for burnout. Working Well Together doesn't mean we have to be together at every moment to work well.

Build Through Vulnerability

Physical touch is an impulsive and vulnerable act that builds bonds of trust. How else can we replicate this? By being more emotionally available ourselves and creating an environment where our teams can feel safe.

Start meetings with, "How are you *really*?" not for uncomfortable details about someone's personal life, but how they're feeling about their relationship to work. That's actually our business. If we don't ask, we'll never know.

Host monthly sessions (no more than fifteen minutes each) where teams share mistakes they've made on the job. Psychological safety is one of our assets. We gain more of it the more we normalize mistakes and create gratitude for the opportunities.

Pair team members together. Make them responsible for check-ins and venting sessions. Make them a part of the workday. This isn't extra work. Ten minutes of blowing off steam in a non-gossiping way will give team members extra energy to attack their challenges. We all share wins and losses, so we need to practice sharing them.

Tune in Together

The research shows us that touch signals our empathy. That's how our loved ones feel our connection. In the absence of touch, we can tune into our own emotions by communicating intentionally with our teams in a way that makes them feel heard and seen.

How?

Normalize active listening. Leaders aren't the only ones who need to listen. Team members have to listen to one another. Train teams to paraphrase others' points while making their own.

Express gratitude at the end of each meeting—one quick moment for each team member. Gratitude is a vaccine for culture. A small dose and we're resistant to cynicism and back-biting.

Encourage phrases like "I hear you," or "I feel you," or "I'm with you" to express empathy. It sounds trite and obvious to say that listening is our most important skill. But only if we follow up phrases like these with action.

Create Spaces to Share Space

Like WD-40 and their "collision zones," physical offices use open layouts to encourage incidental touch. In a virtual office, we've got to use alternate means. Encourage eating lunches together. Not every day. But once a week. Even if team members are in their own homes, they'll get to know one another better. Again, we're not after strict enforcement here. We're looking for ways to express our gratitude for one another in a way that builds a culture that people can step into and feel. We're working. But it doesn't have to feel like work all the time.

Offer virtual yoga/breathwork to sync physical rhythms. It worked for Phil Jackson and the Chicago Bulls. Michael Jordan hated doing yoga at first, but even he had to admit that breathing together was useful. If we don't overplay our hand, our people will feel that the organization has a purpose, not just a paycheck.

In this book, we've seen that barriers fall and boundaries build when we are emotionally integrated enough to express our gratitude for our team members. That's why the absence of touch isn't a barrier. It's an invitation to innovate our connection to each other.

THE RE-CULTURE CURIOSITY QUESTIONS

1. How might you amplify nonverbal empathy in virtual spaces?

2. How could you design "collision zones" for remote teams to create serendipitous moments of vulnerability (like WD-40's open offices) that spark the trust-building of accidental touch?

3. What collective practice could you design that would replace the "ecstatic pile-on" of team wins with virtual togetherness?

THE RE-CULTURE GARDENER

I'd like to introduce you to an HR professional that I'm going to call "K," who is a walking, talking, living, breathing Re-Culture gardener. K is not only my friend, but she also embodies each of the Ten Instructions in every organization that's lucky enough to work with her.

I'm not going to use her name. But she knows who she is.

I used to call K a "culture warrior" because she could be dropped behind "enemy lines" into any workplace culture and have that place trending upward on every metric within thirty days.

But that's not accurate to who K is. Her energy isn't aggressive. She's not going to come in, guns blazing, and set an organization straight.

In truth, she's much better than that. K is more like a culture gardener, who patiently but firmly takes in the state of the soil, the weeds, the dying flowers, and the disorganized landscape, then rolls up her sleeves and gets to work.

That's because K operates from gratitude. She's thankful for the opportunity to work with other human beings. She takes pleasure in helping them and their organization be profitable, productive, and purpose-driven—in the same way that a gardener, to truly bring forth healthy fruits and vegetables, loves the garden in which they tend.

So, let's test K by giving her a toxic garden to tend. And I know just the pair that need a strong, capable set of hands: Josh and Emma. Let's see how K makes their garden bloom.

When we last left our star-crossed team members, Emma had just resigned from the organization due to Josh's mis- (and micro-) management.

K's first order of business is to weed out the mistrust that Josh has engendered with Emma. K begins by initiating something she calls "radical candor roundtables," where Emma anonymously submits concerns to K about Josh's micromanagement. Without sharing the details of Emma's concerns, K pairs Josh with a coach to address his insecurities. Both parties feel heard, without letting the acrimony or the correction play out publicly.

As a result, Emma sees actionable change, which rebuilds trust, while Josh learns empathy and begins to understand how his behavior erodes team trust.

Then, K implements a "values margin call" for when Emma feels pressure to push past ethical or burnout guidelines. All Emma has to do is send a message to K (anonymously), and K pauses the project.

As a result, Josh is forced to pause and recalibrate his "profit-first" mindset. Emma's integrity is validated, reinforcing the cultural values of the company. And the project still comes in on time and on budget.

K goes further and redrafts the workflow chart between Emma and Josh with her "boundary blueprints," clarifying that Emma owns client relationships while Josh oversees AI integration. Decision-making authority is finally coherent to prevent overlap and confusion between Emma and Josh.

With boundaries clarified, Josh's micromanagement diminishes, and his respect for Emma grows while she regains autonomy, reducing friction and allowing her to appreciate Josh's contributions and talents as well.

As a next step, K mandates "renewal sprints," shutting down non-urgent work on a quarterly basis. So, Emma attends her twins' play without backlash. Josh, initially resistant, uses the time for stress-management training and coaching. Freed from the stress of his job, he finds he actually enjoys management and has skills and abilities he didn't even know existed.

As a result, Emma's burnout eases, while Josh discovers his own work-life harmony, softening his "grind-mind" demands.

This done, K moves on to more public means of culture gardening and addressing the organization's (and Josh's) accountability issues. To track this, K installs "accountability boards" tracking team goals. When Josh blames Emma for a failed bid, the board highlights his lack of support. Peer pressure from the rest of the team's metrics forces him to apologize.

Finally, Josh is owning his role in setbacks, while Emma feels empowered to speak up.

To get Josh and Emma working together, K launches something she calls "chaos labs," where Emma's team designs a satirical bidding process using office supplies. Josh, initially dismissive, reluctantly participates, laughs, and lets down his guard.

Cut loose from the pressure to perform, play breaks Josh's rigidity and reignites Emma's creativity. They both see each other as more human.

To stimulate growth, K has Josh award Emma with a "stumble scholarship" to study AI ethics, a skill unrelated to her role, but still within her skillset. Emma shares insights, shifting Josh's view of her as "obsolete."

Josh recognizes Emma's evolving value, while Emma mentors others, rebuilding her shaken confidence.

To really drill down into Josh's fear of failure, K has Emma host a "funeral for flops" after one of his miscalculations. The team toasts his risk-taking, dissecting lessons learned. Josh freely admits his own past mistakes.

For both, failure becomes a collective teacher. Josh stops punitive write-ups and sees the value in Emma's risk-taking.

For the entire team, K institutes a "gratitude grid," and Josh has to watch while the team floods Emma with badges and tokens. Shamed by his own lack of recognition, Josh not only begins thanking Emma privately, but he also begins to display small acts of gratitude to the entire team.

Emma feels seen and sees Josh's gestures of collective support, which rebuilds their rapport.

K runs a "future backwards" workshop, revealing how individual toxicity could kill the organization. She has the team brainstorm "culture guardians" to audit leadership.

Without being asked, Josh volunteers for the guardian role. Emma stays, hopeful her expertise will shape the future.

K isn't a miracle worker; she's a miracle grower. Her culture gardening powers can turn the most toxic, overgrown, weed-strewn garden into a rich, resilient, and healthy workplace culture. If you can find your special K, then hang on to them.

You'll be thankful that you did.

THE RE-CULTURE CURIOSITY QUESTIONS

1. How might you create a culture gardener profile so that hiring one becomes a probability, not just a possibility?

OPTIMISM = FAITH IN THE FUTURE

"It cannot be your duty to do anything that is beyond your reach or your strength at the moment. It cannot be your duty to do anything that sacrifices your own integrity or your own spiritual development."

—Emmet Fox

If trust is the keystone (the last stone laid) of our organization, then optimism is the cornerstone (the first stone laid). Trust is the stone that binds all the other commandments together. Optimism gives us a path forward, where we can dream of a future in which we've laid every stone in its proper place and the project is complete. Optimism is faith in a future we can't yet see.

When was the last time we had faith in the future?

I was born a year after they held the World's Fair in Flushing-Meadows in my hometown of Queens, New York, a mere three years after President John F. Kennedy fired the starter's pistol on the Space Race. Some would say that this was the last time people believed in a future that was better than the time they were inhabiting.

The World's Fair was a dazzling international exposition that celebrated human ingenuity at the dawn of the Space Age. The fair's theme was "Peace Through Understanding," and it showcased an eclectic mix of achievements. More than 140 pavilions and 110 restaurants represented over eighty nations, twenty-four US states, and numerous major corporations, including IBM, General Electric, Ford, and General Motors.

To the people of New York (and the world), it was like walking through a future out of *The Jetsons*. With its futuristic exhibits and ambitious scope, the fair became a powerful symbol of American optimism during a time when the nation was experiencing significant social and political shifts.

Maybe this was the final cultural expression of progress and creativity until the next few years brought the upheaval, war, and strife that would begin to divide us from one another until we would end up where we are now. Divided from each other and ourselves while a clock counts down our doom.

Maybe that's a bit hard, but that's how it feels some days, doesn't it?

The kind of hope in utopia that we felt in 1964 seems almost quaint. When I was a kid walking through the empty World's Fair ground, our biggest enemy was boredom. For kids now? It's anxiety.

Anxiety is the thief that steals in the night when optimism packs its bags and heads to the hills.

> Fear is the question that asks, "What if?" Optimism answers, "Even if."
>
> What if no one trusts me?
>
> What if I forget the mission?
>
> What if I've organized my people wrong?
>
> What if I'm burning them out?
>
> What if I own mistakes and it doesn't help anything?
>
> What if no one enjoys the work?
>
> What if we stagnate and miss our targets?
>
> What if I keep failing because I'm a failure?

What if I don't appreciate the opportunity?

What if I don't believe?

If we go through each of these questions and really answer them in our hearts, then we take the onus off the fear. Because most of us, when it comes down to it, are, as Pittsburgh Steelers Coach Mike Tomlin says, "living in our fears."

What if we answered every "What if?" with its optimistic opposite: "Even if…"

Even if no one trusts me…Re-Culture says that trust takes time. It's earned through humility, transparency, and showing up for others. Little by little, meeting by meeting, day by day, we'll build bridges toward a future we believe in together.

Even if I forget the mission…I'll anchor my decisions to our shared purpose and invite my people to relight the way to where we all started.

Even if I've organized my people wrong…I'll stay agile, rearranging the puzzle with humility and their hard-earned wisdom.

Even if I'm burning them out…I'll change course and instead defend rest as sacred fuel, not a failure of the grind-hustle mindset.

Even if owning mistakes doesn't help anything…I'll own my flaws, because my imperfect attempts at integrity will always outshine perfection.

Even if no one enjoys the work…I'll unearth meaning in the work we do together, because fulfillment often hides beneath friction.

Even if we stagnate and miss our targets…I'll treat inertia as the spark for the kind of reinvention that thrives in paused moments.

Even if I keep failing…I'll rise as a student, because each fall teaches me how to fly higher.

Even if gratitude feels forced…I'll name one small gift from my people because daily awareness rewires habitual indifference.

Even if optimism falters…I'll act as if I believe in our shared future to rekindle conviction.

As leaders, we have to face our fears every single day. Every decision we make and the ones we don't, all of them can bring down our organization.

But fear is the doorway that leads us to optimism. We can't get to where we're going without our fears.

Fear, my friend, is how we get to optimism. An optimistic faith in a shared future is how we get a culture strong enough to withstand the change and uncertainty trying to blow us down.

> "These then are my last words to you. Be not afraid of life. Believe that life is worth living and your belief will help create the fact."
>
> —William James

SOUL AND SOIL

—Captain Yared Getachew

On March 10, 2019, the pilot of Ethiopian Airlines Flight 302 was flying home to visit his mother. His name was Captain Yared Getachew. He was about to turn thirty.

He was born in Nairobi to two physicians. He was the penultimate child of six in a family dedicated to education and service. That's why young Yared was an excellent student and widely respected by all who knew him as a natural leader. Possessing the aura of a great man, one could see him following his father's footsteps into medicine. But, though Yared was a great student, his dreams were sky high.

His father, too, had hoped his son would be a physician like both his parents, pushing him to pursue higher education in Ethiopia. Instead, Yared opted to earn his wings in the rigorous pilot training programs of the United States.

Once he completed his training, he went home to join Ethiopian Airlines as a cadet and immediately made an impression with his discipline and skill. He was a rising star in a national airline that needed bright lights to follow. Yared was an exemplar of national pride. In just a decade, he became the youngest captain in the airline's history to pilot a Boeing 737-800. By the time he took his last flight, he'd accrued more than eight thousand flight hours, and he knew the Ethiopia-Kenya air routes like the back of his hand—specifically, the route called the "UN shuttle" because many of the United Nations workers went back and forth between the country's two major cities.

On March 10, the plane was loaded with the crew and people who worked with refugees, charities, and worldwide health organizations. Families, friends, and strangers.

Just two minutes after takeoff, Yared and his co-pilot responded to a flight control computer error as best they could, wrestling with the controls for over six minutes, and tried to bring the plane back safely to the Addis Ababa airport. They did not succeed.

The plane crashed in a field near the small town of Bishoftu.

Investigations later revealed that the aircraft's maneuvering characteristics augmentation system (MCAS) malfunctioned due to the fact that a sensor had likely been taken out by a bird.

Yared and his co-pilot had not received adequate training on MCAS, and though they followed Boeing's emergency procedures, they couldn't override the system.

Not only was Yared about to turn thirty, but he was also engaged to marry another pilot later that year. His last words were a call to his mother, telling her he'd forgotten his phone but that he'd talk to her soon.

Though Yared and his co-pilot were initially blamed for the crash, Boeing would eventually apologize and settle out of court. Yared's father called the apology "too little, too late" because the family couldn't recover their son's remains. He said, "He is in the soil now in Ethiopia."

We can't forget that culture is people. It would not exist without them. They're the ones who make up the soil and soul of our organization.

The journey of their lives brought them to this present moment, inside our organization. They are in our care. They may be with us for their entire careers. But they probably won't be. It's our job as leaders to leave them better off than when they came to us.

Culture is the soil of our organization. We are stewards who must take care of it so that it can continue to bear fruit for the generations after us.

In some ways, we have to be like Moses, who guided the Israelites through the harsh desert for forty years after their exodus from Egypt, enduring trials and striving to unite a rebellious and stiff-necked people. If we think our work as leaders is difficult! One can only imagine leading a people experiencing freedom for the very first time. Just when things were spiraling out of control, and Moses was about to lose his people and their culture, he went up to a mountain and wrote the code for how to live in harmony together.

In spite of this, Moses was forbidden from entering the promised land. His own imperfections and personal failings cost him his dream. But his people made it.

Just before he died, he was taken up to a high mountain so he could see the country that he would never enter. Forty years of wandering, toil, resilience, and sacrifice, and a glimpse was all he got.

My organizational and spiritual guide, Emmet Fox, writes about the Code that lives inside each of us, "Infinite intelligence is at the core of your being. It will guide and direct your thoughts, your actions, and your words if you will let it. It will bring you the perfect right answer and solve the problem for you."

The Code of Conduct is a singular code for living from the inside out. Re-Culture is how we share it with our teams. I hope that in these pages you've found a way to renew your organization, to make it work, to make it work well, so that we can all work well together.

AI AND RE-CULTURE

"I am an optimist. Anyone interested in the future has to be otherwise he would simply shoot himself."

—Arthur C. Clarke

One of the best culture movies of the last fifteen years is *Steve Jobs*, written by Aaron Sorkin (based on the Walter Isaacson book) and directed by Danny Boyle. The movie tells the story of Steve Jobs, from the launch of the Macintosh computer in 1984 to the launch of the iMac in 1998, which set in motion a course of events that led us to today.

To me, what's fascinating about the movie is that it's about a man wrestling, in real time, with the culture that he created—a culture that flowed from his strength and his weakness. In a crucial confrontation near the end of the film, Seth Rogan as Steve Wozniak says to Jobs, "It's not binary. You can be decent and gifted at the same time."

The culture that Steve Jobs created and codified was based on the binary idea that human failings can be conquered by machines that give us the illusion of humanity.

That brings me to the two huge cultural tsunamis we've faced in the last five years: a worldwide viral pandemic and artificial intelligence.

That's why, before we go, we need to talk about the eight-hundred-pound gorilla in the room that's a circuit board with a human face: artificial intelligence, or AI.

Everybody's screaming about it. The tech bros are selling it like it's the second coming. The doomers are telling us it's Skynet and that we're all about to be terminated. And the rest of us? We're just trying to figure out if it's going to write our kid's homework or take our jobs or steal the nuclear codes.

So, let's cut through the noise. I'm gonna give it to you straight. No fluff. No fear. Just the truth about AI and what it really means for us, for our work, and for the thing that matters most: our culture.

First things first: AI isn't going away, but maybe it isn't the savior many believe it is.

Maybe.

But let's be real. This train has left the station. It's not a fad. It's not the metaverse. It's a fundamental shift, like the internet. But here's where people get it twisted. They think this thing is gonna solve climate change, cure cancer, and probably do your laundry while it's at it. It's not. It's a tool, not a messiah. It doesn't have a soul, it doesn't have a conscience, and it sure as hell doesn't care about your quarterly reports. Pump the brakes on the salvation narrative. It's just…a thing. A powerful thing, but a thing.

Which brings me to my next point. AI is a tool. That's it. Full stop.

Is a hammer smart? No. It's a hammer. You can use it to build a house, or you can use it to smash your thumb. The intelligence, the intention, the purpose—that comes from the human holding the hammer. AI is the same. It's the most sophisticated power drill we've ever invented. It can automate the boring stuff, crunch data faster than a caffeinated accountant, and generate a picture of a bulldog wearing a sombrero on a skateboard. Useful? Sometimes. Magical? No. It's a tool in the human toolbox. Don't bow down to it. Learn how to hold the hammer and wield it when you see a nail. But if, as we've seen, all you see are nails, then you have a problem no tool can solve.

Because no tool can replace humans, the foundation of culture.

Come on, people. I know you're worried. But think about it. Can a really, really smart calculator replace a leader who can inspire a team on a tough day? Can a pattern-recognition machine console a customer who's had a nightmare experience and turn them into a brand ambassador? Can it navigate the messy, beautiful, illogical complexity of human emotion, office politics, or creative conflict?

Of course not.

AI operates on what was. It synthesizes existing data. It's a museum of human creation up to 2023. It can't feel the spark of a genuinely new idea born from lived experience. It can only feed on itself now. Cannibalized data has no nutritional value to you or your business.

A computer can't look at a shaft of light in the late afternoon on a summer day and feel the profound sense of awe that leads to a poem, a policy, or a new business model. It can mimic, but it can't mean. The essence of humanity, our deep intuition, our empathy for the person next to us, our collective spirit in tough times, that's not for sale. Re-Culture is our birthright, and it's firewalled from the algorithm.

This is the big one, the hill on which this entire book is built: AI can't create real culture.

Culture isn't a collection of memes or a playlist algorithmically generated to keep you engaged. Culture is the invisible glue. It's the shared stories around the watercooler. It's the unspoken trust that lets a team take a crazy risk. It's the values that actually guide decisions when the boss isn't in the room. It's the vibe, the soul, the way things are done when we're operating at the top of our intelligence and our empathy.

You think you can prompt-engineer that? "Hey ChatGPT, create a culture of psychological safety, relentless innovation, and mutual respect, and make it funny." Good luck with that. The output will be a sterile, perfect-sounding paragraph of corporate gobbledygook that has the warmth and authenticity of a pet rock.

Real culture is forged in the fire of shared experience. It's messy. It's human. And that is why humans create culture with the work they do well together.

Think about the best team you were ever on. Maybe it was at work, maybe it was on a sports team, maybe it was just a group of friends putting together a disastrous but hilarious fundraiser. What made it great? It was the collaboration. The inside jokes. The way you covered for each other. The late nights when you were tired but buzzing because you were building something together.

That is culture creation. It's the byproduct of human beings doing meaningful work, side-by-side, with trust and a common purpose. You can't outsource that to the cloud. Our collaboration is the engine of our culture.

Now, here's the kicker, the part that separates the thriving from the dying. AI can be used by a strong culture, but a weak culture will be eaten up.

Picture a company with a rock-solid culture. They know who they are. They communicate openly. They trust their people. They bring in AI, and what happens? They use it as a force multiplier. "Hey, this tool can free up our people from drudgery so they can do more of the creative, human-centric work they love! Let's use it to enhance our collaboration, not replace it." The culture is the immune system; it uses the tool without becoming the tool.

Now, picture a company with a toxic, weak, or nonexistent culture. Siloed departments, fear-based leadership, and no clear purpose. They bring in AI as a magic wand to "fix efficiency." What happens? It becomes a weapon. Management uses it to surveil employees. It amplifies the distrust. It accelerates the chaos. The lack of a strong human core means the technology dictates the terms, and the culture, what's left of it, gets utterly consumed. It's a parasite that feeds on dysfunction.

So, is the answer to throw our new tool in the garbage? No way. But it can help us as we renew our culture.

This is the opportunity. AI is forcing our hand. It's holding up a mirror and saying, "Look, all the stuff you've been doing that feels soulless and repetitive? I can do that now. So, what are you gonna do?"

It's pushing us to ask the big questions. What is our uniquely human work? What is the culture we want to build? This is a wake-up call to be more human, not less. To double down on connection, on creativity, on empathy. We can use AI to handle the boring bits—the data-crunching, the first drafts, the administrative sludge—so we can get to the good stuff faster.

That's why I'm telling you, the future of work is bright, because it will be human-centered: It will be Re-Culture.

Re-Culture is the intentional, proactive renewal of our workplaces and our work lives around what makes us human. It's not about resisting technology; it's about celebrating our humanity with technology where it belongs: as our sidekick.

The future of work isn't a dystopian landscape of unemployed humans begging robots for scraps. It's a renaissance. It's a workplace where we finally value the stuff we should have valued all along: critical thinking, collaboration, coaching, creativity, and compassion. The work of the future is the work of connection.

AI is handing us back our humanity. It's taking the robot work off our plates and saying, "Your move." The bright future is one where we stop trying to act like machines and start embracing what we are: brilliant, messy, emotional, and infinitely creative beings who are at our absolute best when we are working together, building something that matters.

So don't be afraid of the tool. Be afraid of not building a culture strong enough to wield it. Now go on, get outta here.

You've got a culture to build. Want help making that happen? Just choose a WORKWELLian (workwelllabs.com) for an assist.

WORK WELL TOGETHER.

Send This Book to Your Boss (Anonymously)

Look, I get it.

You're reading this and thinking, "This. All of this. Adam is in my head. The 'nice' vs. 'kind' thing? The trust equation? Finding my Ringo? The culture that feels like it's slowly suffocating under a blanket of politeness? That's my organization. That's my boss."

You're frustrated. You're tired of the unspoken rules. You're exhausted from watching great ideas get shot down with a smile, or seeing problems get talked around instead of talked about. You know things could be more productive, more innovative, more human, but the thought of walking into your boss's office and saying, "Hey, I think our culture is broken," feels like a suicide mission.

So, you stay silent. You become part of the problem. And nothing changes.

It's time for a different strategy.

This isn't about mutiny. It's not a hostile act. It's an act of profound care for your team, your organization, and yes, even your boss.

It's an anonymous intervention for a culture that's struggling to grow.

In the back of this book, you'll find a pre-paid, pre-addressed shipping label, just kidding! All you have to do is contact *team@workwelllabs.com* and tell us who you want to send a book to; a name and email address, and we'll handle the rest. We'll send a copy directly to your boss, your CEO, your HR lead, whoever you think needs to read it most. There's no return address. No tracking back to you. No recourse. No retribution.

Why would you do this?

Because you care more about fixing the problem than protecting your own comfort. That's the shift from nice to kind in action.

Let's be clear, folks: This book isn't a complaint. It's a blueprint. It's a conversation-starter that you might not be safe to start yourself, but that desperately needs to happen. You're not sending a grenade; you're sending a Re-Culture lifeline.

Imagine if your boss opens this.

They won't see a threat. They'll see a solution. They'll see the story of companies that leapt from the bottom to the top by embracing these exact ideas. They'll see a practical Re-Culture guide on how to build a culture where people truly engage, where trust is rebuilt, and where resilience becomes your organization's greatest asset.

They might even have their own "aha!" moment, realizing that the very aspect they thought was holding things together is actually what's keeping them from greatness.

This is your chance to be kind, not nice. To act, not just observe. To be the anonymous catalyst for a change that will benefit everyone, including the person you're sending it to.

Your move.

And listen, if it backfires and you get fired? Let me interest you in another book: *Pivot: The Art and Science of Re-Inventing Your Life*.

PS: For the Boss Who Receives This:

If you're holding this book, someone on your team cares enough about you and the future of this organization to have sent it your way. That's not an insult; it's a vote of confidence. They believe you are the kind of leader who can hear a difficult truth and use it to build something better. They see your potential, even if they don't feel safe saying it to your face—yet.

Don't look for who sent it. Look at why it was sent. Then, start reading.

Resources to Re-Culture Your Organization

KEYNOTES & WORKSHOPS

The WORKWELL team supports organizations through engaging and interactive in-person and virtual keynotes, workshops, open space meetings and masterminds. Our team of experienced speakers and facilitators will skillfully motivate and inspire your team and attendees. But that's not enough - they will leave with practical and meaningful tools that can be immediately applied. Our support materials reinforce key principles, offer easy to apply takeaways and additional resources to ensure an even more impactful program ROI. Our team handcrafts their talks for your specific audience and your intended results and objectives. View examples of our core talk abstracts at https://WORKWELLlabs.com/Re-CultureKeynoteTopics.

WORKWELLlabs.com/Re-CultureKeynotes

INDIVIDUAL & ORGANIZATIONAL SUPPORT

Adam and his team are dedicated to building thriving workplace cultures, one individual and organization at a time. No matter what type of support you're looking for, we are here to help.

Re-Culture Begins with You

- **Leadership and Executive Coaching:** Our team provides an exclusive and holistic approach to business mentoring and leadership development, expertly integrating personal growth with organizational transformation to help leaders build thriving workplace cultures.

Re-Culture Your Team

- *Work Well Together* Framework Workbook
- Re-Culture Your Team with Bulk Book Purchases
- Organizational Training & Support, including Facilitated Trainings, Workshops & Offsite Retreats
- Consulting with HR and C-suite to Restore Connection, Trust and Collaboration
- Comprehensive Culture Strategy & Programming
- ELT & Group Coaching Programs

WORKWELLlabs.com/Re-CultureSupport

WORK WELL TOGETHER ASSESSMENT

Building thriving cultures and learning to Work Well Together go hand-in-hand. How does your organization's culture measure up? Take our Work Well Together Assessment and find out. Along with your results, you'll receive a link to our Culture Transformation Kickstart Kit, full of information to help you implement the Code of Culture and create environments where everyone can thrive.

WORKWELLlabs.com/Re-CultureWorkWellTogether

RE-CULTURE RESEARCH, REFLECTIONS & REAL STORIES

Podcast

Enjoy insightful discussions with Change Proof host, WORKWELL CEO Adam Markel and leaders and innovators who share breakthrough guidance to fully embrace new opportunities and master today's disruptive marketplace.

Articles

Explore fresh perspectives and actionable insights from the WORKWELL team on building cultures where everyone thrives.

Case Studies

See how organizations worldwide are partnering with WORKWELL to transform workplace culture and achieve measurable results in engagement, collaboration, and well-being.

Research

Access WORKWELL's original research and curated studies on what makes workplace cultures truly thrive.

WORKWELLlabs.com/Re-CultureResources

WORKWELLlabs.com/research-re-culture

ASK AGENT WORKWELL

Ask WORKWELL AI Get instant answers to your culture transformation questions. Our AI-powered assistant draws on thousands of hours of research, case studies, and proven frameworks to provide personalized guidance for your specific workplace challenges—available 24/7.

WORKWELLlabs.com/Re-CultureAskWW

CONNECT WITH US

Team@WORKWELLlabs.com
+1.877.697.4868
https://www.LinkedIN.com/Company/WORKWELL-LABS/

https://www.LinkedIN.com/in/AdamMarkel/

WORKWELLlabs.com

AdamMarkel.com

Acknowledgments

It truly takes a team (and a village, to be sure) to see a project like *Re-Culture* through from start to finish. The promising idea is fragile yet somehow survives the days and nights of inactivity and indecision that might otherwise be its end. And somehow, not squandered at all, the idea emerges resiliently, coming into clarity and even greater purposefulness.

Without the following people and their continued support, inspiration, and friendship this project would have surely been left on the shelf. I am forever in gratitude to Adam Seybold, Michael Palgon, Randi Markel, Deanna Clarance, Lindsay McMorrow, Eden Markel, Chelsea Stein, Max Markel, Steve Farber, Jenna Lynch and the Amazing team at Post Hill Press, Anthony Ziccardi and Lexi Vanatta for nurturing *Re-Culture* to its fullest expression.